es tour bus.
ch Rock 'n' Roll.'

otography by Scott Kershaw

STILL BREATHING

To Richard

STILL BREATHING

The True Adventures of the Donnelly Brothers

'FROM ORGANISED CRIME TO KINGS OF FASHION'

Anthony & Christopher Donnelly
with Simon Spence

Interviews and Research: Becky Seward

all the best

BLACK & WHITE PUBLISHING

First published 2013
by Black & White Publishing Ltd
29 Ocean Drive, Edinburgh EH6 6JL

1 3 5 7 9 10 8 6 4 2 13 14 15 16

ISBN: 978 1 84502 708 7
Limited Edition ISBN: 978 1 84502 747 6

A CIP catalogue record for this book is available from the British Library.

Typeset by RefineCatch Ltd, Bungay Suffolk

Printed and bound by ScandBook AB, Sweden

CONTENTS

If you cannot get rid of the family skeleton,
you may as well make it dance
– *George Bernard Shaw*

To our mum and dad, June and Arthur Donnelly,
and our grandma, Julia Frances Calderbank (Tillot)

FOREWORD

by Oliver Wilson

I can't say I knew Anthony and Chris as a child, but I was certainly aware of them. My dad told me about them and I grew up considering them to be part of the extended family. Along with my dad, you had perhaps two dozen other key people who made Manchester 'Madchester'. Chris and Anthony were in at the ground floor on everything, and there was always a feeling of respect between the people who were – a quiet knowing that you did something important and made things happen.

My first memory of meeting Anthony and Chris properly was in my teens. I was driving through town with my dad and this Range Rover was cruising in front of us. It said 'Gio Goi' on the licence plate. There was a beeping of horns and we pulled over on Liverpool Road near the Museum of Science and Industry. My dad got out the car, so did Anthony and Chris, and they met in between for banter. I remember it being like bumping into dearly loved relatives that we'd not seen in ages. There was clear deep love and respect between the three. I think that's because, in lack of any contractual business agreements between my father and anyone during the '80s and '90s, the family who worked together in Manchester had to rely on a bond: a gentleman's handshake perhaps or a heartfelt agreement that they were there to do the same thing, that they were on the same level, brothers in arms. I saw this bond in the way they were together that day on Liverpool Road.

That bond got passed on to me. Anthony and Chris have been extremely supportive of me in all my endeavors and continue to look out for me and help me in whatever way I need. Not just Chris and Anthony, but Tracey and Arthur and June too. Like I say, it's a Manchester thing. You don't need to know someone intimately, but there is a common spiritual bond between people of the same mindset and orientation.

Now there is a very special thing about certain people from Manchester. Anthony. Chris. Alfonso. Pickering. Brown. Ryder. They all have it. And no one from any other city has it. The underdog who wins against all odds, backs against the wall – that's how we do better than anyone else. What I say is what's right, what I think is what's right – a true self-confidence. Give us nothing and we'll build an empire out of it. We made the impossible possible and laughed while we did it. That is why Chris and Anthony, and the other people I mentioned, did so much from nothing. They found their own building blocks – themselves. The crucial point, however, is that none of these qualities are used with any kind of arrogance or in a way that is derogatory towards anyone else. There is no posturing that comes with any of these qualities and as such they are entirely honorable. The point is that none of it is said, or even thought. It just is. There is no arrogance . . . there is no self-affirmation required. There is no bullshit. You see the essence of life is doing.

So this special thing is something unspoken. That is why it is so incredibly powerful. It exists only unsaid in the moment, which gives it a spiritual luminance. It gives the people who possess it a strong, warm glow. Anthony and Chris are a living embodiment of this very rare, mystical, spiritual Mancunian quality.

Oliver Wilson,
son of the founder of Factory Records
and The Hacienda, Anthony H. Wilson (RIP)

PREFACE

Damien Hirst, artist: I met the Donnellys at Glastonbury years ago when they were always hanging out with uncompromising madmen like Bez and Keith Allen. Their story is fucking insane but just goes to show what you can do if you aim high and don't compromise – with a heart of gold and balls of steel, coming from nothing doesn't mean you can't become something mega!

Ian Brown, The Stone Roses: The first time I met Anthony and Chris was at Genevieves in Manchester after Spike Island. We went back there for an after-show and I ended up drinking a bottle of Wild Turkey with Anthony, supplied by Matthew Cummins, Gareth Evans' brother-in-law and co-manager of the Roses. At one point Anthony told me if I needed anything at all to come and see him, whether it was 'a bag of weed, a Kalashnikov or a tank'. 'Russian or American?' I asked. 'I will get you a Martian if you want, pal' was the answer. Still making me chuckle twenty-five years on. Looking 4ward to the book. All the Georgie Best. ianBROWN 1LOVE PAL X

Bernard Sumner, New Order: I love Chris and Anthony. They were always good for a laugh and a party. I can't repeat what we got up to at The Box – Peter Gabriel's home and studio. It was an old converted watermill. Still makes me laugh thinking about when they tried to push their bus out of the mud and it couldn't get over the bridge to the house. Great memories.

Max Beesley, actor: The first time I met Anthony and Chris was at the G-MEX Centre. I was on stage sound checking for a Take That gig when two lads came strolling down the isle, shouting, 'Beesley, we've got some gear for you and the band to wear for tonight's gig.' It was Chris and Anthony. I couldn't believe the balls on them. They marched through security whilst we were doing a private rehearsal and basically dictated what the musicians were going to wear that night. I think they may have mentioned getting the Take That lads in it too, but that was going a bit far! They turned out to be good mates for many, many years. My dad knew their dad and somehow we were all interrelated through history and friendships amongst the elder fellas. That was at the beginning of my music days as a session musician, so I would meet up with them and pick up loads of gear to wear on *Top of the Pops* or any other music shows I was doing at the time with Jamiroqui, The Brand New Heavies, Paul Weller . . . whoever. If the lads were fireworks Anthony would be an Air Bomb and Chris a rocket. Both of them have got fire in their bellies, both are career-driven and very smart. They've both got a spark! They are charismatic and good lads that are very, very loyal to their friends – something that hardly exists anymore.

Howard Marks, Mr Nice: As a criminal myself, I would say Anthony and Christopher's history definitely helped them in a variety of ways. Criminals are generally anti-establishment (excellent for cool street cred) and have ethics that extend beyond signing contracts and the like. We tend to have self-made laws (no rip-offs, no grassing, helping those less fortunate than ourselves, standing by our colleagues, etc.), tenaciously abide by them and have hope and faith that we shall always do so.

Graeme Park, DJ: They were always in and around The Hacienda. We used to have a lot of after parties and they were always there, two of the faces that were always in the thick of it. Manchester now is an amazing metropolis and a fantastic place to live and work, but in the late '80s it was a really grim place, very grey. The combination of Acid House, The Hacienda, Factory Records and that distinct Manc attitude of sticking two fingers up to everyone created this amazing scene. The Donnellys were right at the heart of it all with their attitude: 'Why don't we just make some clothes and go and rave.' They embodied the whole 'do it yourself, let's get on with it' attitude of that time.

Chase & Status (Saul and Will): The 'Blind Faith' video was hands down our favourite video we've done, and the filming of it was just as fun as it looked. It really felt like we had gone back to 1991, the vibe of the warehouse, the ravers and the clothes. It captured the nostalgia we're always searching for. The video touched a lot of people, young and old, and is very special to us. I hope we can do something as exciting again together in the future.

Graham Massey, 808 State: That entire 'Madchester' scene was about merchandising and the T-shirts was really where you made a lot of money – if you could keep control of it. The Donnelly brothers were known bootleggers – they were right on the edge of the darkness. There was something kind of uncomfortably over the line about them. They were completely fearless.

Darren Partington, 808 State/Big Unit: From '88 'til the present day tearin' it up front centre the Donnellys goin' all the way and built on pure passion tearin' the arse out of high street fashion brotherly love taken to the extreme Acid House one love yer were livin' the dream.

Tom Meighan, Kasabian: I met Anthony and Chris a few years back now in Leicester. There always seems to be an angle with them, whatever they are doing. I mean, look at this book – how the fuck do they pull it off? Fair play to them – they seem to get where water can't.

Jimi Goodwin, Doves: I first met Anthony and Chris in '87 or '88 when I was grafting T-shirts around Europe. Some of my fondest memories are of playing pool and smoking weed in The Firbank pub with the lads. Also, they put on the best party I've ever, ever been to at their family farm. Must have been the summer of 1989. By nine o'clock in the morning, anyone still there had retreated outside to gather their shattered minds. I was walking round the garden in a daze and there was still music playing . . . I popped my head around the barn door. There were only two people in there, still dancing, still communing with the spirit, facing each other wild-eyed . . . Anthony and Chris.

Deadmau5 (Joel Zimmerman): When I was working on Your Own Clothing with Chris and Anthony it was a give and take situation. They helped me out massively with 'I Remember'. They help me and I help them – it's simple.

Tom Stubbs, Sunday Times Style: I went to meet them in Manchester. It was like a cross between a really picturesque scene of wholesome rural middle England and a little bit of south central LA. They came out to meet us on the forecourt – there was a lot of sportswear, baseball caps . . . a firm, basically. I think I fell out of the car in front of them all and that was that really – so much for being the flash London bloke. As ever, their hospitality was amazing. It was genuine warmth and you can get lost in that very quickly. The party went on for days. If you're into your clobber you sort of head to toe everybody to work out what they're about, and it was easy to tell that they knew their stuff. They were immersed in men's street style and they had pedigree. Anthony and Chris just shoot from the hip and do what they feel. Because they started where they did, they've got stylistic integrity. They're the real thing. They won't be swayed, no PR or strategy meeting's going to change them. Anthony has a visceral approach, an eye for clobber and how things should be perceived. Chris is your philosophising Manc, the combination works and 'it is what it is,' to quote the boys.

Clint Boon, Inspiral Carpets, XFM: Anthony and Chris Donnelly in many ways are typical of a large section of recent Mancunians. A working-class generation who, inspired by the spirit of punk rock, went on to do things themselves, in their own way, on their terms. Sometimes just for the crack, more often to survive. To have a life. Make no compromise. Take no prisoners. Some fell by the wayside. Some didn't see their dreams come true. Others, like Tony Wilson, Tom Bloxham, the Gallaghers, architect Ian Simpson – and indeed the Donnelly brothers – took that punk spirit and the spirit of this amazing city and ran with it. They donned those Mancunian wings and flew above everyone. Sometimes, in Anthony and Chris's case, even flying above the law itself.

Scott Kershaw, photographer: I showed them some pictures, then a week later I was on tour with Babyshambles. I had to go back to my mother's afterwards to recover. The pictures I ended up shooting were really successful and really got me noticed. I also nearly died at one point. We'd finished a shoot in Ibiza and I went on a bit of a bender in Amnesia. I ended up falling through a corrugated iron roof of a hotel in San Antonio and landing in a Spanish family's washroom. That's definitely one of my nine lives gone. Nothing has been like Chris and Anthony before or after. Nobody works like those two.

Cass Pennant, Casuals, author/filmmaker: Whenever our eyes meet not a lot needs to be said. It's one of those 'Yes, Mr Pennant, we've got a CV too, except what you thought you knew about us you don't and whatever you heard you heard wrong,' because until now they have never told and that's this book's unexpected twist.

Ben Drew, aka Plan B: It was when we were launching the *Strickland Banks* album back in 2010. It was the first live gig we'd done and we'd hired out the Cafe De Paris in Soho. We were filming the gig and we wanted the crowd to be dressed correctly, we didn't really want people turning up with hoods but we knew we couldn't really control that. Anthony and Chris got involved, and as people were coming through the door Chris was giving out polo shirts and other items of clothing for everyone to wear. It was compulsory that people would try and dress in that old-school Northern Soul way, and the clothes they had at the time really leant itself well to that. We managed to get the whole crowd looking like it was from a bygone era. It was exactly what we needed. From that we really struck up a relationship. I was just into their stuff and it seemed perfect. If you find a brand you actually like and they want to work with you it's always going to be a good fit.

Matthew Comer, photographer: I was shooting Wu-Tang Clan and I saw Anthony and Chris outside in this massive car. Anthony said, 'Oi, have you got any good photos of them wearing our brand?' Wu-Tang and the Donnellys seemed like a good fit. Most fashion houses will set up a proper, full-on shoot and arrange all the models to come down. These guys are just like, 'Right, we've got some T-shirts, let's take pictures of them now.' Everything's rapid. I'm going to have to quote one of the most Mancunian phrases and it definitely sums them up . . . mad for it.

David Bianchi, band manager – Carl Barat, Echo & the Bunnymen, The Libertines and more: No trip to Manchester for a gig is complete without a post-show knees-up with Anthony and Chris and the boys. They seem to know my clients before I do!

Dominique Vidalon, Reuters: It's been a rollercoaster ride for the Donnelly brothers. I met Anthony and Chris at the time of the Pete Doherty/Gio-Goi collaboration and we bonded over our common love of rock 'n' roll.

Miles Kane: I've got great memories of all my nights out with them crazy fuckers. I met Anthony and Chris when I was in The Rascals. I came off stage and somehow ended up with them in my dressing room getting right on it. Every time I see them it's always a laugh. At the Benicàssim festival 2012 they were with the Roses and it was mayhem, carried on for about three days, but you know how it is . . . what happens in Spain stays in Spain.

Eddie Prendergast, fashion icon, Present: Back in the '70s there used to be a travel documentary called *Whicker's World* presented by a bloke called Alan Whicker. He was the original jetsetter; he used to go around the world to all these exotic locations. No matter where he was, his reporting style was always very droll and nonchalant. One of his most famous lines was, 'I'm here in the West Indies where things are slightly different, where good is bad, and bad is the best you can be.' Now let me tell you a story. Years ago I was in Manchester setting up some agents for the north of England and I was talking to a friend of mine who knew Chris and Anthony very, very well. He was telling me a story where he and Chris had gone to a church function earlier in the month (not his usual environment) and afterwards they were stood around talking to the vicar, who was bemoaning the fact that the roof was collapsing and the church was falling apart. He was thousands of pounds short of being able to save the church. Several days later, the vicar rang my friend to inform him that someone had anonymously donated the funds to fix the roof. *Where good is bad, and bad is the best you can be.*

John the Duck (who has now grown into a beautiful swan): The first time I worked for Anthony and Chris was at the big Live the Dream rave. They asked me to go in to the middle of the nearby lake to hand out a flyer. I did it, going beyond the call of duty. I officially became part of the firm that day and remain a good friend.

Gordon Smart, The Sun, XFM: Manchester has a thing for producing brothers with a bit of swagger. I'm proud to call myself a friend of the most infamous the city has ever produced. My only regret is that I never knew them when they had hair. Did they ever have hair?

Stephen Graham, actor: I first heard about the Donnellys when I was a 'Raver' back in the day, when I was a teenager jumping around in a field in an unknown location. Me and my mates always thought they were an urban myth! Many, many years later, after my raving shoes and whistle had been well and truly hung up, my mate Brownie called me up out of the blue and asked me would I do a music video for a DJ [*Deadmau5*]? When I asked who was involved in production, he said, 'The Donnellys' . . . my response was, 'No fucking way, they're not real!' In the video I had a chunk of dialogue that consisted of 'The Ten Commandments of Rave'. This sums the brothers up to me – they are a cross between Robin Hood and Laurel and Hardy and for that reason alone I fucking love 'em!

James Barnes, Director, Pete Doherty In 24 Hours, MTV: As the entertainment industry grows ever more corporate and cautious, very few real rock 'n' roll characters remain. Anthony and Chris Donnelly are two such characters. Despite working with the most unpredictable star in music – Pete Doherty – and having to marry TV production with their somewhat unorthodox methods, not for a second did I think they wouldn't deliver.

Juliet Denison, Executive Producer, Pete Doherty In 24 Hours, MTV [now Head of Development, Talkback]: It's been said that 'Life is either an adventure or nothing,' but for most of us life isn't one long adventure, more a collection of incredible moments we accumulate, giving us great memories that we'll talk about forever. I worked with Anthony and Christopher on MTV's *Pete Doherty In 24 Hours*, but to describe the event in a step-by-step account simply won't do it justice. What I will say is that the making of *Pete Doherty* has taken its place in my collection of moments. The Donnelly Brothers took me on a one-off, unconventional, funny, reckless and brilliant adventure that I've never repeated and will never forget.

James Barton, Cream: Going to their first offices at Imex House was like going to a gig, music pumping out and Ian Brown hanging around. Andy Carroll and me were the main guys running clubs and playing house music in Liverpool, and the boys had connected with us. Everything is a little hazy from back then, but my overriding memory of both of them is loyalty. They are the type of people that once you become friends, it would be for life! Which is exactly how it panned out when they reconnected with me many years later for the re-launch of Gio. Anthony was telling me that he was planning to sue Giorgio Armani for using Gio for his cologne range. I was thinking, 'Fuck he's still got the biggest balls around.'

Stuart & Mark Knight, Toolroom Records: Working with your family can be tough . . . but it can also create one of the strongest forces in business. Myself and Mark can draw parallels with the relationship Chris and Anthony have, and I think this is what made it so easy to get along and work with the guys. They hustle to make things happen and are constantly ahead of the curve – something we have massive respect for at Toolroom.

Mike Pickering, DJ, M-People, A&R Sony: I've known them from the early '80s and they're not a million miles away from what they were. Still lovable scallywags, but they're clever in their business dealings. They almost know instinctively which artists are going to bring them the most publicity and who will represent the clothes the best. The thing with Doherty, for example – if you think that the only two brands that collaborated with him in the height of his fame were Gio-Goi and Dior, that really sums it up. Look at the Chase & Status video. It's absolutely brilliant. When I first saw that, I didn't realise Chris and Tracey were involved, I remember going mad saying to people, 'Who has done this, who's the director?' It was so real. The Donnellys always had a reputation for organising the best events, great attention to detail, even when they first started Gio and the T-shirts had 'Dodgin' the rain 'n' bullets' on the inside. Anthony always looks for an angle or a way to forward his business. Chris is very stylish and quite artistic, that's why it works. When they do things it's done with a lot of tenacity. They just keeping moving on, I never see them moping around . . . they're always on to something bigger and better. I was at Ibiza Rocks with Kasabian and Noel Gallagher, all of a sudden this big Range Rover flies round the corner at breakneck speed and it's Anthony and Chris with a car full of clobber. It was hilarious, they can't just arrive there like everyone else . . .

Pete Doherty: I have written a libellous account of the Donnelly / Doherty collaborations in sartorial and social history and will send it soon. Here's a taste . . . As the TK Maxx buyer hit the kerb, a Mancunian voice said, 'Just checking I still had it in me.' [*Doherty never got round to sending his full libellous account – quelle surprise!*]

Andy Rutherford, Music and Sports Industry Management: I first met Anthony and Chris in the Gio-Goi office in about 2007. One of my best memories is of a video shoot we did in an old warehouse in Manchester. Your Own Clothing sponsored the shoot. It was a great day and amazing creativity from the Donnellys.

Gordon Mason, Filmmaker **– They Call It Acid*****:*** I travelled up to Joy from London on a coach for North meets South. It was a really friendly vibe and an amazing venue. Seeing people dancing on stone walls and worshipping the sun as it rose over the hills on the Sunday morning remains a favourite party memory.

Mani, Primal Scream/The Stone Roses: Anthony and Chris have my utmost respect. They're shaking up the fashion world like we want to shake up the music world.

Mike Moran, MD Mojofuel: It was about 2004/5 when I met Anthony and Chris. It was through some fashion designer friends. I remember being told, 'Be careful. They're very connected and not to be messed with.' I had heard the urban legends about the Quality Street Gang, but on that day they were just two fellas – one was loud and brash, one was quiet and creative. Both had incredible presence. In the years since we've filmed and photographed all sorts – we've blown up cars, broken into warehouses, filmed on scooters, bikes, jeeps, whatever it took to get what we needed! I love working with them over any other fashion brand. Red tape doesn't exist, rules are meant to be broken and we won't ask for forgiveness or permission. That said, they do also have a soft side. I was lucky to be the producer for the 'I Remember' Deadmau5 video and on the day of the shoot I got a manic phone call from my wife, saying that my infant son was being flown in an ambulance to Alder Hey Children's Hospital. He was really sick, on death's door. I had to drop everything and leave. Sixty extras, twenty-five crew and a really tight deadline! The Donnelly family gave my wife and I so much support that day. The video didn't matter, and I will always remember that. These days I'm proud to say that I count them both, and the rest of their family, as very good friends.

Keith Allen, Actor: My first words to Anthony were, 'Can you untie me, please?' We have been close friends ever since.

Scully, international man of mystery: As long as I've known them, Anthony and Chris have been great fun. They have smashed the fuck out of an industry that can at times be a snotty closed shop. Good on 'em – I know as long as they are about I'll be laughing too. Anthony's relationship with money even makes me laugh; the first deal I ever did with him he said, 'We can split the readies right down the middle three ways.' It was proper Del Boy stuff. Anthony has the ability to sniff money out like a pig looking for truffles. He seems to be able to tell that I've got a deal lined up or am on the brink of doing one and wants to be involved, even though he doesn't know what it is – like a psychic Donald Trump.

Carl Barat, The Libertines: The Prince of Wales was always a beacon of debauchery. When the beacons of Camden finally dimmed, my last memory of that place was a fashion show in which my dear old buddy Pete Doherty strutted his stuff on the catwalk in Gio-Go for Anthony and Chris. It was quite a place for a while when the brothers had it. It was the same place Adam Ant used to drink – also where he shot a gun through the window. The thing I remember is they never had any ice in there.

Alan Erasmus, legend & Factory co-founder: 'It seemed like a good idea at the time.' Buona sera. AE

Kenny McGoff, Head of A&R Sony NY: I first met Anthony at Ibiza Rocks. It was when I was head of A&R at EMI Music Publishing and I had the Arctic Monkeys and Kasabian playing. I knew I had met a friend for life when we walked through the kitchens and blagged a table full of booze at Pacha. I met Chris shortly after and have been family ever since. They work hard and play hard. Every time we meet it makes me smile. The working relationship is always second to the friendship. I've always loved that. When my brother took ill and we needed to get him into an emergency hospital, the guys were the first to put their hand in their pockets, and that is something I will never forget.

Karl Nielson, Director AEI Media: There are two key aspects to Anthony and Chris's success. The first is that they are men of their word; if they say they are going to do something then that is that, final, they deliver. The other, and probably the reason for their longevity, is that they remain current because they care, and are always working with the latest acts destined for big things.

Dean Skarratt (Will Not Be Televised) Manchester's No.1 Hip Hop promoter: The only men I simultaneously fear working with yet can't avoid . . . Chris and Anthony Donnelly – Don 1 & 2

Peter Hook, New Order/Joy Division: The Donnellys are a HUGE part of Manchester's history. If this book contains ANY of the stories I know about Chris and Anthony, it will be a very entertaining read! These two rascals are a big part of what I, and the world, love about Madchester's music and fashion!

Colin O'Toole, filmmaker: Anthony and Chris have a genuine interest in things and a unique way of going about things. They keep reinventing themselves and their drive and enthusiasm doesn't ever seem to waver. They have that uncanny knack of being in the right place at the right time. They worked with Deadmau5 before anyone knew who Deadmau5 was, and a couple of years later he was the biggest electronic artist on the planet. At the time I just thought, 'What? This kid's a joke, he's got this stupid mouse head on,' and Chris convinced me he was going to be this big DJ and artist and it turned out to be true. Some of the schemes you think, 'Why are they interested in that' and then it turns out to be massive. It's really interesting to watch.

Bez, Happy Mondays: I've known Anthony and Chris for over twenty-five years. The explosion of Acid House brought loads of different people together and there were a lot of lads going out in town from different areas. We all came together through the love of dancing, believe it or not. Chris and Anthony are proper characters. The most amazing thing about them is where they are now, proper entrepreneurs. It just goes to show what you can achieve with a lot of hard work. You can come from nothing and build something important that's relevant to the rest of the world. As kids growing up we were all into our fashion – they came along and had such a good understanding of the market, the lads and where we were all coming from, that they were able to capitalise on it early on to make the clothes that were relevant for the time.

Leo Stanley, Identity: . . . AND ON THE SIXTH DAY, GOD CREATED MANchester (. . . and then Chris & Anthony Donnelly). Thanks for twenty-five years of mayhem, love and dance. Nice one!

Matthew Greenhalgh, screenwriter,* Control *and* Look of Love*: I was on the scene in '88/'89 so I'd heard of the Donnelly brothers – but only being sixteen I was never part of the cool crew in The Hacienda which they definitely were with the Mondays. So we share that mutual experience of those ecstatic years that lasted 'til about summer 1990. Those years changed our l ives – I wouldn't be a writer if they hadn't have happened. We got lucky that that was our youth culture – especially when you consider all this corporate fucked up festival shit that kids get rammed down their necks today. When I first saw their Gio-Goi stuff I was like, 'Gimme some of that,' it was like our own label for Manchester. They fitted perfectly, as in baggy and vibrant – I had one of those sweatshirts with 'Dodgin' the rain 'n' the bullets' on and never had it off my back. We met properly and became friends a few years back when I heard they were behind the 'Blind Faith' video for Chase & Status that Dan Wolfe directed. I've got a film script with a similar theme that I wrote in the late '90s and was interested in what they thought. So I gave them the spiel: story lines, character arcs, plot twists, cast suggestions . . . and at then end of laying it on thick I looked at them both for a reaction. I was trying to read them but both were poker-faced, then Chris went, 'So . . . does that mean you want some dough?' I cracked up – because he was right. When I chat with Chris and Anthony they remind me why I've never felt comfortable in London.

Jon McClure, Reverend and The Makers: Well there's an old quote, isn't there? 'If you're all right with them, they'll be all right with you.' This definitely applies to the Donnellys. Their whole life reads like a movie script. They are old school men's men.

Pat Carroll, Central Station: We met Anthony and Chris in the late '80s when we were working on all the Happy Mondays and Factory artwork – we got on like a 'negligee' on fire (this will make sense in a bit). They were fucking hilarious and proper ambitious. Pretty much straight away we started talking about setting something up together . . . which ended up being Gio-Goi. We started doing Tee's, got the right people wearing 'em and created an instant myth – with everybody talking about a clothing company that hadn't made any clothes. Eventually we were ready to launch at London Fashion Week. We wanted to make a statement, so we decided to make the show an art installation on a massive scale. The only problem was we needed a space big enough to create it in. Anthony and Chris knew about this old, abandoned church on the edge of town. Pitch black – fucking candles and everything. We brought the paint and boom box, they supplied the fizzy drinks and the Colombian party food. We created these giant paint bombs and ended up dragging each other about in bin liners like human paintbrushes. It was like a Jackson Pollock, acid-fuelled, cultish, sacrificial ritual that makes the end of the film *Kill List* look normal.

One of our other 'business' meetings started out in Dry Bar . . . we moved on to The Hacienda, while Anthony jibbed back to the hotel he was staying at, where he accidently set fire to his wife's negligee and burnt it off her! Anyway, no harm done, and Anthony turns up at The Hacienda in time for last orders and to offer us a lift home – his mate was driving. So we were halfway home doing 120mph, running every red light, when he tells us the mate who's driving has dropped fifteen window panes!

Shaun Ryder, Happy Mondays: I was at one of the Donnellys' legendary parties . . . I said, 'Why not have a go? You know what we like to wear.' The rest is history.

Adrian Hunter, Pete Doherty manager: I first met Anthony and Chris at the Birmingham Academy on a Babyshambles tour when they had come along to shoot Peter for a Gio-Goi campaign. They drove past the tour bus and straight to the top of the multi-storey car park. This perplexed me a little until I realised that they simply didn't know where they were going. They were running Gio-Goi and I was managing Babyshambles. Peter was the face of Gio-Goi so I became involved with them professionally. Obviously after all the business was over we have kept in touch socially – always good to see the boys. Criminal history?!?!? Is there something I should know about?

Keith Dyson, solicitor: Anthony and Christopher have been arrested by the police on several occasions and have used me as their solicitor. I have been involved with numerous high-profile court cases like the one against the Donnelly brothers. I also acted for Curtis Warren at the time he was the UK's and Interpol's number one target. Curtis was eventually arrested in Holland and reputed to be worth £145 million, appearing in *The Times*' 'Rich List'. I thought that the 'Operation Bluebell' case against Anthony and Chris was an improper use of police powers and as such was an abuse of the courts process – the police targeted Anthony and Chris on a speculative basis. They posed as wealthy businessmen with cash to spend.

Curtis Warren, entrepreneur: A great book by the Donnellys showing what life was like in northern citities after years of government neglect and indifference in Thatcher's Britain.

PROLOGUE

'STYLE PAIR ACCUSED IN DRUG RAID'
Manchester Evening News – front cover splash
Thursday, 6 October 1994

Two fashion gurus were due in court this afternoon following the seizure of Ecstasy, heroin and guns by armed police, who raided several homes. Brothers Anthony and Christopher Donnelly, bosses of trendsetting Gio-Goi at Ardwick Green, Manchester, were charged with drug offences last night. The pair, billed as the UK's answer to Dior and Yves St Laurent, joined top designers at a Paris exhibition last month.

Their designer gear is so highly rated it is worn on tour by top pop bands including Happy Mondays. They have been described as the Sex Pistols of the fashion world, 'radical and magical'.

They splattered paint over their stand at Earls Court and threw a party for friends like Happy Mondays and Stone Roses. The brothers organised the first rave parties in Manchester in the late '80s and made top contacts in the world of music.

They were held in custody last night after being charged by serious crime squad detectives who raided several homes in Manchester yesterday.

Anthony Donnelly, 29, a company managing director of —— — was charged with conspiracy to supply drugs. Christopher Donnelly, 26, of ——— was charged with conspiracy to supply drugs. The brothers' father, Arthur Donnelly, 52, a scrap dealer, from ——— faces six charges of conspiracy to supply drugs. Michael Carpenter, 40, a builder, of ——— was charged with conspiracy to supply and possession of drugs. Jonathan Faulkner, 20, of ——— was charged with conspiracy to supply drugs and supplying diazepam.

A police officer from Stockport was released on police bail after detectives questioned him. He was facing possible suspension from duty today and was consulting lawyers. An accountant from Worsley was also bailed after questioning by detectives.

1
EXPECT THE UNEXPECTED

Anthony Donnelly: If it was not for our dad, Arthur, nobody would know who Chris and me were.

Arthur Donnelly: When I was growing up in Wythenshawe, we had no money. As a kid I used to go with a pram down the railway lines, collecting coal for the fire. We killed chickens and pinched potatoes out of the fields. We'd rob the milkman, otherwise we'd have no milk. My dad, James, was a bricklayer, a good one, a very hard-working man, but he was a drunk. My mother, Ellen, was a bit psychotic. She was religious, a member of the Mother's Union [*international Christian charity*], and would clean the church for free. She put three of us, my two brothers, Johnny and Jimmy, and me, away in St Joseph's in Patricroft, Salford [*a home for orphans and children under the age of twelve whose parents could not look after them*]. We were sent there when I was about seven, Jimmy was a year older and our Johnny was about three.

St Joseph's was not a nice place. I had my first fight in there. I saw one of the nuns who ran the place give the other lad the cane and then kick him down the stairs. I thought I was in there for months and months and months, but I was only in several weeks. The nuns would beat us. There were beatings all the time. The dining room was a long, narrow place in the basement and if you didn't eat your dinner, they'd put the pudding on top.

My family life was no good. My father was drunk every night. My mother was a good cook, good housekeeper, everything very clean, but she was nasty. She was always rowing at home. There were always broken windows, blood everywhere and smashed furniture. That's how I was fetched up – so when it came to it, I looked after my family.

Anthony: We're all originally from Ireland. What we were told was there were forty of the family who left Ireland and settled in Liverpool. One of them killed somebody in a pub fight and then they dispersed all over the country. Some went to Australia. The only relatives we know, or are hands on with, are the ones who settled in Manchester. Our dad's dad, James, had helped build Wythenshawe when it was first put up in the 1920s. It was a big housing estate on the south side of Manchester, supposed to alleviate inner city squalor. That's where my dad grew up in the '40s and '50s.

Arthur: I was away *all* the time when I was young, approved school, borstal and prison. It was Jimmy, Johnny and me who brought the police to the door. Before that the family had never had anything to do with the police. I was a Teddy Boy. They put me in borstal for three years for a load of lead – three years for lead that wasn't even stolen! I got put away in approved school for three years for stealing a bottle of lemonade from a café – from a back yard. I did one job breaking into Brookes Biscuits. We got a load of chocolate and fed the pigs. We nicked blocks of chocolate as big as a table – we couldn't eat it all. We used to thieve all the time. Yes, we were villains – always in trouble. I was put in Strangeways [*prison*]. They used to hang people there back then and I used to clean the cell they were in the night before they were hanged for a bit of extra duff [*pudding*].

Arthur's partner in crime was often 'Little' Albert Gibbons. He was the nephew of the well-respected Davies brothers, 'Ginger' and Georgie – young men who drove Bentleys and had interests that included car dealing, haulage and pubs. Little Albert was also sometimes known as 'Albert the Blade'. In 1965, he stabbed to death Pat Fallon, a doorman at Manchester's Stork club, in a fish & chip shop.

Arthur: Georgie Davies did ten years for shooting a policeman and when he came out I was with Albert Gibbons. I was eighteen. It was the guys younger than the Davies brothers who I knocked around with. Albert was only small and he always had big knives. I was good with a knife myself – and the axe. I never missed. Albert and me worked on the horse and carts as Rag and Bone men. We used to collect dunnage, good second-hand clothes. I used to go on Smithfields market, in the city centre, and sell them. There was a firm called Cohen's and all they bought was rags by the tonne – cottons and wools. It was my idea to sort out the good clothes and take it on the market and sell it. So we had a garage full of clobber in Whalley Range. That was the 'Rag Trade'. We took it one step further and we got nicked. It was a new idea to go round door to door, put a plastic bag out and say you were collecting for the Benevolent Fund. 'Any old clothes, please give to the blind' or whatever. It was when I was working on the market that I met June.

June Donnelly: I was born and bred in Ardwick [*inner city Manchester*] in a two up, two down with a toilet in the back yard. It was a very happy place to grow up. I met Arthur at the Plaza dancehall when I was sixteen. He was very shy and very particular about his clothes. He used to get his suits, shirts and shoes made by an Italian tailor. I set my sights on him. They were Wythenshawe and we were Ardwick. I got pregnant [*with Tracey*] and then we got married. We had a house in Ardwick at first, with all my family and cousins. We were very close knit until the slum clearance separated us all.

Arthur: We always got in everywhere free, all the clubs. Never paid. Be it Ginger or Georgie, the older fellas who were the governors then, we always knew someone to get us in. It was a well-known thing – any trouble in the clubs the lads would sort it out. They weren't on the doors. They had that much respect that club owners rang them up to say someone has had a go at the club. Then they'd go sort it out for them. They'd look after everybody. There was no trouble in the clubs, all taken care for, one big happy family . . . right through the '70s as well. But June and me had no money when we lived in Ardwick. I used to go to town and steal gear. Little Albert and me went out one day, went in a coffee bar and walked out with the jukebox – in broad daylight.

In the '60s, Jimmy, Johnny and me started a company together: Donnelly Steel Erection Company. We worked for ourselves putting up steelwork. In the beginning we'd go working away with no money and you'd try and borrow a car and steal petrol. The business grew and we got one job at Stafford Airbase that would be worth £5 million in today's money. June worked in the office at one point. We did all Comet Discount warehouses, ICI and Cammell Laird Shipyard. We were travelling and fighting all over the county, in pubs and clubs. I worked in a coalmine in Barnsley. I slept in the coalmine. Jimmy also had a construction firm, doing houses in Stockport. I'd put in the sewers and build the interior walls. We knew then, at that young age, that the country was fucked. We knew what the situation was in this world: that the working class was trodden on and all the fuckers in the Government were robbing everyone and getting away with it. When we did the steel erecting we used to meet people all over the country and give them back handers – one or two thousand pounds. How else do you think we got the work? We used to get false Union cards . . . how else could Jimmy and I go in ICI working on a big job?

Arthur and June's second child, Anthony, was born in February 1965. He was born in June's mum's house, the house she had grown up in, on Carmen Street in Ardwick. June was pregnant with Christopher when the family left Ardwick and moved to Wythenshawe – the council estate Arthur had grown up on – in 1968. Christopher was born in May 1968 at the same Manchester city centre hospital as his sister Tracey, St Mary's on the corner of Oxford Road and Whitworth Street near the future site of The Hacienda. The post-World War Two slum clearances of inner city Manchester, places such as Ardwick, saw Wythenshawe grow to be the largest housing estate in Europe. By the late '60s, the estate had been split into nine named areas and covered eleven square miles, with an estimated population of 70,000. Unfortunately, in 1970, shortly after moving to Wythenshawe, Arthur was sent to Walton Jail [now HM Prison Liverpool] for two and half years for conspiracy to commit robbery – involving a jewellery salesman and Albert Gibbons.

Anthony: At home, whilst my dad was away, we went to bed with candles – we could not afford the electric. Either that or there were strikes. Mum had three children under five to look after. The DHSS paid for Tracey and me to go on holiday to Dr Garrett's Memorial Home in Conway [*north coast of Wales*] for six weeks. It was supposed to take the pressure away from the single parent. My mum only let us go on the understanding that me and Tracey would not be split up but that was the first thing that happened to us on arrival. They put me in a room with a kid with a glass eye. Every night he would take it out and leave it on the side. It would stare at me all night. As soon as he was asleep I was out of bed and ransacking the crisp box. I knew from an early age that I wanted stuff. I felt I had to use my imagination and my hands to get it.

My dad's dad, James, died when I was very young, before Chris was born, and we never got on too well with Nana Ellen, my dad's mum. My actual earliest recollection is of Chris being born. I ran in the street shouting that I had a baby brother. When we moved to Benchill [*one of the nine areas of Wythenshawe*] we lived in a three-bed council house, the corner plot, on Benchill Road. We thought Wythenshawe was a beautiful place, the bollocks, surrounded by lovely green fields. Back then I believe there was only a small network of criminals in Manchester operating.

On my mum's side, our granddad, George, was a labourer. It was our Grandma Frances on my mum's side that helped raise us when my dad was in the nick and all through when we were kids. I was very, very close to her. She was a seamstress. Later, when I got into punk through our Tracey, I asked her to make me a mohair jumper. If you had an electric blue mohair jumper you were somebody. It came back as an old fisherman's Aran jumper – the correct style but wrong type of wool. I also asked her to make me a straight-legged pair of trousers that came back making me look like I played polo – tight at the bottom and baggy at the top. Although she had a job in the fashion industry it didn't shine through. We loved her, though.

The night before my dad got out of prison, my mum decorated the house from top to bottom. She bought new clothes for me and Chris and Tracey. I had braces on and a pair of short pants. My dad screeched up outside the house in a Ford Corsair with all his boys inside. He gave me ten pence and took me to the shops. I was proud as punch walking with my dad to the shops. I was six and everyone on the estate had a dad except us. He'd made a gypsy caravan out of matches in jail. That was in the house for a long time.

Christopher: People were dispersing from Ardwick because they were regenerating the whole area. They sent almost everyone, the overspill, to Wythenshawe. It was the Promised Land at the time . . . it was all green, lots of grass and trees, farmland. My mum said she had never seen anything like it.

We were very close to our grandma. When they knocked the houses down in Ardwick she moved to Hattersley [*ten miles east of the city centre and, like Wythenshawe, another overspill council estate*]. We used to go up there and stay with her. She was like a proper grandma. There was a lot of love there. She remarried after George died. Her new husband, Jack, was a nice fella. Grandma was funny. She'd come to all the family parties and body pop or moonwalk. She was ninety-one when she died. She used to smoke and drink Gold Labels [*a very strong barley wine beer up to 12% alcohol*]. For Christmas I'd buy her a crate of Gold Label and a bottle of whiskey.

My mum had a bleached-blonde beehive. She's from a 100 per cent hard-working family. Her brother and sister are the most strait-laced, normal people. We have always been close to my aunty Norma and her husband, Uncle Alan, and Uncle Ray and his wife, Aunty Sylvia. Sadly my aunt Sylvia and uncle Alan have passed on.

My dad is the middle child of seven, four sisters and two brothers. His brothers Jimmy and Johnny and their families have always been a big part of our lives. My mum's life changed when she met my dad, who was a complete rogue.

Albert Gibbons lived just up the road from us in Wythenshawe. He was always at our house. He was a top geezer.

June: Their dad was back but things changed – the routine changed. Chris used to sleep with me every night while Arthur was away. The day his dad came home he decided to sleep with Tracey and Anthony. He was only young, but it was his own decision. Arthur went to work and worked away most of the time. He is a very hard-working man. While working at Clarks [*putting in steel shelving*] he brought a big bagful of shoes home. Every shoe was a left shoe. I kept them because maybe I thought we'd get the right ones some day.

Tracey Donnelly: We used to have a cubbyhole under the stairs. My dad came home one night with a load of shoes and they got put in the cubbyhole. After about a day I realised they were all left feet. And I used to sit in there with one shoe on that I really liked, thinking, 'I wish I had the other.'

Our dad would surprise us. When he worked away doing the steel erecting he'd come back with posters and albums. You always knew you were going to get something when he came back. Our dad's a workaholic, that's his thing. He always provided.

Arthur opened his first scrapyard – Donnelly Auto Spares – in the early '70s in Ancoats, on Ancoats Lane, a former thriving industrial area of inner city Manchester gone to seed. It was a culturally rich but stubbornly poor area – sometimes known as 'Little Italy'. Squatting on derelict land, Arthur ran the Ancoats Lane scrapyard successfully – becoming an expert on motor engines. There were also a number of car pitches nearby run by friends, and the area became a strong powerbase for this clique.

Arthur: My first scrapyard was in Ancoats, then I had one on Hyde Road [*Ardwick*] and then I wound up with one back in Ancoats, on Hoyle Street. The one on Hyde Road I camped on the site for seven years. At the start, I gave two grand to a couple of kids to fuck off. There was a lump of land across the way with four or five cranes parked up. I fenced off the land so it was ours and I took the engines out of the cranes – Gardner Engines worth about three grand. In the end the kid who owned the cranes paid us ten grand to move his cranes off the land.

Then I started ripping all the bushes out of the yard and building a wall. I was putting a footing in when this kid walked up with a clipboard. He said, 'I'm from the bank.' I said, 'Lovely. What you doing? Selling insurance?' He said, 'We own this land. Do you want to buy it?' I said, 'How much is it?' It was a lot of money, thirty grand, something like that – so I said I'd think about it. Then I moved around the corner and got someone to tip three or four hundred tonne of bricks and shit on this land. The bank rang me up again and said, 'Do you want to buy it?' I said, 'Have you seen the state of it down there?' They said, 'Well, what would you give for it?' I bought it for thirteen grand. The day I moved back on there, I got the machines and pushed the mountain of shit across the road onto the croft next door. When you see an opportunity – take it.

Anthony: We grew up around scrapyards and car pitches. We were walking down the road in Ancoats one day and we found a pigeon with a sore wing. My dad wasn't in the yard so we took it to the bloke next door who wears three ties because he can't make his mind up which one to wear. We asked him if he could fix the pigeon. He's sat with a dirty old hat, a sheepskin jacket, just like Arthur Daley, next to an old steel bucket with holes in with flames coming through the holes. He said he could fix it, then took the pigeon off us, wrang its neck, pulled its head clean off and threw the body in the bucket, spitting blood out. That's what we grew up with. Always expect the unexpected.

We lived at 5A Benchill Road back then until we moved next door to 5 Benchill Road. Number five was a bigger house. The family who lived there was involved in a house swap with someone – and we sort of jumped in the middle of that. We sent the people moving to number five to our old house. You'd go home at night and there'd be five big boxes of biscuits in the kitchen from somewhere or other – so you'd be the kid at school the next day selling fifty Penguins or Jaffa Cakes. Or there might be 800 *Jaws* T-shirts in the front room.

Christopher: My dad had been to approved school – he didn't have much growing up and was trying to make something out of nothing. When we were very young there wasn't a load of money. It wasn't until my dad developed his business through the scrap and the engines that we started to see money. My dad used to buy engines for reconditioning and send them all over the world. We lived on the edge of the estate next to what is now a motorway, the M56 – at the time it was just fields. There were always stacks of tyres and engines in the garden. There was a string of nice cars and wagons full with oily engines, dripping oil onto the road. We were the family no one wanted to talk to unless you knew us. Even the police – when they came to our house, they'd throw stones at the door or window. Or they'd come down the path, knock on the door and then run back to the gate. They were frightened to death of us. My dad would run out with a spade and threaten them. We saw all that when we were very young. The police wouldn't leave my dad alone. We wondered why.

My first experience of the police was when I was in the infants in Benchill primary school. There were uniformed police and detectives stood outside the classroom with the head teacher. I knew they'd come for me. The head teacher shouted me out of the class and told me I had to go with these men. I went home and my dad was handcuffed. One of the police said to me, 'Right, Christopher, can you tell us where the gun is?' I knew then, right then at that very moment, that we were different – I was different to everyone else in the class. And I knew even then, at that early age, not to tell them anything. There'd been a post office robbery and my dad matched the description of the culprit. I looked at my dad and he said, 'Go get the gun.' So I got the gun. I knew where it was hid. There were always lots of guns about the house. They may not have worked and some may have been antiques. My dad would come home with random things. He'd come home with big chains of bullets or German helmets from the war – I had a massive collection of World War Two helmets and gas masks.

Anthony: There was a real gun – a sawn-off shotgun. We watched someone hiding it and they had not seen us. I've always been fascinated with guns. My cousin and I went to a place next to my dad's yard and lifted up the boarding where it was hidden, moved a few stones and it was there in a plastic bag. We were test firing it through a piece of wood and we hit the scrapyard dog in the arse. We ran off leaving the dog with an arsehole like a blood orange.

At the scrapyard me and Chris used to burn copper wire out of the cars for our spends; rip the wire out of the dashboard, put it in a bucket on fire with holes in the side, melt all the plastic off, wait for it to cool down, chuck the copper in a wheel barrow, walk it to Silverman's, tip it onto the weighing scales and the geezer would say there's three quid or a tenner or whatever it was.

I was in the scrapyard one day trying to impress my dad and a guy came in saying he'd left his tools in the boot of a car that was going to scrap. I put my hand up and said I knew where his tools were. I made this bloke climb six cars high and forty cars along. To me it was an adventure. When I got there, I opened the boot and there was nothing in it apart from a spider jack. This geezer called me a wanker. I went back to the office where my dad and all his mates were with their steel toe-cap boots on, all covered in oil, and I told them what the man had called me. By this time the bloke had walked out of my dad's scrapyard and into my uncle's car pitch next door – he sold second-hand sports cars. They kicked him to fuck, kicked him through a wire fence and they were screaming, 'Say sorry to the lad!' I had to stand there and watch them leather him. I was made to watch and in the end I actually asked them to stop.

Christopher: We were allowed to drive cars at the yard. We used to drive a car forward and backward, smashing into other cars. On the six-weeks holiday, if we weren't going away we'd spend most of our time in the scrapyard. I'd smash every mirror in there. My dad would come home on occasions and we used to play murder in the dark with a knife or 'split the kipper'. He's an expert knife-thrower and he'd throw the knife at us. You'd start off with your feet together, throw the knife on the floor, then put your foot to the knife; the other person gets the knife and throws it further away from your feet. The first one to fall over or get the knife through their feet would have their 'kipper split'. Another one he used to do was get your hand on the table and stab between your fingers. It might sound a psychotic thing to play with your kids. I'm sure there was a minor bit of safety somewhere but not that we could see.

None of our pals' families had money like us, we'd come home and there'd be bags of cash on the side, always bundles of cash. My pals would come around and they'd be just looking at it like, 'What the fuck?!' My dad was unpredictable. He would turn up at school, come into the classroom, pull all us kids out and take us to an outdoor pool at the Galleon in East Didsbury. We'd have a great day. Or he'd come home and say, 'Right, we're going on holiday' and that was us – we were gone. 'Pack your bags, we're going on holiday now.'

He brought a fox home for a pet one time. We were on holiday in Anglesey once and we had to dump the car. Someone turned up with a new car. We had to book into different digs. That was our family holiday. We were different and we lived differently.

Arthur: These kids grew up around scrap and the people coming to see me – all the main people in Manchester. And they notice, don't they? They get wider, don't they? I was over at the scrapyard and I'm watching our Jimmy trying to sell this car, he's desperate for money. There's a kid there looking at the motor and he's at it, I can see his finger going. So I walked over and I went, 'Fuck off,' and hit him. He went down. Our Jimmy had a petrol can and he battered him with a petrol can. The kids have seen me fight a few times. Terrible when you think about it. That's how we lived. You hired a car for a day and disappeared for month. We used to get a nice car to go on holiday in. Then the police would be looking for it. We did that a few times. I would buy and sell anything.

June: The scrapyard was always full of characters. They used to come to the house as well. There was Jimmy Wingy – he weighed twenty-five stone. They all had a nickname – Johnny Two Ties, Bill the Clutch, Dummy or Cadbury. There were always American cars in my driveway, flying machines. Arthur was and is his own person. As far as I'm concerned, he's working – he's doing his business, but obviously got other involvements.

Anthony was a very happy, loving kid. You could hear him coming home from school: he would sing all the way home. He'd sit in the toilet singing, he was always singing. Then he just went off. He was a lot of hassle.

Chris was headstrong. Anthony was more emotional. Tracey was the thinker. When Anthony started getting in trouble, Arthur would murder him. He threw him out. Anthony ran away. But he did do some naughty things. I don't know why. And then he'd be in public phone boxes phoning me up, or he'd write me little notes, 'Sorry Mum, couldn't help it.' He was a mixed bag.

One time we went to Wythenshawe market and Anthony wanted these black and white motorbike gloves. I told him no. He stole the gloves. I found out later he had a big hole outside my house in a tree and he had all his loot in there. I tried and tried. But I was not in full control.

The first thing with Anthony and the police was trespassing. We had the railway police round. I tried to keep the boys safe and right, but it didn't always work. I did most of it on my own. Arthur was away a lot. I was very young, very naive. I did the best I could.

Looking back you think, 'Why didn't I do this or that for them?' They were all bright kids. Chris was more creative. Anthony was sporty, but he was a bugger. Chris was a bugger, but Anthony was more out with it. You knew what you were up against with Anthony. Chris was quite good but he probably did his own thing. Anthony's always had that funny streak. He is his father's son.

At the back of ours, on the industrial estate, they had the Mr Kipling factory. Everybody used to be there, robbing it every night. There were Kipling cakes all round the estate. There were lots of factories in the area: Paxo was another – so there'd be plenty of stuffing going about at Christmas. But that was just part and parcel of living there. It creeps up on you and it just becomes the norm. There always seemed to be people moving furniture from house to house, beds strapped to roof racks, chairs on top of prams, somebody always needed it.

Anthony: Mr Kipling would get robbed every night and you'd always find someone else's boxes of cakes in what we called 'scallywag canyon'. We'd go to the crisp factory in Sharston [*Wythenshawe*] where they'd throw the burst packets of crisps in a skip. Someone would drive past and three heads would pop up from the skip. You don't think at the time, but that's pretty bad eating out of a skip. One day a Wall's bacon wagon tipped over round the corner and the cab landed on the driver and killed him. He's under the cab dead, the police are on the scene but because it had skidded for 300 yards there's all pork joints and packs of bacon all over the road. Women from the estate were running there with trolleys and bags. No one cared about the driver. The estate smelled lovely of bacon for a week afterwards – or was that the local police station?

I was constantly playing pool at the [*estate*] youth club. I was going in the youth club four years before you were allowed in. You had to be eleven to get in. I was seven. So whenever I went out with my dad I was always playing pool for money – I'd tell my dad, 'Make me play.' The money was mine to keep if I won. I had my own cue. I was a very determined child. We were the 'sons of'. We were getting noticed on the estate as 'his boys'. My first charge sheet was walking up the railway line throwing stones through people's greenhouses. Vandalism. Petty crime. With the gloves, Mum said, 'No you can't have them' because she wanted to keep me in check. So I stole three pairs. That was just how I was. No one was telling me I wasn't having something.

Christopher: 'Scallywag canyon' would take you from Sharston right through to Northenden [*Wythenshawe*] past all the industrial estates. There was Vimto, Paxo, Smith's Crisps and Mr Kipling. I used to go down to Kipling robbing it all the time as a kid. I took it a step further. We'd sneak past the security guards and go into the factory. I'd come home with a shopping trolley full of cakes. It was a strange way to grow up. We were very independent kids.

The local pub was called the Anvil. We'd climb over the back of the pub wall and nick the old soda bottles. They'd give you two pence if you brought them back, so we'd steal them and sell them back. We'd then go and buy sweets from Flanny's.

Our dad was grafting hard. He bought me a motorbike when I

was six or seven and my mum kicked right off. It used to run on a car battery, big heavy thing it was. The steering was shite and I smashed straight into the school gates. I was full of cuts. Mum wouldn't let me have a motorbike after that, but my dad bought me another one – we had to keep it in secret. But my scariest moments as a kid were when my dad kicked off.

Anthony: I was robbing tins of beans and bread out of the house and feeding my pal Colin, who lived six or seven doors up. He was living with his granddad and his uncle and he didn't have anything. Talk about poor: their dog – a huge monster – used to shit all over the house. I'd go round and there were old turds laying about with mould growing on them. At Christmas me and Chris used to wrap our old presents up and give them to Colin. I used to go fishing with him. One time we saw some kids who had Mitchell 300 reels that cost twelve quid. So we took all the fishing gear off them. We got caught and charged with robbery. I got a fine but Colin was put in care because of his situation at home.

I started taking my mum's rent – finding the money in the pot. Then it escalated: pinching from the purse, the jar for the meter. It wasn't bad. It was fun. With the rent money I took the whole street to the local shopping centre and bought everyone pudding, chips and gravy. I robbed one of the neighbours. The son had a Sovereign ring I wanted. It was an older boy, and I think he stole it off one of the other lads. He robbed us, we robbed him and we robbed his bike as well. I couldn't be told no. I was locked in the house for a week – in my room with my food passed in.

Arthur: This is Anthony. At that time I was smoking a pipe and he came in and said, 'The fella across the road said he'll stuff that pipe down your throat and kick your arse. You've got to do something.' So I said, 'All right, come on son, come with me.' We cut through my garden and confronted this guy. 'You're going to stuff this pipe down me throat, are you?' He said, 'Art, honestly, I didn't say nothing at all.' I've thought, 'Thank fuck for that' because he was a big fella. But that was Anthony – he made it up. That sums him up in a nutshell.

Another time he burst a blood vessel in his nose and was smearing blood all over house. I came in and didn't know what the hell was going on. I thought somebody had been killed. To look at them, you've never seen three more beautiful kids and Anthony could be a lovely kid but he was a one-off. If you took him to the cinema he'd turn round looking at people instead of the film, same at the football, watching the crowd not the game. But you couldn't control him. And I was always a snapper. I've chased after them firing a shotgun in the air. I always go off at a tangent. I've always been a bit of a nutter. It was when you got married and had children that you realised your own dad wasn't as bad as he was painted.

Tracey: Even though our dad was starting to earn good money now, we were, and are, a working-class family; the only difference was we had a video, we had this, and we had that. In some houses something goes on and they say, 'Ooh, guess what?' But in our house, there's already another event that has happened – there's never a dull moment. There was all sorts going on. At about ten, eleven, I joined the church choir and that was my way of rebelling because I used to go to these happy clappy events at the Free Trade Hall. On a Sunday I'd go to church. I was up and gone and I used to come back and they'd all be in bed.

Our dad worked away for most of our childhood – he could be gone for two to three weeks at a time. So if we were up to no good or being cheeky, our mum would threaten us with telling him when he returned home. Very rarely did she tell him, as she couldn't cope with the aftermath. I think due to our dad's own childhood he didn't really know how to discipline so it would go from nought to 100 in seconds. That's probably why the boys got away with a lot.

Arthur: I used to put my money on the mantelpiece and they'd all help themselves. They had fortunes. It was straight cash – it wasn't hooky cash. I'd live like a gypsy for weeks on end. I'd pull up in a wagon and buy engines from scrapyards all over the country. I'd travel through the night, get there at eight in the morning, and have my burning gear, my tools, my diesel and start cutting engines out. I lived in the wagon. I washed in rivers. I lived in yards sometimes if there was money to be earned. Every morning, before half ten I'd have earned two hundred and fifty quid – go to a scrapyard, get under a van, take the gearbox off – hundred and eighty quid! That's what I used to do. We had a scrapyard in the Gorbals, Glasgow. I was buying British Leyland gold seal engines for reconditioning. I'd earn two grand in a day: exporting engines all over the world. Every week I'd send a forty-foot trailer down to Manchester.

As kids they knew what an onion bhaji was when every other kid in Wythenshawe had no idea. They used to eat in Chinese and Indian restaurants when I came home. They had the best food, the best gear. While I was living like a tinker, they were right as rain. They were well looked after if you compared them to the other kids on the estate. I bought them a motorised go-kart. They had everything. If I could afford it, they could have it.

Anthony: If there was a school trip and it was a hundred quid most kids would bring in 50p a week until it was paid off. I'd come in with the hundred, in cash, the next day and just pay it. We were always different. We had a VHS, one of the earliest ones, five or six years before anyone on the estate. My dad would come home from the scrapyard with tens of thousands of

Arthur and June on their wedding day, 24 August 1963.

Brothers Johnny and Arthur with his best mate, Albert. Looking sharp in their tailor-made suits.

5A Benchill Rd, Wythenshawe, 1968:
Anthony and Tracey meeting baby Chris.

Anthony, June and Tracey at Caernarfon Castle in Wales, 1970.

Anthony, Chris and Tracey with their grandma Julia Frances. Arthur was locked up but the kids were always well dressed for Whit week at their grandma's.

Anthony, Arthur and Tracey, 1970.

Anthony, Arthur, Chris and Tracey at London Zoo. Another holiday, another dumped car.

Chris on Christmas Day 1978. Finally got his saxophone like Zoot from the Muppets in his new Man U kit.

At the house of family friends, the Withers, where the Donnelly kids would often turn up after a police tip-off. Anthony (far left), Chris front row (far left) and Tracey (far right).

Portrait of Arthur drawn by Anthony, aged 7, while Arthur was in prison.

On holiday in Benidorm, 1977. Chris, Nuño, Anthony and Eduardo, the two Portuguese boys who Chris once claimed were behind the name Gio-Goi.

Arthur, Anthony and Chris.

Arthur, Tracey, Chris and Anthony on their first holiday abroad – Benidorm 1977.

5 Benchill Road, 1978: Anthony, June, Chris and Tracey all sporting flick haircuts.

Stephen Yates and Chris, wearing a sheepskin coat, around the time Chris started following Anthony into crime.

Tracey's prized ticket.

Anthony, Chris and Tracey on holiday in Spain. Anthony wearing his Sex Pistols T-shirt.

Family holiday in Corfu where Anthony robbed the cash box in a shop and loaned his dad, Arthur, some holiday money.

Anthony, aged 21, and John Molloy before they left for Europe where they had to escape over the border twice. Once after rifling a safe in France and again after being arrested for an assault on a police officer in Gibraltar.

Chris, aged 13, and Anthony, 16, at Benchill Road.

1986, Gibraltar, Inter-Rail trip. Fitz, Anthony, Chris, John, Stephen, Sean, Beano, Malley on the beach. Chris and Anthony treating the lads with the money they'd just had off in France.

Chris with the 'Smugglers' van on the ill-fated trip to Wembley with Anthony that saw 17-20 of the boys nicked in Coventry for rioting in a pub, resulting in front page headlines and the lads being escorted out of Coventry by a convoy of police.

Tracey, aged 21, at Swing in 1984. Swing was the hairdresser's underneath the stage, in the basement of The Hacienda.

Jason and Chris in the Firbank pub.

Anthony in Swing with Stephen Yates seated.

New Year's Eve 1986:
Chris and Anthony in
The Hacienda before
Acid House.

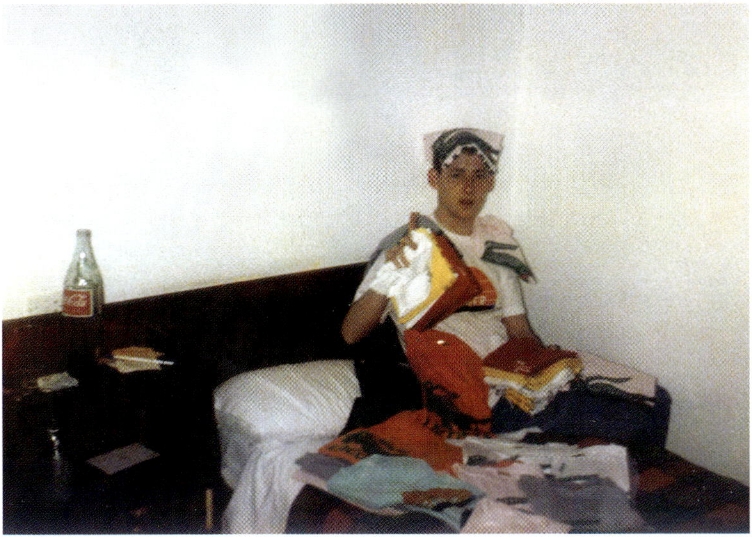

Shoplifting from
the Lacoste shop
in Ibiza to pay for
the holiday.

Chris and Tracey
at The Hacienda,
Christmas 1986.

Chris dancing in Amnesia back in the day when it had no roof, 1988.

Anthony and Tracey in the VIP area of Amnesia, Ibiza, 1988.

Chris and Natalie in Ibiza out of season, 1988.

CHRIS'S 21ST

Birthday party invitation designed by Central Station.

The birthday crowd, May 1989.

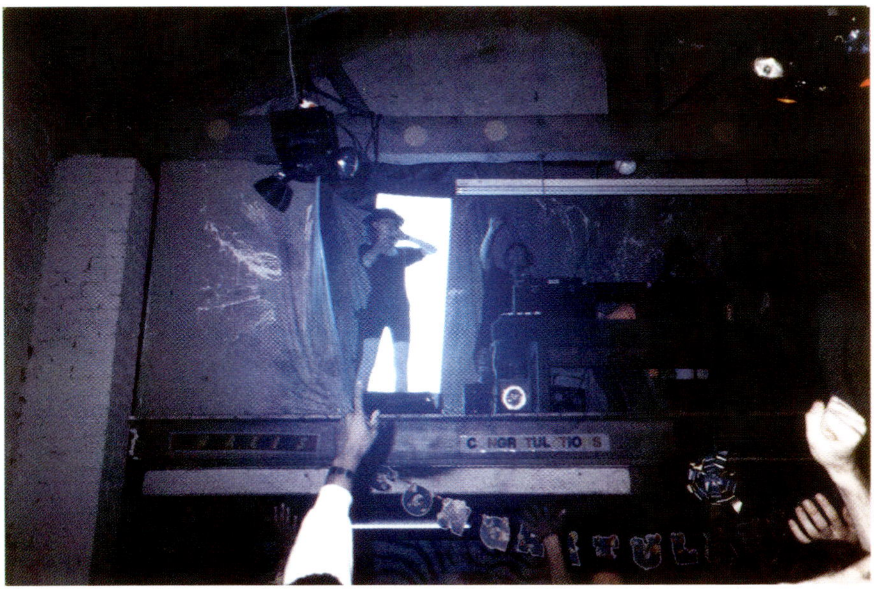

The infamous sunbed that was used to light the show in the barn.

CHRIS'S 21ST

Tracey and Anthony.

Jon DaSilva DJing and getting a tan at the same time off the sunbed lighting rig.

Kesta and Chris. Chris looking pure Acid House.

CHRIS'S 21ST

June and Reni from the Roses.

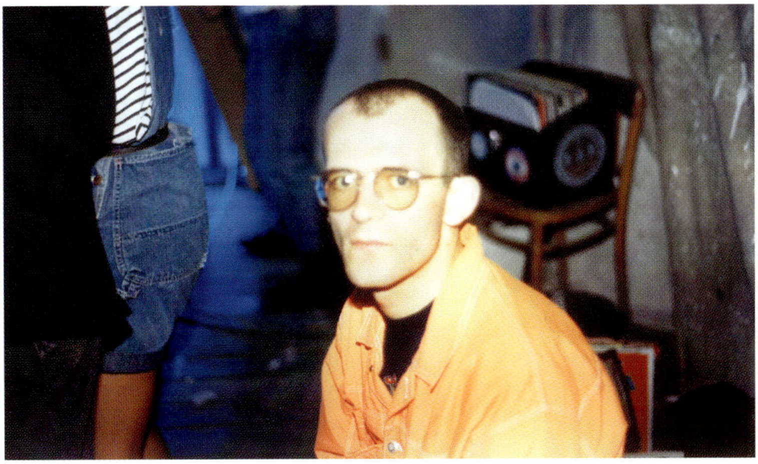

A youthful-looking Graeme Park.

Anthony and Chris. Blowing whistles was cool at the time.

JOY

Joy, 5th August 1989, Ashworth Valley, Rochdale. The membership card designed to avoid prosecution for the organisers. A private members' party or an 'illegal rave'?

Natalie, Chris's wife, getting ready to party.

Anthony surveying the ground and stage. Note the mobile phone in his back pocket – a Motorola Brick.

Chris – with his back to the camera as no faces were allowed to be photographed.

The merchandise.

Chill out time.

Thunderdome's Steve Williams on the decks.

Party in full swing.

JOY

Chris still up partying at 2pm the next day with a serious hairdo (featured in the film *They Call It Acid*).

Jon DaSilva and Laurent Garnier.

Chrissie Pagnotta and Andy Wilson in attendance.

Anthony and the boys in Amsterdam after leaving the country to escape the investigation of Joy and watching *Sky News* reporting on two friends who had been decapitated after falling off a motorbike.

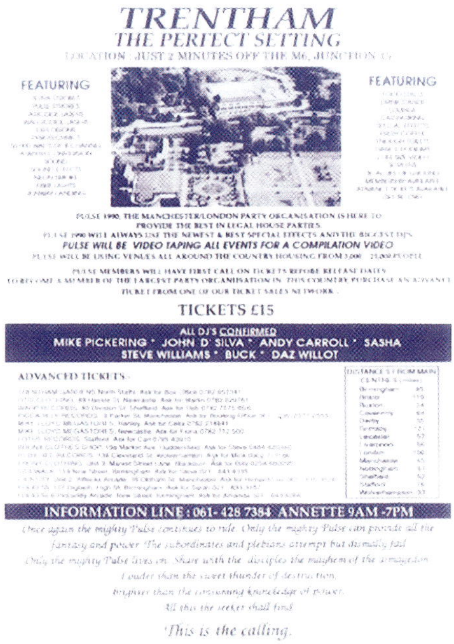

When Anthony and Chris tried to go it straight with a legal Acid House party, the police shut it down due to their reputation from the early days.

The end-of-tour party Anthony and Chris put on for the Happy Mondays. Front and back of the flyer.

Flyer for Sweat It Out, the Donnelly brothers' first Acid House warehouse party – the very start of Madchester.

Mike Pickering, Jimmy, John Brennan, Bernard Sumner, Heather, Tracey and Sarah Sumner at New Order's party at Peter Gabriel's Box studios in Bath.

Anthony at the New Order party at Box held because New Order had been missing the Acid House scene whilst recording *Technique* there.

pounds. So pals would come round and you've got a video player that they've not heard about, ten grand in cash on the side, loads of stolen biscuits and T-shirts. You would want for nothing when our dad was there. My mum was still out working. She was at the Golden Garter [*a venue in Wythenshawe's main shopping strip, the Civic Centre, that hosted bands such as the Drifters or Showaddywaddy*] laying and clearing tables. She was a proud woman. She wasn't blinkered but she would definitely turn a blind eye. She wouldn't have known all that was going on. As far as she was concerned, my dad was a rogue, fair enough, but he's got a scrapyard, he's out doing what he's doing and he's coming home, bringing the money in. There was loads of weird stuff.

One time he took me to a proper bombed out Mancunian wasteland and we were throwing away perfectly good paintings. You'd go home and there's a geezer with 700 gold chains stood there. I started putting two and two together.

Tracey: We loved it when our mum was working at The Golden Garter. All the big names of the day would play there on the cabaret circuit. The acts would be booked for a full week and on a Monday they would do the sound check. As our mum worked in the days setting the tables for the evenings, we were able to go in watch them sound check. As young kids this was so exciting, we got to meet loads of people. I used to take my autograph book in and get them to sign it. My mum and dad took me with their friends Peter and Eileen on my first official grown up night out there to see The Chi-lites. I had mithered them to death to let me go. I never forget walking in there that night, I had only ever seen the club in daylight, so to see all the tables and the club lit up was magical.

Our dad used to buy albums off the shoplifters each week for us. We would get about twenty at a time. He would arrive home with this pile of LPs and we would divide them up. There would be some rubbish ones, but you would also get some real gems. There would be everything from the *Top of the Pops* album to Brook Benton and Iggy Pop. It was stuff we wouldn't have necessarily have bought at that age . . . a great introduction to all different types of music.

Christopher: My dad was bringing cars and caravans home and all kinds of mad stuff, and one day he turned up with a horse. He brought it back from Scotland. So we cleared the shed out in the back garden, got some hay and we had a horse living in the back garden of a council house. It used to stand at the kitchen window and look through the window. Sometimes it'd come in the kitchen and sit down. While we would be walking in with our plates for dinner it would also be there. Somebody reported us to the RSPCA. They came to visit and went away perfectly happy – said the horse was well cared for, no problems!

I was in school one day and this kid said to me, 'I've just seen your horse running up the road.' I ran out of school and followed the horse tracks on the grass to a big public green area. The police were already at the scene trying to catch it. So I said, 'I've got this leash at home.' The police made me run all the way home to get the leash. By the time I got back the horse had gone. My mum was getting her hair done in the hairdresser's at Unit 7 in the Civic Centre and the horse was on the Civic marching about with all these police trying to catch it. I was like, 'Fuck.' I managed to get the leash over the horse's head and then I had to walk it all the way home. My mum had seen me chasing it all over the Civic while she was sat there with her hair in rollers. She probably thought, 'I'm not getting involved in that one!' Eventually the horse went to a horse farm. My dad realised that we shouldn't be keeping horses in a small council house back garden. I thought it was pretty cool.

2
BENCHILL BOYS

Anthony: The way I was described in my school reports was, 'Anthony could always do better, he's lacking in concentration. His mind is somewhere else.' I was always five years in front of myself. I was always in a different place. The teacher asked the class, 'What do you want be when you grow up?' Everyone else was saying I want to be a postman; I want to be a fireman. I said, 'I just want a big fuck off till and I want to sit behind it taking dough all day – not a till as in a shop, I just want everyone in here to pay me.'

Christopher: At school for me it was, 'Lazy, lazy, lazy, lazy.' I just wouldn't do anything at school. I wasn't interested unless it was sport or art. When I joined school they used to have these books called Wide Range Readers. They put me on Range 1 and I was still on Range 1 when I left four years later. I would just not read it and they couldn't make me read it. I just wasn't interested in it. They couldn't do anything for me [*it was only as an adult that Chris discovered he had dyslexia*].

Anthony: I got a lot of accolades playing football when I was young. My dad never turned up for one game! I played football at Wythenshawe Park later on for the local pub and we weren't your normal team – it was basically every criminal off the estate. People called us the 'Strangeways eleven'. At half time we used to have whiskey and spliffs. We had a manager called Joe who used to keep shouting instructions onto the pitch. He was like a social worker. Joe was shouting at my mate Basil off our estate and the next thing Basil stopped running towards the goal, turned towards the sideline, ran over and butted Joe and knocked him unconscious. It was hilarious at the time.

Christopher: I used to run for south Manchester and my dad never turned up at a race. When I got on the football team my mum took me to the Civic Centre and bought me a pair of football boots with yellow Gola stripes on the side. I went to school and I was buzzing my socks off with these boots. The next week my dad came home with a pair of Adidas Beckenbauer but not with the white stripes – with yellow luminous stripes! Where the fuck did he get them from? You just couldn't get that sort of shit and then my Timpson boots were elbowed. That's how it was. I had the best boots going but he still never came to watch me play football.

Tracey: My mum went to the football games when she wasn't working. I'd finish school, go home and go back out to see them play football. My dad was wrapped up in earning a living; home was mum's domain. Our dad couldn't tell you what school we went to. He'll know the primary school because it was across the road but he won't know anything else, really. I know he regrets not being as involved as he could have been when we were growing up. They were very young parents and they definitely didn't conform to how things should be done. My dad never took anyone's word as gospel. I suppose you could say he had a problem with any authority. Through this we had the freedom to make our own decisions and forge our own way.

Anthony: You were dealt your cards . . . whatever life threw at you. I had to know how to react to violence because of my dad and my experiences at the scrapyard. I had to understand that it could happen so I had that installed in me. That was just the way it was. There weren't really any dark moments for me apart from I was always being threatened with being put away in a children's home – that was my number one fear, getting caught. The family was famous on the estate. We were the kids who were getting run over by our own dad, being shot at by our dad, always fighting, always involved with the police . . . notorious people.

My dad bought my mum a café called Tony's Café in Moss Side on Claremont Road near the Claremont pub. As well as the scrapyard, he also had a tyre shop on the corner of Kippax Street [*which ran alongside the then Manchester City ground*] called Kippax Spares. We also had a butty [*sandwich*] bar in town, in the Northern Quarter, called the 'Butty Bar'.

All the [*Manchester*] United and [*Manchester*] City players would come down to the Ancoats scrapyard to visit: Stanley Bowles, Georgie Best, Martin Buchan, Lou Macari. My uncle was hanging out with Muhammad Ali, Angelo Dundee and Phil Lynott – so it was not unusual for us to see famous people.

Christopher: There was a man called Shine who had the newsagents opposite the yard. He was a top, top geezer, Jamaican. I was mad for a saxophone because of *The Muppets*. I got one for Christmas and my dad sent me to Shine to learn how to play. I went down there on Sunday afternoons, with all these black geezers jamming. I was in the middle with my saxophone. I came home saying they were all passing a cigarette around. They were all stoned out of their minds. I never learned saxophone but I had fun. The geezer who used to take me to Shine's was called John and he lived above the café we had in Moss Side. He was really, really camp – he wore pink flares like John Inman in *Are You Being*

Served? Then he just disappeared. Three months later I saw him in a town eating out of a bin. It was a very bizarre but very open upbringing.

Anthony: Crazy Steve was another character that was around. He wore a crushed velvet suit – black geezer from Moss Side. He had top of the range cars and was nuts. We saw him one day in Moss Side running with a baseball bat, with his hat flopping and his leather coat and velvet flares. He stopped when he saw us. He'd just battered four people with his bat and then he started having a normal chat with us, 'Yeah, I've just fucked some people up.' Crazy. The windows in his car were smashed. He was dressed like something from *Starsky and Hutch*. He had the ribbon round the hat and a baseball bat dripping with blood. But he was part of the jigsaw, as were Tommy and Georgie [*Davies*], Ginger's sons. They were the same, crazy, driving the best cars but you knew they were up to no good. I idolised Tommy and George.

Christopher: We drove through Moss Side when I was child and Crazy Steve was lighting and throwing bangers at people out the window of the car. The Dummy used to work for my dad at the yard. He was built like a brick shit house but couldn't speak. He was deaf and dumb. It wasn't very PC calling him the Dummy. He used to take me to the shops for toffees. Every dog they had in the yard was called Sabre. If one died they'd call the new one the same name, Sabre.

Anthony: We had one dog that was a killer. Only one man could feed him. They had him in the shed with a chain on his neck. My dad used to feed him with a pole. The chain was buried in his neck. He had to get the flesh off it and get the vet out to stitch his neck up. It was ferocious a dog. It loved eating dashboards.

Christopher: I saw that dog rip someone's arm off. It was on a chain but a bloke came in the yard and he was warned, 'Don't go to the back of the yard, the dog's down there.' Next thing I've heard a scream. The dog had him on the floor and was dragging him by his left arm. From his wrist to his elbow you could see bone. He kept passing out. We phoned the ambulance and then my job was, 'Quick get the paint out and get a load of "Beware of the Dog" signs painted.'

Anthony: Everyone had something going on but it was my dad and other friends who owned nightclubs, car pitches and pubs who were 'the firm'. [*Suspected of being the most powerful criminal group in the city's history – Manchester's top 'faces' – and under almost constant police surveillance.*] My dad was always like the man on the ground doing the work. The name Quality Street Gang comes from an old advert for Quality Street chocolate [*a limo rolls up to a bank, men with long coats, fedoras and dark glasses march in and the frightened cashier hold up her hands. A man with a fat cigar slips his hand inside his overcoat and pulls out a box of Quality Street chocolates*]. I heard some of the old firm walked into a bar in town one night and somebody turned round and said, 'Look at them, they look like the Quality Street gang.' It stuck but it was a label given to them by other people. They never advertised themselves. Chris and I have been brought up in and around it. They don't call themselves the Quality Street Gang – they've all bought and sold off each other all their lives. They've all relied on each other and they've all watched each other's backs. If that's what people want to call them I'm not here to destroy the myth. But as kids, we would know the name Quality Street, yeah, course we would.

Christopher: It wasn't something to aspire to. Your family's associated to this thing – yeah, so what? It wasn't something that governed our lives by any means. I'd go down the yard and some of them might be in a Rolls or some in a Jag. Someone's got a bag full of swag that they're selling and there's loads of cash knocking about . . .

Arthur: The police thought we were up to all sorts, but I was buying and selling houses. We employed half of Manchester; we looked after everybody. We weren't notorious for knocking people about; we were notorious for earning money. We'd only fight when we had to. There was the odd policeman: always somebody taking a back hander. The Quality Street Gang, if you want to call it that, probably goes back to the '30s, it is fathers and sons in Ancoats. The police were jealous. They knew we were grafters, entrepreneurs at the time and they didn't like it. They didn't like it when you answered back.

Anthony: What we were seeing and experiencing was affecting the way we were developing. I always say we were cultivated by violence, music, money and fashion. I was a difficult child. I was stealing – or making – money from wherever I could to pay to go away with my friends. I was always hanging out with older lads. I was only eleven and they were all on YTS schemes, they had wages. It was becoming impossible to control me. I was growing up very fast. I was an adult but my parents still saw me as a child. So there was a war between my mum and dad and me. I knew every crack in the pavement, every window to escape from. I was observant. I bought a ticket for a coach to Blackpool to go and watch City. When my dad found out he ripped up the ticket. I was furious. But then he turned round and said my friend does trips for football – why don't we organise something? Better the devil you know. His friend was a probation officer and he took United fans away on his bus – they called it the Wythenshawe War Wagon. The bus was considered to belong to United's hooligans.

So when I was eleven, I took every football thug from Manchester City to West Ham's ground – including some of United's boys – on that bus. It was not unorthodox for United and City to team up and go away together – it depended on your circle of friends. Chris was always United but he went to as many City games as I went to United games.

On the way down to West Ham, we found all the United firm's craft knives in the ceiling of the bus. Before we even got to London there were two stabbings at Knutsford services. Service stations would often be frequented by opposing fans heading for away games and we bumped into another mob from a rival club that night. We drove through the night and got taken to a house that belonged to another probation officer. They fed us. They were hippies, they thought they were doing a good thing, taking the kids to football, but they didn't know we were armed to the teeth. At the house we found a tool bag and we took hammers and blades. We were the thing they were trying to change – poor, uneducated no-hopers – but they were never going to change us.

We decided to go to West Ham's ground early in the morning. We were the first there. We sprayed the ground, it was a big thing to put your mark up – just Manchester slogans and 'Fuck West Ham'. There was a wine shop and we robbed it and then we sat in the park drinking. Word must have got out that we were there and this mob came over and said, 'Are you from Manchester?' I had a large pebble [*the size of half a house brick*] behind my back. I pulled out the pebble, ran toward this kid and threw it. It went off. It was a famous football fight, evidenced I believe in another book.

Football was always a weekly thing. It was an activity; there was nothing else to do. We lived for football. To go to the football and search out the opposing fans' lads . . . that was it. Leeds, Liverpool – it didn't matter. The objective was to cause as much trouble as humanly possible. I would go anywhere with anyone, but we were never affiliated with any one hooligan gang. Our little firm was a bit aloof. Wherever the violence was there was usually theft. While everyone was fighting we were the ones putting billboards through the jeweller's window. In 1977 Man United beat Liverpool in the FA Cup final. When they were parading the cup in the city – the homecoming – I took Chris on his first day out stealing. My intention was to go to town to cause trouble. When we got home we had hats, scarves and posters. We went to town with nothing and came back with all this stuff. Nobody asked where it came from.

Tracey: Anthony got into football and by going to football he was never interested in being with kids his own age – he was knocking round with kids five or six years older than him. So I think that's what kind of turned him into a bit of a hooligan, robbing and everything. But that was his thing and it was all about how you looked and how much money you had in your pocket. Bands and magazines – that was my thing. I just really got into going to gigs. I was massively into a Wythenshawe band Slaughter & The Dogs. Through them I went to the Sex Pistols at the Free Trade Hall [*in 1976*] – not the famed first gig but the second one. I used to drag Anthony to gigs at Cavendish Hall [*Manchester Poly*]. If there were any big acts in Manchester, they'd stay at the Posthouse Hotel in Wythenshawe. I'd be twelve or thirteen and Roxy Music were staying there. We hung about all night just to get in. We sat with the band and they put us on the guest list for the gig.

Anthony: It's all dropping in at the same time . . . football, punk, the Sex Pistols on the television with Tony Wilson. In my head I just wanted to be older. That was how my life was, always spent wishing it away. I went to the Anti-Nazi League Rock Against

Racism gig in Alexandra Park. It was a nice day out and all the football thugs were there, drinking beer and smoking pot. Then they were going on to clubs that I couldn't get into. But I could get into gigs. It was all happening very fast at that time.

At Rock Against Racism I saw two kids from Ardwick that I knew from football, Bobby Gillette and Barry Valentine. They had straight-leg jeans and plastic sandals. That's when I wanted my plastic sandals. The next time I saw them was at a Buzzcocks gig at Belle Vue. I was the punk joke – twelve, very slight, all the gear on. I'd made this badge board out of a piece of wood and foam. One of the older lads, Pubby, had given me badges to sell. You have money creeping into all aspects of our lives.

I could see that the same people who were attracted to the football were attracted to the music, the style and the money. You had the normal kids on the estate in flares like David Essex, and then the five or six of us who were punks – my pals and me. We were into anything that was anti-authority and punk had violence and attitude.

Christopher: I was nine or ten going out with all these punks. I was in school with my Doc Martens on, a pair of jeans all ripped up, a Mohair jumper, our Tracey's school blazer all ripped. I was dressed like a punk rocker at school. We were punks – obviously all down to Tracey. But I was into clothes at that age. After primary school, all my mates went to Yew Tree [*High School*] and I went to the school Anthony went to, South Wythenshawe – which then became South Manchester High School.

My mum and dad took us suddenly on holiday for six weeks three days before I was due to start there – so when I got back people had made friends. I turned up with a tan, a pair of Indian moccasins, button-down shirt and a pair of electric blue cords – I was suspended from school twenty times over the cords. I took the school uniform letter into the headmaster. 'It doesn't say you're not allowed to wear cords, it says blue – it doesn't say what shade of blue. I've got blue on.'

The first year, I was hardly ever there . . . never went. Then I started driving to school in a Hillman Imp. I was driving at twelve. My grandma had a New Year's Eve party in Hattersley and my mum and dad got absolutely legless. My dad put me in the driver's seat and I drove them home to Wythenshawe. We were wild, when you think back.

The teachers gave up on me. If I turned up for history, the teacher would say, 'What are you doing here, you might as well go.' If it was triple games I'd be there. I was put in one of the bottom classes out of the whole year because I was so unruly and I was constantly bored in class. But I had the best trainers, the best whatever. I was always the coolest kid. I would sign in school in the morning and then get off. I was out doing a bit of thieving. I got into the Mod revival so I was turning up to school in two-tone suits, a trilby, Fred Perry and fishtail parka. I'd be coming home late at night through the Civic Centre and there was still 'Joy Division' and 'Buzzocks' sprayed on the walls. Our house had 'Buzzcocks' right down the side of it.

Anthony: I was causing a lot of stress. I was sent home from London, found by the police jibbing trains on Euston Station with Eddie Beef and Ivo, who were a couple of United's main lads at the time. I ran off to Blackpool. I was with kids that were older than me. We raised money for a phone call and some chips. When I rang home, it was eleven at night, no buses and dark. I was pointed in the direction of my dad's pals – the Mancinis, who were from Manchester and had bought a big hotel in Blackpool. There were three of us. We went over, the night watchman let us in and then he fell asleep so we helped ourselves to the bar of booze. In the morning we'd been given the bus tickets by the night watchman to get us back. He was left in charge, and as he was getting ready to drive us to the bus station, he opened a garage at the back of the hotel. There was a big bottle of champagne and he had his back to me so I took the champagne and ran off. I sold the champagne and just went off again. My dad got a phone call saying, 'Your son is wild and out of control.'

I was into football . . . I just didn't go to school. I left school at thirteen. The family would be sat in the front room and I would literally run through the front door with the police behind me. I would go out the back door, jump over the fence, run in to next door's – Anne and Jimmy Heydon's – and just stay in their house. They would make me a cup of tea. It was that normal. At quite an early age the police knew us.

Christopher: I was doing the same sort of thing but at a much younger age because I'd seen Anthony doing it. I was out doing a lot of things and quite clever at keeping it away from my mum and dad. I very rarely got caught, and we were out thieving every day. They knew I was up to something because my best friend, Stephen [*Yates*], would always get caught (Stephen would freeze at the sight of a police dog) and we were inseparable. The police became an everyday occurrence. Whoever they would come for we'd all bail out. One time when they came for me, my mum kept them busy while I got out of the bedroom window and down the drainpipe. Of course it was down to the family name – they'd been coming for my dad for years and years. Now they were coming for Anthony and me.

I used to hitch it to London when United were playing at Wembley. My dad would give me a fiver and a fork or a knife and say, 'If anyone tries or says anything, stab them!' I used to get the bus to Altrincham, go drinking, get a train to Knutsford, more drinking, go to Knutsford services and hitch it from there. I've been arrested for all sorts of things but I've not got a conviction.

The first thing I ever got nicked for – I was ten – was for robbing a bike from the airport. We used to go to Manchester Airport, my pals and me, and get on the roof of the airport. We'd watch the planes and mess about. One day there were three or four bikes there but they weren't locked up so we just took the bikes. We got back to Wythenshawe and the police pulled us, took us to the police station. My mum and dad had to come and get us out. My dad was taking the piss; it wasn't exactly the Great Train Robbery. We had to go back and get a caution. If I'd gone out to steal the bikes I'd never have got caught. I wouldn't have been peddling down the main road.

Tracey: You'd get a phone call and you'd be told you're going to get turned over. We'd all have to go for a walk, go to sit in our mum and dad's friends' houses, no questions asked. The police would come for my dad and he'd be eating his tea. He'd take his tea in the back of the van with him and he'd be like, 'See you later,' and we would just carry on with what we were doing.

I got a Saturday job when I was twelve. I used to get my wages and buy my mum a box of chocolates and Chris something to wear. He was always crazy about his clothes. I loved buying him stuff. Mum tried her hardest to get me to school but I wasn't interested. So what I used to do was sneak in school in the morning, get the register, put my mark in, and go off for the day. I used to wag it and go on to the Civic Centre, or the museums and galleries on Oxford Road . . . they were great places to hide and I figured I wasn't completely wasting my time.

Anthony: We went on holiday with my mum and dad to Corfu in 1978. My dad was running out of money because he was spending like mad. I was wearing a Sex Pistols T-shirt, and a pair of bang-on trainers. I left my mum and dad at the pool and headed for town. I'm an active criminal now. I took Tracey and

Chris and made them keep dog outside the shop. True to form, I had a sneak around, found the money and took it. Tracey got a treat and then I went and bought a load of Lacoste from the Lacoste shop. I also loaned my dad some cash, as he was short of money, to pay for the remainder of the holiday. It was bizarre. Chris is looking at all this going on. I was never questioned about where the money came from.

We were way beyond our years. The lads I had seen in the plastic sandals and the skinny jeans at the gigs were a lot older. The football hooligans I hung out with were twenty, twenty-odd, and I was thirteen. Chris and I were in the thick of everything. We were making our money – our ill-gotten gains. We would be out purchasing the clothes with the money from wherever we got it from.

There used to be a shop called Paris Dix-Sept on Deansgate [*in Manchester city centre*] where Martini jumpers were eighty quid. The owner had a white Rolls-Royce. He was nice to us. But, again, we were fuckers, scratching his car on the way out. We were not nice people. I was driving a 1300 Morris with a flick haircut, and wearing the best gear – for instance, a pair of Marco Polo jeans, a Martini jumper, Lacoste polo, a pair of Kickers or Fiorucci, college shoes, FU jeans, Innega cords, Farah slacks, sheepskins and Sovereign rings. Going out to the youth club and robbing sportswear shops on the Civic Centre, every shop, anything and everything.

Girls were now firmly on my mind, as well as football. 'Teresa the Pleaser' – it's self-explanatory. I went round at midnight. She let me in her back bedroom. I was just getting on with doing the business when her dad shouted from the next room, 'Teresa! What's going on?' I was that thin I got on the window ledge between the curtains and the window. I knew I fitted perfectly because every night I used to sneak out of my mum's house. Her dad got out of bed and started walking to the room so I jumped out of the top window. There was a kid called Lunno nicking their double gates. I actually helped him pick up one of the gates and carried it to his house with him. They fitted perfectly. Lunno's driveway looked miles better with his new gates.

Our little gang was christened the 'Benchill Boys'. Growing up on an estate, we all knew each other from the age of three. We knew everything about one another – whose parents had split up, who was getting beat up at home, whose brothers were in prison. That gang mentality – it was needing each other. I was fourteen [*1979*] when I saw my friend get killed. He was my mentor, Coxy [*Anthony Cox*], the person in the group I looked up to. He was tough as old boots and would fight with anyone. He was only seventeen but he could have been forty. Everywhere we went our crew were blacklisted. I was the worst out of the bunch. We gate crashed a party in Northenden and as I walked in a kid put a cig out on my chin. So we started fighting with him. We were heading back to our area and the police came into Wythenshawe Park and chased us all. Coxy went across the motorway and he got hit in lane two by a taxi. I was a minute behind him, I heard the bang and I got there and my mate Beano was sat with him on the road but he'd gone, he was dead. It said in the newspaper Coxy died on the way to hospital but we knew he was dead at the scene. There were some people in a van that were on their way to sing Gospel and they had to slow down. They saw the accident and they screamed, proper screamed. That was kind of a turning point for my pals and me.

Tracey: At Benchill, we had what we called the parlour in our house that was always mine – where I had my music. Then my dad brought a pool table home, a proper pub pool table, so everybody from the estate was in our house every night playing pool. It was devastating when Coxy died. He had always been in the parlour with us playing pool, we missed him. He was the first of many of our friends who died young.

Anthony: We'd have twenty or thirty of our little firm in the house, my mum cooking dinner for everybody. There were always people living with us, our pals. If there were any strays they lived with us. We had one pal living with us for five years; he's a coach at United now. Another kid, Julian Bradshaw, lived with us for a time. We all loved him. It didn't matter what he did away from the door, he never came back to our door and did it there. Julian was eventually shot dead on his eighteenth in Moss Side, blasted twice with a shotgun. It was a really early shooting in Manchester – one of the first [*1987*]. On another occasion a few kids we knew took Temazepam and broke into the butcher's. The police found them chopping meat with white coats and the butcher's hats on. They had thrown a bin through the window to get in. There was blood and guts everywhere and they were just chopping meat up, drooling on Mogadons and Tamazepam, barbiturates. Nothing shocked you.

This was a hardcore council estate. There were a lot of lads having problems but they always knew there was a bed at our place. Anybody that absconded from Rose Hill [*remand home for juvenile offenders in Northenden*] would ring our number as soon as they got out asking for me or Chris. Our number was posted on the wall at the home next to the phone – sort of like a helpline: need to escape, call the Donnellys. I was forever giving clothes away to them – kids were from Blackley, Collyhurst and Moss Side. That's how we met a lot of friends from all over Manchester.

Christopher: Everyone who ran away from Rose Hill came to our house. They knew they could get some bus fare. The Sunday dinner was in a pressure cooker, the kitchen full of steam, me mum squealing like a cat singing Frankie Valli all day and Anthony and me coming in and out with pals and getting extra dinner made for friends. There was always enough food. Our dad would come home from the meat market with meat by the tonne, or salmon, whatever was going in Manchester. That's when we started meeting up with other little groups like our own – kids from Woodhouse Park or Sharston and north Manchester. They were into the same thing and we started interlinking and crossing over. Our gang got bigger and bigger. This is the time when we would rob absolutely anything – the clubman, the coal man, fucking anything. We'd all go to football and then to Brewster's [*club*] in town. I was going to Brewster's at thirteen. On the way home you'd go to the Reno, an after-hours club in Moss Side. Our cousins would come into town so our friends would be meeting with their friends. But our immediate thing was still us and based around Wythenshawe.

Anthony: We were becoming more popular. They would come from all over to our house. It was becoming a place to go. Come round to ours and drink beer and play pool. Once the door was closed in that parlour we got up to all sorts. It was our club. You'd come home round the back garden and there'd be thirty or forty people sat there, and in the house the select few. The police were always at the house for someone. It was not uncommon to see the police coming down our path.

Christopher: I sprayed on the wall as you entered the estate, 'This Is Benchill, Enter At Your Own Risk'. That was on there for ten years. A bloke pulled over when we sprayed it. He opened his car window and said, 'What the fuck are you doing?' We stuck the can of spray in his car and sprayed him in the face.

I used to go to a pal's house, usually after court, to get stoned and listen to Pink Floyd and Frank Zappa. When it got to that bit on the Pink Floyd album, 'Would you like to see me fly,' my pal used to jump out of the top window and come flying past the window downstairs to make us laugh. He did it one night and landed on the fence . . . busted his balls. Then his trick became showing you his giant, bruised bollocks for a month.

I'd go to school, sign in and then go out causing mischief. DER, the shop, did rental TVs and videos for people to pay on the weekly. They used to park their vans up doing their deliveries. We'd be monitoring quite a lot of DER vans – looking inside to see if there were videos and tellies. Me and my best pal Stephen [*Yates*] nicked this video and we wanted to get rid of it – you could get £250 for a video then. Stephen said, 'Sell it to your brother. He's connected.' We gave Anthony the video but as we passed it to him he shouted, 'Police,' and threw it in a bin and ran off with us. He doubled back and got the video, sold it and kept the money. He went and bought this white Martini racing jumper, thinking he was the bee's knees with his flick haircut. So we all agreed, me and my pals, to leather him. I attacked him and they just stood there and he battered me up and down the road.

After the football we'd come into town for the night out. We'd go into Woolworths first and they used to have ends of lines, proper old raw denim Levi's and Wranglers, not flares – semi-flares. We'd change the labels and price tags and buy them all. I remember having a pair of jumbo cord Wrangler semi-flares. That was not robbing, that was just getting some jeans while we're in town at a reduced rate – I mean, we all love a bargain.

Anthony: Whatever the trend, we weren't following the trend. We were starting the trend. We were getting the brands, the labels. The firm that was from Liverpool and the firm that was from Manchester were going away to Europe following football and stealing internationally, bringing back watches and clothes. There was nothing here. The boys from the council estates from Liverpool and Manchester were looking for greener grass. You had two different squads all chasing the best brands and it was all about who could outdo each other. I remember Chris going to Italy when he was twelve on holiday with my mum and dad and bringing me back a Marco Polo sweatshirt and a pair of Fruit of the Loom jeans and Fiorucci sandals. It was a very, very small amount of people involved. If Liverpool came up to Manchester for the football it would be like a fashion show. You would have the absolute nuts on – they would be able to spot you and you would be able to spot them. Then we would go to war with one another. They put it down as 'Casuals' but it seems to me that was only a term that's come out with nostalgia years later. I never knew any other firms in football, not personally. They were all naming themselves like the ICF [*West Ham's Inter City Firm*]; that was never for us, we were undercover.

Christopher: I'd go to Old Trafford with my own pals. We'd be knocking around with the main hooligans but we were very young, just coming through, on the fringes. They started getting into doing the tickets [*buying and selling*] at the football. I did for a bit but I couldn't get into it – it seemed like hard work to me, stood there asking people for spares all day so they could sell them on – although some of them made a lot of dough. My immediate friends and me would be out helping ourselves instead. It just seemed easier.

Anthony: It was standard for all the boys from our estate to get to the football early on a Saturday afternoon and buy tickets at face value or less and sell them for more. Chris didn't fancy it. I did. I'd do anything for a few quid. I was there. Then we moved up a gear and went to a pop show and started buying and selling tickets. I was queuing outside Piccadilly Records – buying 200 tickets. We'd take kids from our estate and make them queue up to get their full allowance. It was an industry. We'd be going overseas doing it. Then it was the merchandise – another revenue stream. I already did the badge board. It went to a poster, then to a T-shirt and a programme. Before you know it, you had an industry. We did the Royal Wedding [*July 1981, Charles and Diana*]. We worked a programme for that. This is when we were getting an indication of how big the merchandising is – filling in, working for someone else. You'd get to London and be given 500 books and have to return £1.50 per book but you'd be selling them for £4. As things progressed we'd be overseas stealing anyway, so let's go and sell T-shirts at that gig and on the way home open a jeweller's window and take the watches, take a diamond ring – then stay in a hotel, creep into the room where the safe is and rifle it. We were like the police force; we didn't have any time off.

In 1981 I went away stealing with my mates. They'd been to Turin for the football [*1980 European Championships*] and they were arrested for violence, but while they were there they had some money away. So they said to me let's go away stealing and head for Italy. I was only sixteen. We were sort of aiming for a holiday and thieving throughout the holiday, as opposed to going on a working holiday to Austria or Switzerland that would be pure theft. We wanted to go and have break. We ended up at the port of Brindisi. We were not making any money in Italy so I said to the boys, 'I know where there's money in Corfu,' because I'd robbed a shop in Corfu while I was on holiday with my mum and dad years earlier. For some strange reason in my mind I thought because I took the money from the middle of the pile it would have gone unnoticed, or maybe they thought it was a discrepancy. So we bagged up. I was always the one who used to do the villainy. I was very, very able, very confident and game. So if there was a tiny widow I could push through it. I would be sent in. We now head for Corfu to rob this place. The ferry ride was full of Italians and Greeks and it smelt of good food. On the top deck there were hippies playing guitars. We'd never seen anything like it. This is the life . . . it was a dreamscape. We were having all these new experiences – going abroad stealing broadened our horizons.

We got off the boat, hired motorbikes, drove to the place in Corfu town, went to the store, the same box was there and I opened it, but this time I took every penny. Then we went to stay in Gouvia. We went there by coach with a load of partygoers. The coach driver left his takings on the dashboard of the coach. I nicked the wallet and the bag was full with all the ticket money. There was 500 quid in the wallet. I had to go back in to pull the older ones out and say, 'Listen, I've just robbed the coach.' I had to hand the wallet to the leader of our group. They bought me a spaghetti dinner for nicking it and the money paid for the rest of the trip. Eating spaghetti in the restaurant without my mum and dad, paying for the waiter to serve us, was bliss.

Christopher: On another occasion Anthony and co went away and when they came back they got a taxi to Royals [*a pub in Wythenshawe*]. As they pulled up to Royals, which was a massive building, one of the lads went to Anthony, 'There's your Chris.' Anthony's looked up and I was coming down a drainpipe, four floors up, with a telly between my legs.

Anthony: It was the done thing to travel to Europe, to sneak about and rifle safes. It was like being a professional criminal for a lot of people. There was a group of extremely talented lads doing it. My forte was being able to identify where there was money, being able to smell money. They used to call me The

Count off *Sesame Street* as a kid, count the money. The elite wasn't fighting at the matches. We were more advanced than that. We were not thugs; we were extremely well-dressed international entrepreneurs.

3
SWAG

Anthony: For my sixteenth birthday [*1981*] I got weed and speed as a present from a family friend. Whether the objective was to sell it and return money I don't know. I presumed it was, but it ended up getting consumed. My dad would try and get me to work. He left me to run the yard and I back chatted him one day. He told me to 'fuck off' so I told him to 'fuck off' and as I'm walking off up the road he hit me on the head, from about thirty yards, with a half brick. He knocked me out in front of his pals. It was a cracking shot, though.

Christopher: Every night, while my mum was working at the café in Moss Side, Anthony would be waiting for me behind the front door and when I opened the door he'd blast me in the face. Every night. We'd fight and fight until you couldn't breathe. The last fight we had was over a tin of beans. I'd cooked this half tin of beans, he came in and said it was his. He then came round the back of me and whacked me in the ear and knocked me on the floor. I got up. He was stood there. I put all my might into a punch and blasted him in the teeth. I bust all his lip. Then we had a proper fight and that's the last fight we ever had. I was small but I got up one day like Tom Hanks in the film *Big*. I was big! And that was when we started collaborating together. I was fourteen. He started coming out with my mates and me. My nickname was Donzo and his was Mad Dog.

Anthony: That was the last fight I wanted. He hit me and it came up like a bauble on my chin. We were always close, but after that fight things really started to change. I took him out for a drink and introduced him to my scene. Before that he was happy-go-lucky, doing his own thing with his friends. We were like two mad dogs. We could have a two-way conversation without talking, just by looking at each other. We would go to a pub called The Church in Northenden. I was absolutely mental on cannabis and booze. The pub had to employ twenty security. We used to smash it up every night. It was the best pub I've ever been in, it was like the monkey house in the zoo. It was the key to the madness. I loved it.

Christopher: We'd all be smoking weed in there. The dad of our friend Geoff ran another pub we'd go to called The Firbank. We spiked him with acid once. He was running around looking for chickens. He barred Anthony and Anthony sent him a pig's head in a box. The pub shut at 1am and every weekend we'd nick a car from outside or in the immediate area just to get home in. It was normal. One time we nicked this taxi and on the way home we saw a load of lads we knew. Stephen [*Yates*] leaned out the window and shouted, 'Hey wankers!' It turned out that it was one of the lad's dad's taxi. Stephen dropped me off and then my other best pal, Jason, went out in the taxi. He drove it through a neighbour's garden wall and into the house. By the time he got home the police were there and he couldn't understand why. Obviously the kid had gone home and told to his dad that Stephen had nicked his taxi.

June: Me and Arthur were downstairs watching telly, the next thing the police came in full blast, took Chris in his pyjamas, said he'd been out robbing cars, handcuffed him and took him out. It was pretty regular – visits from the police. They'd search the house and I'd say, 'Well there are no cars under the bed.' At night, when the lads were out, the police used to shine these massive torches in my bedroom and then knock on my door to tell me, 'We know they're out and we'll have them.' They did give my lads a lot of hassle but there's no smoke without fire. Another time I was sat in the living room when the police scooped up Anthony's car, a white Ford Escort, and put it on a low loader. He never got it back.

I lent Anthony and Stephen my car one night to go out in, a gold three-litre sport Capri. They got pulled and the police took the car. I was always at the police station. I got Anthony out and they kept me in to interview me about the car and kept it for three months. There were millions of incidents. Too many to recall.

We used to have a lot of hassle with Anthony. When I went to work in the morning, I had to take the fuse out of the kitchen that ran all the appliances. I had to – this is before I went to work – go in the bedroom, pack up Chris's trainers, his favourite T-shirts, whatever. I took everything to work with me so that Anthony wouldn't wear them. I had to take the rotor arm out of the car when I came home from work so they wouldn't pinch my car.

Anthony: There were the good times on the estate when someone would come back with a raise from overseas. The pub would be on fire. John Sullivan, international jewel thief, absolutely mega. He used to go away grafting and you would see him walking through the estate with a £2,000 cashmere overcoat on and a pair of brogues, dressed slick like an Italian with the hair greased back – the full look. Everywhere he went he had a key that would work in one in ten jewellery cases in dealers all over Europe. He went on the Amsterdam diamond tour and took his key for this jewel box. It's just that beautiful Mancunian thing – chancing your arm. He stuck his key in and it fitted. He rinsed the Amsterdam diamond centre and carried on with the tour. By the end of the tour he had something like twenty-seven watches. You would see him in the pub and he would have grands and grands in cash – party time. Unfortunately, like a lot of our pals, Sully passed away.

Chris would be going out with his group of pals and I'd heard they'd been putting each other in a bin and throwing each other through shop windows. They'd all run in and grab what they could. They'd be coming home with £20,000 of leather jackets. It was wild. Fashion was everything to us. It was all about the look. The problem was we didn't have the money.

Christopher: There was a bit of a trend where a few of the lads off our estate would go into town and kick the shop doors off or throw bins through the windows. They'd run in, grab the clothes, then get a taxi and go home. It happened on dozens of occasions. I got arrested for robbing Jack Crème on King Street. I was found in the street with a big pile of clothes. The police smashed me in the face. I was nicked for burglary and me mum and aunty Rita had to come and get me out because I was a minor. I told the police I'd found the stuff in the street, which I did, of course. My mum took pictures of my face and we made an official compliant. In the end I got acquitted of robbery in court and I dropped my complaint against the police.

Tracey: My best friend Cath Berry's brother, Andrew Berry, was setting up a hairdresser's called Swing in the basement of The Hacienda; he'd got into Tony Wilson [*the founder of Factory Records, home to Joy Division and New Order, and The Hacienda club*]. I'd been going to The Hacienda since it first opened [*in 1982*]. Andrew offered me a job doing the reception for Swing and I started work there in 1983. It was a crazy period for me. Andrew is one of the most innovative people I have ever worked with.

We'd have days where we would shut the doors to customers and do stuff like paint showroom dummies and hang them from the ceiling in Swing. It was an amazing place to be working. New Order's Rob Gretton and Bernard Sumner, The Smiths' Mike [*Joyce*], Johnny [*Marr*] and Andy [*Rourke*], Vini Reilly, The Fall – Mark E [*Smith*] and [*his then wife*] Brix . . . all these bands used to come in to get their hair done. Our space was also the changing room for the bands at The Hacienda, so you'd get Divine or Culture Club coming in, all the bands of the time, and some of them would wreck it. Everyone was welcome at Swing. People would turn up to hang out for the day. I met a lot of the friends I still have today at Swing. There were some casualties but a lot of them went on to do some great stuff: [*Author and DJ*] Dave Haslam would be there selling his fanzine, Rebecca Boulton worked at The Hacienda and went on to manage New Order, drummer Simon Wolstencroft played with many great bands . . . the list goes on and on. Anthony and Chris got to meet a lot of interesting people there.

Christopher: At the time we were into football and we used to go to Brewster's, the main club. The music they played was Jocelyn Brown, Luther Vandross-type music. All the lads from all over were in there. It was only small, very dark, a weed-smoking place. Tracey was totally into The Hacienda and that was an indie club back then. We would sometimes go over to The Hacienda dressed, for want of a better word, like terrace lads. We would be going into Swing and seeing all these weird characters. One time I'd acquired a load of leather pants from somewhere so the obvious place to take them was down there, to Andrew Berry and his crowd.

Anthony: We'd frighten them to death. Tracey went off on a mission: she wanted something different, she wanted to be part of the music and art scene. But via her we were constantly tapping into that type of world. We'd go to The Hacienda to see gigs such as Gregory Issacs or Grace Jones. Tracey was into clothes, music, art and making these little movies with The Weeds [*Andrew Berry was the band's singer*]. She was really 'arty' and coming from our area that was pretty far out.

Christopher and me were more terrace – that's the word our friends used to describe us. Britain was getting a touch more switched on to the new type of sneak thief and thievery. So we would spend more time in Europe, where they were a bit more backward, and end up having grands in our back pocket. We'd live a real, real good life. No complaints. We were having bang-on holidays all over the world. Going abroad – there were always trips grafting. We all went to Eindhoven with United. On the ferry I was arrested for theft on the boat and was put in the brig. On another trip to Amsterdam we went with this nutcase. He had a dog back home and they cut its ears off. One time he threw it in the back of a post office van with a goat. You could hear the goat running round while the dog was trying to kill it. They used to feed the dog sheep's heads. These kids were nutters. One of the lads was shagging a bird from our estate. She had a flat in Stockholm. We stayed there and went into a jeweller's and copped for a parcel of diamonds, a big parcel. Then we went on the piss. On the way to Germany, on the twenty-four-hour Love Boat, this nutcase goes missing. I heard loads of clapping, loads of Germans, Swedish and Dutch people, all round the fast food alcove section of the boat. My mate is sat there setting his balls on fire with 100% Vodka. He pulled his knob out, put 100% Vodka on it and set his knob on fire. He kept getting standing ovations.

So we're on the boat, each with about twenty women's necklaces, diamonds and pearls, and he's setting himself on fire. He was that drunk, he was uncontrollable, so we put him in the boot of the car. At customs, he's kicking the boot, shouting, 'I've got ten kilos of coke,' but the custom officer was laughing. He walked round the back and said, 'Now, what've we got here then?' We said, 'He's just double pissed, we just need to get him home. He's been a nuisance in the car so we've put him in the boot.' Customs told us to get on our way. It actually worked in our favour.

Christopher: There was a period where a lot of post office vans were getting robbed. They used to carry a green bag and everyone found out the green bags were full of money. It was the worst kept secret. You'd just hear random stories: someone's had a post office van off and copped for however much. [*Overall, crime in the North-West rose by 40 per cent between 1981 and 1986. Armed robberies almost doubled. Manchester was dubbed the crime capital of the UK.*]

Anthony: I was nicked for a robbery on a post office van. I was arrested and identified as being the person who took the bag. I was arrested in Manchester on another charge and Staffordshire police came and picked me up and took me back to Stoke. They kept me there for three days. It was on a post office van in Hanley, Stoke on Trent. I think I did seven or eight ID parades and only one person picked me out and that was the bus driver who had allegedly seen me take the bag. The Crown Prosecution decided not to charge me because there was only one witness. My mate got three years. There were all kinds of innuendo and accusations about what we were and were not doing. You'd get pulled in for questioning for all sorts of offences.

Christopher: Six of us went up to Newcastle for the football. The kid driving had just passed his test so he was driving in the slow lane all the way there. Another kid had this Newcastle scarf that he said had belonged to his great-granddad, like a family heirloom, and he was flying it out of the car window. Anthony was smoking a joint and went to open the window to throw the roach out and somehow the scarf was blown away. One hundred years that scarf had been in the family and we were all too stoned to notice it had gone. Then we got to Newcastle and it was snowing – we were all in sheepskins, whereas the Newcastle fans were just in their Newcastle shirts. There was a firm of about 200 lads and one of them copped our accent. We started to walk away, faster and faster, and then broke into a jog. This whole mob started chasing us, hundreds of them, it was like a scene from *Braveheart*. We legged it toward the car but the kid couldn't get it started. This mob was charging towards us and we were shitting ourselves. We thought they would eat us alive we were that far north . . . finally the car started and we got away.

Anthony: Another time I organised a van to go to the Charity Shield final. I borrowed it off my dad and it had up the side of it 'The Smugglers'. We went to the supermarket and stocked up on beer, loaded it into the van. By the time we'd got to Coventry we'd drank it, seventeen of us. We went from the motorway into an area of Coventry town centre to get a wine shop and to have a drink in a pub. We walked into the toughest boozer and we were in there singing United songs. They rang all the other pubs in the area and the main crew from Coventry came down. They gave us a proper fight. Chris got stabbed, somebody ended up with a fractured skull. We were fighting for our lives in this pub. We gave them the best fight they've ever had. Then the police came and arrested us all. They kept us in custody until the following day because they reckoned we were too violent and pissed to be let out. The next day they released us and the press were outside. We were the first people to be arrested after Lord Popplewell began his investigation into hooliganism. It was front-page news. We had to drive out of Coventry with police motorbikes escorting us.

Christopher: I was United but when you were abroad it didn't matter. You'd meet all your pals from all over town over there looking for money. Everyone was doing the same sort of thing and probably still are. If you're a man in our family you have to earn. It's not a spoken thing but there's a massive pressure to make the grade and to stand up and be counted. I can remember my dad saying you'd never get rich working for somebody else. When I left school at fifteen, he gave me £400 in cash and a transit van. I had two men working for me and I used to go out collecting scrap around Manchester then go and weigh it in. I did that for while. Then I had a seven and a half tonne wagon doing the same thing. I worked with my dad on a couple of houses: buying them, doing them up and selling them, but that was hard work because he was going through a mad period. He stressed me out so much I got psoriasis.

Anthony: Chris and me we're out one day doing the scrap and we picked up this Holland's pie van off my dad to collect scrap engines. Chris was driving and I was sat in the passenger seat. We got to the lights and the brakes have gone. So we're flying through the lights and Chris is messing with the gears to change down and the gear stick came off in his hands! We've got no brakes, no gear stick . . . eventually we got back to our dad's yard and he said, 'What's wrong with you? Just put it back in and get on with it.' I said fuck this. I was not suited to this type of work. My attitude was: I need money and I need it now.

Christopher: On one occasion my dad sent me on the train to Inverness to pick up a wagon. It was one of those trips I did quite often – since I was thirteen. He used to put me on the train with fifteen grand or whatever it was to pay for the engines. Someone would meet me at the station; I'd give them the money and get the train back. I'd get fifty quid for the day's work off my old fella. So I've gone up to collect this wagon. I had no licence. He told me there were a couple of animals to pick up as well – a goat and a goose. So I'm thinking it's going to be a box van or something. I get there and it's this flat back wagon with grass all over the roof and a bird's nest on the engine. I rang my dad and said, 'What do you want me to do with this goat and goose?' He said, 'Just put them on the back and tie them down.' I said, 'You can't tie a goat and goose down to the back of a wagon and drive 400 miles. Are you mad?' I already knew the answer to that. So he said, 'Put them in the cab with you.' That was an everyday occurrence, being asked to do the most ludicrous things. He had a network of scrapyards round the country that'd buy in engines for him. He'd tell them what he needed and then he'd go round and collect it. Then he'd take it to the people he was selling it to. They would then send it to the Far East to get reconditioned and the whole thing would start again. There was loads of money in it. We used to buy alternators and starter motors if they had a certain serial number. There might be 20,000 cars in the Far East that needed a certain type of starter motor so they paid top money for them. So we'd go round the scrapyards looking for these things – pay £2 for them because it was a bit of scrap. My dad would give us £10 and to him it was worth £25.

My mum and dad were trying to get us to go to work. We must have driven them mad because if we wanted to go off somewhere, we'd just down tools and go. We did little bits of scrap metal dealing but we were always into something else.

We went to Ibiza in 1984. Anthony had been and came back saying how great it was, so we just booked a flight. We had some friends already there on a package tour and we jibbed in with them. Every day Anthony and me would go out and rob ten pairs of brand new espadrilles, ten pairs of shorts and ten T-shirts. We'd hand them to our friends and go out for the night and cause mayhem.

Arthur: I worked our Chris to the fucking bone. I had him doing the houses and scrap. I sent him to Essex to meet Moaning Bob, a friend of mine, buying engines for export. Moaning Bob was on the doors. Chris lived with that crew for three weeks. Moaning Bob was a raving nutter. Chris went down there working, met them all, including Essex's finest. Him and Anthony made lots of pals down there that they are still in touch with. I'd send Anthony to the yard we had in the Gorbals – he'd be less trouble up there than he was down here. They were a pair of villains at that time. True to form, Anthony was sent home; he was causing trouble up there as well.

Christopher: It was that time when all the lads older than me and older than Anthony, the cool thing – or they thought it was cool – was to get into heroin. All the major lads who you looked up to were smoking heroin. But then the next thing they were all fucked and became smackheads. [*In the mid-'80s Wythenshawe was awash with a tidal wave of cheap heroin and it became a well-known destination for those seeking to score.*]

Anthony: Someone had put a sawn-off shotgun through someone's letterbox in Wythenshawe. I was in the back bedroom at home with some weed and a grand in cash with thirty police, some armed, outside the house. It was half five in the morning, they were banging on the door and they got no answer, so they crashed the door. They burst in the house and came up the stairs. When they came in the bedroom, I'm screaming at them to 'fuck off'. They're telling me to lie down and I wouldn't – they wouldn't put the guns down. It was a screaming contest. We were all wrapped up together – my mum, my dad and me. They found nothing. I was only worried about my readies. I didn't want them fuckers grabbing my hard-earned cash. Me and my dad got taken to the police station and then we got bailed. We were asked about the gun. There was a gun but it was a replica – there was a daft Mickey Mouse gun floating around the estate and there was nothing more to it.

Christopher: The armed response came through the door in the house looking for me. I was at Natalie's, my girlfriend's, house, asleep on the couch. There had been some trouble with a local drug dealer in Wythenshawe that day. I'm surprised my mum didn't have a nervous breakdown. The police were looking for me for armed robbery on a smackhead. It wasn't me, obviously. I handed myself in for it because the police said it was. It was a case of mistaken identity and all the charges got dropped because the kid never turned up for the ID parade. He had moved off the estate in a rush apparently.

June: That was very scary. We had to keep Chris away for a week. The armed police don't knock. They turn you upside down. It's terrible. And if you don't know anything about what's going on, that's even more terrible. We'd just had the local bobby previous to that, or perhaps the CID. But this was something else – they're armed and everything. I think it was about a week later Chris handed himself in with a solicitor. That was it.

Christopher: That was the kind of shit going on all the time. I had a friend, who'd been in my class at primary school, who got into drugs and burned himself to death. He was drinking spirits and set himself on fire by accident. Things were happening every single day all over the estate that would make your hair turn grey. It's a dirty drug, heroin, isn't it? Nobody wanted it on the estate. Nothing surprised us anymore.

Arthur: I moved from Wythenshawe. The police were terrorising us over the boys. No one knew where I was for two years. Nobody.

The police finally got me over an MOT on my wagon in the city centre – they swooped mob-handed. They got me to a police station, knocked fuck out of me. They said, 'There's a funny MOT on the wagon.' I said, 'What a fucking pisser, that's how I bought it.' But my new address was now known to the police.

Whereas once the Quality Street Gang (QSG) had been so secretive it was said they didn't exist, in this period, as a result of a purported association with John Stalker, Deputy Chief Constable of Greater Manchester Police (GMP), they found themselves on the national TV news and splashed across newspapers from The Observer *to* News of the World. *All police surveillance on them in the past had been unsuccessful, but now it was suggested that the newly formed Greater Manchester Police Drugs Intelligence Unit had been set up purposefully to investigate the QSG. During this brief and unfortunate period in the public glare, the QSG were linked to armed robberies, fraud, drugs smuggling cartels and gunrunning for the IRA. Despite this intense period of surveillance, nothing was pinned on the QSG – leading to the police once again wondering if the QSG existed at all.*

Christopher: I didn't know what my dad was doing. All I can tell you about is the stuff I was doing. I know my mum was ill with the police constantly kicking the door off. It was making her ill – the police coming every day for my dad, Anthony or me. She wanted to get away from the area. They found somewhere out of the way with a bit of land. Although we moved away from the estate, all our pals were still there and we drank in the pubs round there every night. I was eighteen when I moved away from Wythenshawe. I was seeing Natalie, who I'd been seeing since I was sixteen. She's now my wife. When we arrived at the farm we were like the odd family all stood in the window together when anyone walked past, thinking, 'Who the fuck is that out here on the lane?' Looking back, I bet the person walking past must have thought, 'Look at them fuckers in the window looking at me' – about seven of us, like *The Hills Have Eyes*.

Anthony: We had got nowhere to live in Benchill; we were ostracised from our mum and dad. I was seeing Annette [*with whom Anthony has two children*]. I was living at her mum and dad's in Woodhouse Park [*Wythenshawe*]. I'd been dating Annette since I was sixteen. Chris found out that some fella was having his house repossessed and I was given the opportunity to buy it. All I had to do was get the deposit to move myself up a gear. Annette was pregnant. I found the money.

Tracey: I was working in Swing and then I started doing the tickets for the gigs and merchandise at The Hacienda. Then they started asking me to answer the phone for The Hacienda. Next I got a job working in the Factory Records' offices on Palatine Road. They had starting this new manager, Paul Mason, at The Hacienda. He'd come from somewhere in Nottingham and was starting on Friday night. It actually coincided with Anthony's twenty-first birthday. So I said to Tony [*Wilson*], 'Is it okay if they all come in The Hacienda?' I went in to work on the Monday and Tony said I'd been totally inebriated and that my brothers and their friends had been fighting at the door. Anthony and his friends had been refused entry and the whole reception area and the doormen got smashed up. I was held responsible as I had arranged it all and was suspended from work at Factory for a week on full pay. Tina, who I worked with, was quite rightly annoyed, as it left her on her own in the office while I had what she saw as a week's holiday. There was a definite divide between The Hacienda people and your Brewster's people. If you went to The Hacienda you were a 'weirdo' but Anthony and Chris were really cool with my crowd. They had already got to know a lot of them through hanging out at Swing. The Hacienda would be empty some nights and a bit boring, so I'd leave and walk to Brewster's because I knew Anthony and Chris and my cousins would be in there. It was from one extreme to another for me.

Mike Pickering, Hacienda DJ and Factory A&R: I met Tracey working at Factory. I met Anthony and Chris shortly after. Anthony's birthday was my Friday night at The Hacienda. Anthony had planned to get a coach-load of his mates down but in the meantime Paul Mason had got the job as manager. I remember Paul coming up to the box going, 'There's a load of people outside; they're saying they're with you? I can't let them in; they look like a bunch of thugs.' It was Anthony and Chris. So I let them in and Paul Mason and me had a huge row. There ended up being quite a bit of trouble that night. Anthony and Chris were always getting in trouble. They've calmed down a lot since then.

Christopher: We had Anthony's twenty-first in the RAF club in Wythenshawe and then we all got a coach to The Hacienda. We got there and they decided they didn't want to let us in. So we ended up having a riot on the door with all the doormen and left. This didn't help our cause with Factory or Tracey at that point. Tracey was a big influence in our lives – probably the most significant. She was the catalyst. She inspired us and introduced us to a different type of person. The people who were running The Hacienda and Factory saw something in Tracey. Anthony and me would go to The Hacienda to see her but we were always known as Tracey's 'Scally' brothers and that's what we were. Most of our friends wouldn't go there. We were going between the two worlds – between The Hacienda and Brewster's.

Tracey tried to get me a job as a roadie for [*Factory band*] James.

I liked the band but I turned up in my dad's XR3 Cabriolet. The band were a bit posh, a bit New Age – not like me. I lasted a day. My mum and dad had moved to the farm and I had an argument with me mum over not working. The next thing my dad appeared and pinned me up against the wall. We were both screaming. I was shouting, 'Go on then, do what you want.' Mum pulled him off. I'd had enough. Our pals were living in Gibraltar so Anthony and me decided to go away. We nicked our dad's car. We took my best pal Stephen [*Yates*]. We were going to jib every train and steal our way across Europe. We ended up in Lyon with about fifteen quid left. Outside the train station was a massive big kiosk that sold magazines and different things. So we stood outside and Anthony said, 'There'll be readies in there, cash.' Stephen and me got the women out and Anthony got into the safe. There was a load of coins in rolls. Anthony took about 150 quid. We were all laughing and we ran for the train with the money. But we missed the train – it was pulling out. We said, 'That's an omen.' So we went back and pulled the same trick. This time we were going to search the safe thoroughly. He came out of the kiosk and he had his hands under his coat running through the square. And we were going, 'Have you copped? Have you copped?' He just went, 'The bag's loaded.' There was just short of about twenty grand in cash, so instead of getting the train we booked into a hotel across the road and decided to go on the piss. Bad mistake.

We should have left town immediately but we crashed in a hotel across the road from the safe we had robbed. The following morning the first shop we walked into was a leather shop and we put a leather on each – we just couldn't help ourselves. There was no shopkeeper there. As we were walking out the postman was walking in and he's obviously seen that we've all got tags hanging off our leathers. He started shouting, 'Thieves!' We managed to blag a taxi and got away, got our bags out of the hotel and took a taxi to the next town. It was one of the most enjoyable times I can remember stealing money. We travelled to the next big town and boarded a train heading towards Spain and the border.

Anthony: And then we turned up in Gibraltar. Our pals were starving and living in a cave on Miami Beach. So we hook up with our friends and go out in Gibraltar town centre and get pissed. There was an argument with this soldier and his mate. We were fighting with them and a policeman came over and someone chinned him. Chris got off and escaped over the border back into Spain, to La Linea, where our hotel was. I got remanded in custody with Stephen and a pal called John Molloy. We were charged with assaulting a police officer.

I represented myself and the others in court. At the end of the small trial the court usher came up, shook my hand and the judge gave me a £60 fine. The usher said I did really well defending me and my two pals. We part-paid the fine and we were released immediately. Obviously the rest of the fine remains unpaid.

I've always known that we're talented at getting money. Around this time we were starting to seriously do black market tickets and band merchandise in a big way. We were making money doing anything we could turn our hand to.

Christopher: We were doing the concerts, working the passes – the swag. We were smoking loads of dope and drinking. There was no plan – it was just a case of getting a few quid from where ever you could. A lot of kids were doing what we were doing at that time – kids that weren't doing nine to five, earning money other ways. You'd get a knock on the door, 'Do you want to come to Germany? Do you want come to Switzerland?' You might turn up in Germany for, say, Michael Jackson and you'd have us there, a firm from Wilmslow, which was Ritchie and Jimi Goodwin [*of the Doves*], a Scouse firm, a firm from Southend . . . everybody knew each other but you were in your own little mob. We'd all buy our T-shirts from this one firm of older geezers.

The common enemy was the security and the police because they were tying to stop you selling merchandise in the streets. So you could end up all teaming together and have a running battle with security for Pink Floyd, Queen, U2 or Springsteen – whoever it was. We did all those tours. You'd have all the different firms, all driving around Europe, taking anything that wasn't nailed down and then all converging on a pop concert for two or three days. We were young, travelling abroad, having a laugh getting stoned, drinking, making money. Anthony was leading the way on that.

Anthony: It was a way of life. There was a concert on and that was your job at the time. I'd drive the van and there'd be thirty of us Mancs all night outside the stadium in whatever country, selling tickets and T-shirts. I used to drive everywhere, all over Europe. I loved it.

Christopher: Anthony had the foresight. He said, 'Why are we buying T-shirts to sell off other people? Let's make our own.' I mean, Anthony would always get a good deal off whoever was selling the T-shirts, but making our own gave us control. It was a great idea. Nobody could stop us doing that. No matter what age we were. Anthony ended up in this warehouse on Oldham Road with all these Littlewoods' seconds he'd got off these fellas that our dad put him in touch with. Our pal, a designer, got this U2 T-shirt made and all the other concert sellers paid to use his artwork. It was shit hot, just as good as the official T-shirt.

Anthony: We would always challenge people. We've always had a 'fuck you' attitude. It was all our friends who were selling the

T-shirts for other people [*the established manufacturers of bootleg T-shirts*] so I knew I already had the workforce. All we needed was the product. We get involved in the design and the quality of the merchandise, sourcing it. We worked the [*U2, 1987*] Joshua Tree tour – to the point I became quite friendly with The Edge and Bono. They used to spot me outside and pull the window down and talk to me, ask me how I was doing with the tickets.

Christopher: You'd get different firms, on various scales, doing this. We might print a thousand T-shirts but then someone from Miles Platting might come and get a run of a 100. So Anthony would have a price on that: a wholesale price and a worker price. For Michael Jackson we got a coach to Sweden, fifty-two people – the official bootlegging coach. Then you have to monitor them, restrain the lunatics. There was a lot of fighting breaking out. We ended up in Germany and went in this shop and came out all in new yachting gear. There was a burger van and you could see the cash box. Someone jumped over, passed it to me and I put it under my jacket. We got about £200 out of it. Anthony got the hire car towed away. He'd parked in a disabled parking zone with about six grand in the boot. We got it back. He'd hidden the money inside where the indicator was. There was always drama and adventure on tour, always a tall story to tell in the local pub on our return.

Anthony: We were doing okay but we didn't make a lot of money off the T-shirts. We were losing as much as we were making. Trading Standards in every country would try and grab the T-shirts off you. Then you'd be fighting with the security. It all had to be done with military precision. You'd turn up in a bus and hide two mile from the venue. Then you'd distribute the T-shirts evenly – 1, 2, 2, 1, one small, two medium, two large, one XL. Someone had a pen and paper and booked it out. Then the twenty people go off with the merchandise and only nineteen come back because Billy's gone missing with his money, spent it in the pub, bought weed and met a bird – she blew him off round the back of the stage and now he's fucked off and is living in Austria with this new woman – this shit really happened. So you get people MIA, missing in action. Then there was the ones that came back and said, 'Listen, I've sold 140 but Trading Standard's seized twenty so I'll weigh in my 140 but can I have another forty to go and get the money to pay the fine for the ones that were seized?' It was a business. The book was closed and we'd pack up to go to our accommodation – that's where the fun begins. It was a rock 'n' roll band. We were on tour. We'd book into a hotel, get a double room and then fourteen lads would be up the fire escape. At the service station, you'd take the table nearest the till and twelve dinners would go round the back and two got paid for. You were on tour. It was the most fantastic life ever. We were the unofficial side of the band's tour. We worked Michael Jackson in Europe. But we printed a T-shirt with Michael Jackson's face on that we could only sell at night because the ink had run green. I suppose we were before our time with Jackson.

4
DANCING GANGSTERS

Anthony: This kid called Eric Barker started wearing silk pyjamas and a Moroccan hat at the football. We asked him why he was dressed so freaky and he said, 'Because I don't care anymore – I'm just into music.' We all thought Eric had lost his marbles. He was not a hard-core hooligan – he was on the periphery. He wasn't into putting jewellers' windows in or fighting; he was the nice kid who you could talk to about football, music, fashion and clubs. He was like an academic, from our point of view. I got talking a bit more to Eric at the match. He said, 'You have to get on this,' and he invited me to a club called Stuffed Olives. I turned up and he gave me my first Ecstasy tablet. I was beered out of my mind and holding onto a banister as it hit me. It was like a rocket. Eric was saying, 'Let go of the banister.' Once he prised me off the banister, my hands went up in the air and I was on the dance floor. It was amazing.

In very early 1988, Eric Barker was at the very forefront of what would become the Acid House revolution in Manchester. His nickname, coined by Bez of the Happy Mondays, was 'The Wizard of E'. The club, Stuffed Olives, was a well-known gay bar in the city centre that was transformed on a Sunday night into the city's first major Ecstasy venue.

Eric Barker: In the beginning I was dressed like any other normal geezer on the terraces at Old Trafford – in a pair of jeans and a Fred Perry polo shirt. But we'd be coming out of Stuffed Olives with steam coming off us, soaking wet from dancing so much when we were out E'd up. I just thought, 'This clobber is not up to this.' I'd been to Ibiza and seen someone there dancing in silk pyjamas like what old men used to wear in the '60s, with nice patterns on them. So I started wearing them. Soon enough, everyone started changing their clothes and wearing baggy stuff rather than tight fit.

Stuffed Olives was like a preacher's meeting. It was a very select crowd. Everyone started to ask about it and we had to call it 'Gaff X' to put people off the scent. It only held 150 people. It was semi-illegal. Everyone was out of it on E. The rush of proper MDMA powder – when you'd not had anything like that before – was exhilarating. It used to start at the bottom of your legs and go, whoosh, right up – this warm feeling. The next thing you know, you're thinking on a different plane and you start dancing because of the beat of the music. It made you feel so good. All your problems, whatever shit was going on in your life, just disappeared.

At The Hacienda there was only a handful of us at the beginning – the Happy Mondays were part of it. The rest of the club would be just shuffling along and our corner would be like a freak show, bouncing and dancing. People were asking, 'What's going on here? What are these people doing?' Slowly more people got enticed into it until it reached a tipping point, and then the whole club was on fire with Ecstasy. But at the start there was probably about twenty or thirty of us in the corner. The scene in those early days was full of duckers and divers, all unemployed working-class scallies. Everyone knew Anthony and Chris as a couple of villains. I mean, if you didn't know, then obviously you weren't in the know. Everybody from the street, shall we say, knew what Anthony and Chris Donnelly were about.

Anthony: After taking Ecstasy, I went back to our pals on the council estate in Wythenshawe and for the whole of the next week I was saying to Chris, and everyone, 'You've got to do it, you've got to do it!' I was absolutely convinced. They formed a queue. But to score E you had to know one or two or three key people – supply was extremely limited. Our friend ordered a load for our own use. It was sent from London because he knew some people in Brixton. They sent it by Red Star [*Red Star Parcels, owned and operated by British Rail*]. The pills turned up in a video case in bubble wrap and each tablet was individually wrapped. They were called California Sunrise and had originated in the States. We took the tablets and we went to Stuffed Olives.

From being pot-smoking and drinking scallywags, we were transformed. We didn't drink beer for twelve or eighteen months, not a drop of alcohol. The pills were given to somebody in a pub in Ancoats called The Angel. They knocked the letters, A, N, G and L, off the pub sign and were calling the pub, 'The E'. The pills had been distributed from there. So we're at the boozer the following weekend trying to buy some gear back. It was only a week since that parcel landed but it had all gone.

Christopher: Stuffed Olives played a massive part in Acid House history in Manchester. Everyone thinks The Hacienda was the club but it was Stuffed Olives first. There were probably a hundred people in the whole of Manchester that were into Acid House and Ecstasy and that's where it happened – on a Sunday night at Stuffed Olives. It was open from ten o'clock until four a.m. and that was *the* place. You'd pull up round the corner and there'd be people in the street with their hands in the air because they were already up on E. No music, all outside, all dancing. They gave out little tickets when you walked in – I later pulled the slogan off the ticket for one of our Gio-Goi T-shirts: 'Ecstasy, once is all you need but it's seldom enough'. There was no alcohol. Everyone used to hold on to this banister when they first took an E and you had to get them to let go. We used to put poppers in the smoke machine. It was great! They'd play James Brown or The Commodores' 'Brick House' or 'I Know You Got Soul' by Bobby Byrd. You could buy half a tablet in Stuffed Olives for £12.50 and the geezer would bite it in half in front of you and put it in your hand. After I'd had the E, I was in town the following week and I walked into a [*clothes*] shop called Identity [*in Afflecks Palace*]. They had this music playing – Acid House. I went up to the geezer at the till and asked, 'Where've you got this? Can I buy this?' He said, 'No.' It was just one tape. Our Tracey did us a copy of that tape. Me, Anthony and all our pals all had this one tape. No matter whose car you'd get in, it was just like 'the tape'.

Anthony: I heard an amazing Acid House tape at a party at [*New Order singer/guitarist*] Bernard Sumner's house. It was the only Acid House tape in the town then. [*Actor*] Keith Allen was also at the party [*Allen was making a TV series in Manchester called* Making Out *and New Order were doing the music for the show*]. About twenty of us went back to the house and Bernard was handling this tape like it was a piece of precious jewellery. It was new and it was like the Holy Grail. I spent the night stoned with Keith Allen and Bernard listening to the tape. So there was now E and Acid House music and we know what it is and where we can get it. We need to build on it. There were ten of our firm on the Acid buzz and it was going off for six months at Stuffed Olives like you can't believe and it was getting a little bit bigger. The Hacienda was warming up for it and there was a real hard-core building.

Christopher: Ecstasy made that period what it was, without question. That was what brought the Acid House explosion to Manchester. [*Hacienda DJ*] Mike Pickering was bringing [*Acid House*] music back from Chicago, but it was definitely the combination of house music and Ecstasy that made The Hacienda blow up. From our area there were ten of us and it spread: you'd convince someone new, then see them an hour later on the dance floor and there was no words spoken – it was just eye-to-eye. All around Manchester the same thing was happening.

At The Hacienda in the corner underneath the balcony there'd be a hundred people going off. It would be like a zoo. Eric Barker was on the podium, whistling [*with his fingers, leading to the popularisation of whistles on the dance floor*]. People would come in just to watch this corner. They would say, 'Have you seen these fuckers all throwing their arms in the air?'

I went from wearing a pair of hiking boots, a pair of jeans and a polo shirt – all this heavy stuff – to, the week after, shorts, T-shirt and [*Converse*] All Stars. I also used to wear quite a lot of paisley shirts and a headband because I grew my hair to my shoulders. I looked like Cochise, the Native American.

Anthony: The people who I'd grown up with knew me as a thief and a scally and a football hooligan and now thought I'd gone mad. But once they took the tablet, they joined in; they were mad as a box of frogs too. I have a mental image of Chris and me sitting in a car and we had All Stars and smiley face T-shirts on way before all the masses had them. At The Hacienda, by the summer of 1988, Wednesday night's Hot [*started on 13 July 1988, with DJ Jon DaSilva*] and Friday night's Nude [*DJs Mike Pickering and Graeme Park*] were wild – really unbelievable. We ran The Hacienda for the next two years but you were the elite of the E scene if you had been to Stuffed Olives. We ran The Hacienda from the front door to the emptying of the bars – we'd take the bar to our Acid House parties. Leroy, who ran the bars at The Hacienda, would let us walk out with the stock; they would pass it out to us for our raves. It wasn't intimidation – although we

The trip to Stockholm where jewellery went missing along the way, balls were set on fire and Customs were evaded.

Dave Lawrence, Chris, Jelly Universe, Natalie and Mark Whittaker at MAB trade show at Earls Court, London – the first Gio-Goi exhibition.

Matt Carroll, Chris, Anthony, Pat Carroll and Dave building the stand for Gio-Goi's first trade show.

A part of the MAB stand: a fantastic piece of art by Central Station.

The F*cked Up warm-up jacket which was the biggest seller from the early days and the jacket that Alex Higgins was wearing when he appeared on TV with Terry Wogan.

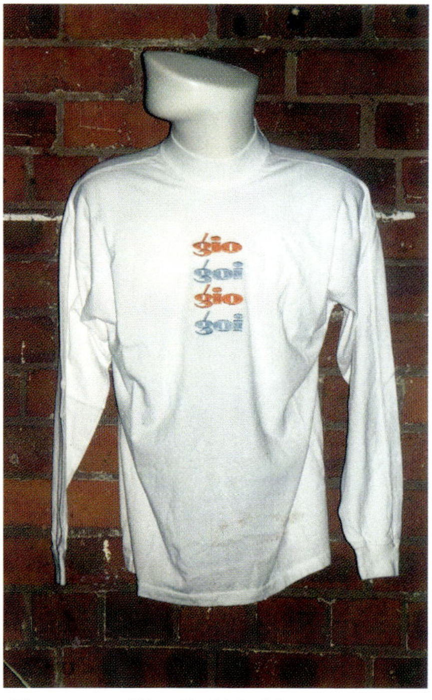

First ever Gio-Goi T-shirt to appear on TV – as worn by The New Fast Automatic Daffodils.

Gio-Goi warehouse, 1990. Rumour has it this was where the bulletproof vests were tested.

The F*cked Up range.

The Gio-Goi office, 1990.

Anthony and Chris, 1990, in the Gio-Goi office.

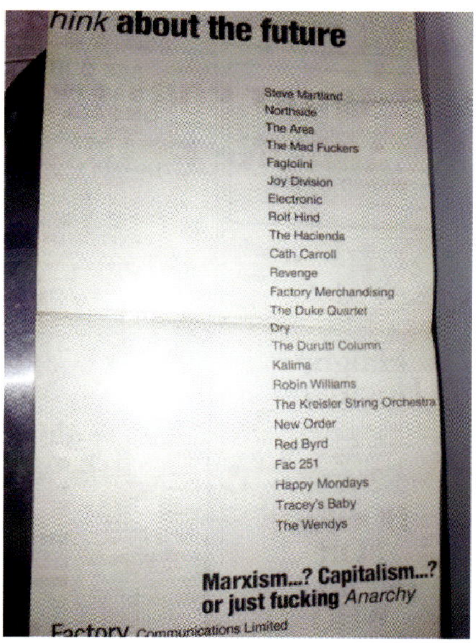

hink **about the future**

Steve Martland
Northside
The Area
The Mad Fuckers
Fagliolini
Joy Division
Electronic
Rolf Hind
The Hacienda
Cath Carroll
Revenge
Factory Merchandising
The Duke Quartet
Dry
The Durutti Column
Kalima
Robin Williams
The Kreisler String Orchestra
New Order
Red Byrd
Fac 251
Happy Mondays
Tracey's Baby
The Wendys

Marxism...? Capitalism...?
or just fucking *Anarchy*

Factory Communications Limited

Tracey leaves The Hacienda to work for Chris and Anthony at Gio-Goi. Factory Records announce Tracey's baby, Paris.

The Gio-Goi office. Tracey standing, Natalie sitting.

Chris and Anthony in Arthur's scrapyard being interviewed for *The Face* magazine.

Chris about to go running to clear his mind.

Paul Davis (Happy Mondays), Chris, Anthony, Andy Barker (808 State), Andy Rourke (The Smiths). The opening of Parliament in November 1992. The most violent club in Manchester.

"We don't look like the sort of people that run a clothing company, we look like the sort of scallywags that sell hotdogs outside Old Trafford!"

ACTION CLOTHIN

blags to riches

Gio Goi have managed to combine the fashion world with the Manchester underworld to produce clubwear fc the moment: this is street fashion with *real* attitude.

INTERVIEW BY **MANDI JAMES** PHOTOGRAPHY BY **GRANT FEA**
MODELS: **BOZ-EYE** (TDA), **YATES** (PREVIOUS), **H** (TAXMAN), **DALE** (TDA), **GILLY** (DON'T GIVE A FUCK) AND **PARIS** (NO PREVIOUS)
ACCESSORIES FROM BIG BLUE, 14 ROYAL EXCHANGE, MANCHESTER

The tale of Gio Goi is a ripping yarn of blags to riches set slap bang in the grimy streets of Manchester. Fronted by Anthony and Christopher Donnelly, who've threaded a needle in their lives, and fashioned by design demon Jonathon O'Garr, Gio Goi's rapid rise is something of an anomaly. Not only have they made their mark in the midst of a heavy recession when most designers are struggling to make ends meet, but, as the Donnelly brothers are the first to admit, when they started out less than 18 months ago they didn't have "bastard clue" what they were getting themselves into.

"Young people these days can achieve things, they care and want to get involved," rants Anthony. "Nobody wanted to back us when we started out, so we just went ahead and did it ourselves, rewrote the rules to suit us."

Gio Goi is the latest in a long line of schemes and scams the Donnellys have been involved in. In the acid house haze of '88/'89 they were instrumental in creating some of the longest convoys and organising some of the giddiest parties in the North-West, attracting people from all over the country, national media attention and the ever-watchful eye of the law. Soon after, Gio Goi rose out of the ashes of a burnt-out Manchester scene to kick against the shoddy scally image of fuck-off flares and hooded tops.

"Basically we got fucked off with seeing Joe Bloggs and that market stall mentality coming at us from everywhere. We knew we could do better than that, make the type of clothes we liked, we knew our mates would be into."

The first Gio Goi was a T-shirt with the logo 'Bloe Jobbs' in Joe Bloggs letraset emblazoned across it, which raised a few hackles and made people sit up and take notice. What they lacked in practical experience they made up for with front and blagging power, building their public image by tapping into the contacts they made during party time. The buzz spread round a ready-established network, whilst samples of gear were given to local heroes 808 State, Electronic and Happy Mondays, who gladly advertised Gio Goi's wares.

With their bright stripes, coloured denim, padded waistcoats and sharp graphics, Gio Goi clothes are on the same wavelength as Chipie, Duffer Of St George and Chevignon. They champion the casual but calculated ergonomic style of the '90s, but are far from just another bunch of amateur copyists. Where Gio Goi differ is in their attitude and background, which permeates everything they lay their hands on.

"Our clothes are different 'cause we're different," opines Anthony. "Your Mr Chipie and Mr Chevignon, I don't how old they are but they're not out there, they're not going to any clubs or parties where people wear that type of gear, whereas we're bang into it. We know exactly what's going down."

Taking pride in the fact that they are 'upfront and out there', Gio Goi have "Dedicated to those dodgin' the rain'n'bullets" stamped across their cards, loaded messages like 'Gibraltar' (Gibraltar = rock = crack, drug of choice of certain Manc gang types) printed across the chests of their shirts and a fuck-off-and-die, almost kamikaze attitude which grates against the usual cosy cliques of the fashion world.

"There is still a certain stigma attached to being from the North, despite having the best football teem in the country," shrugs Chris. "We get reps and businessmen come in here, they expect us to be sat there in a suit and tie and we've got 'Bad Trip Mother Ship' sprayed on the office wall." However, Gio Goi's belief that they will build a fashion empire is supported by the fact that not only are they already distributing their goods worldwide, but they've been badmouthed in the press more times than they care to remember - a sure sign of success is when you're pissing people off.

"We've been accused of all sorts," shrugs Chris. "And what people don't know about us they make up, when the truth of the matter is we come in every day with our butty boxes and get on with it."

"We don't have any competition, at least not anybody that we consider a threat," continues Anthony. "We ignore people who badmouth us, don't mean anything to us 'cause we're out the and we're doing it. Everybody paints us in a b light, but people will eventually learn to respect t fact that we are businessmen and nothing els We're the underdogs, we know that, but everyo who boots us just gets fucked, 'cause we ju bounce back. They used to say when we was doi parties we had steel balls 'cause we got hassle many times, but we kept at it."

Gio Goi believe in moving with the times, no ma ter how quickly they shift, constantly changing th line and steaming out limited editions. They pr duce most of their garments abroad because Briti manufacturers are "up their own arses and unre able". Etiquette has been thrown right out of t window, Gio Goi are treading on toes wherev they walk, but nothing can stop them.

"What the fuck is fashion anyway?" laugh Anthony. "I always thought it was good-lookir people strutting up and down the catwalk. B what about the likes of us? We've got to we clothes. The models we've used on this pho shoot are just lads off our estate. People can relate to geezers with square jaws, fuckin' bull holes in their chins, marchin' about loving them selves. What we want's a little bit of a beer belly, mad freaky face, and if they look alright in the gea then every other fucker can."

The rise of Gio-Goi as portrayed in *i-D Magazine*.

Some of the lads from the Wythenshawe estate modelling Gio-Goi in Hulme where the illegal acid house den The Kitchen was. The hearse was brought to deliver Gio-Goi stock for a laugh – although some people didn't find it funny.

Johnny Marr and Bernard Sumner on a photoshoot for Electronic, in Gio-Goi.

Havely Circle, Benchill. The boys are modelling Gio-Goi at Flanagan's (Flanny's), our local shops on the estate.

Our pals the Bowrys modelling Gio-Goi.

Susy Franco, Anthony, Natalie and Annette having lunch at Sehm in Paris on the Gio-Goi stand. Susy translated for Anthony and Chris on trips abroad – she was invaluable.

Anthony, Tracey, June and Chris at June's 50th.

Arthur, Nigel Benn and Chris.

The family with their friends in Tenerife who opened the shop in Las Americas.

Chris and June having a laugh in Tenerife, 1993.

Carlie, Anthony and Daryll on holiday in Calahonda, Spain.

Annette, Carlie & Daryll on holiday at Disneyland Paris.

Stephen Yates's mum Janet with Chris at Chris's house in 1993.

Anthony and Rhianwen, his long-term girlfriend, in Mexico. Still going strong with a beautiful boy, Dylan.

Opening night at Parliament was hostile. All the firms from all over Manchester turned up and stood around the dance floor, leaving a gaping hole in the middle like a school disco.

Parliament in Ardwick today, abandoned. Anthony and Chris wore bulletproof vests on the way in and out of this place – it was an asylum.

Jeff, Chris and Stephen outside the Church pub, Northenden.

Chris and Darren Jones at Chris's 30th.

Arthur's scrapyard where the investigation Operation Bluebell started.

Bonfire night on the farm before the arrest – the lads all wearing Gio-Goi.

Anthony, in Hacienda T-shirt having his hair cut, with daughter Carlie just before he was arrested.

A FRIEND DROPPING IN

Manchester Evening News

38,962 THURSDAY, OCTOBER 6, 1994 30p

19 PAGES OF JOBS

Woman: Driving force of drama Page 12

On the Heartbeat Page 35

STYLE PAIR ACCUSED IN DRUG RAID

■ Christopher, left, and Anthony: Held overnight after arrests

TWO fashion gurus were due in court this afternoon following the seizure of Ecstasy, heroin and guns by armed police who raided several homes.

Brothers Anthony and Christopher Donnelly, bosses of trendsetting Gio Goi at Ardwick Green, Manchester, were charged with drug offences last night.

The pair, billed as Manchester's answer to Dior and Yves St Laurent, joined top designers at a Paris exhibition last month.

Their designer gear is so highly-rated it has been worn on tour by top pop bands including Happy Mondays.

By Steve Panter

They have been described as the Sex Pistols of the fashion world, with designs regarded as "radical and magical."

Gio Goi burst on the fashion scene four years ago at London's biggest menswear show.

They splattered paint over their stand at Earls Court and threw a party for friends and celebrities like Happy Mondays and Stone Roses.

The brothers organised the first rave parties in Manchester in the late 80s and made top contacts in the world of music.

They were held in custody last night after being charged by regional crime squad detectives who raided several homes in Greater Manchester yesterday.

Anthony Donnelly, 29, a company managing director, of Whitehouse Farm, Hazel Grove, Stockport, was charged with conspiracy to supply drugs.

Christopher Donnelly, 26, of Kingsway, West Didsbury, was charged with supplying heroin.

The brothers' father, Arthur Donnelly, 52, a scrap dealer, from Torkington Road, Hazel Grove, faced six charges of conspiracy to supply drugs.

Michael Carpenter, 40, a builder, of Parsonage Road, Heaton Moor, Stockport, was charged with conspiracy to supply and possession of drugs.

Deborah O'Neill, 29, of Gladeside Road, Benchill, Wythenshawe, was charged with possession of a revolver without a firearms certificate and supply of drugs.

Jonathan Faulkner, 20, of Bedford Avenue, Whalley Range, was charged with conspiracy to supply drugs and supplying diazapam.

A police officer from Stockport was released on police bail after he was questioned by detectives.

He was facing possible suspension from duty today and was consulting lawyers.

An accountant from Worsley was also bailed after questioning by detectives.

The front page of the *Manchester Evening News* the morning after the arrest.

Fashion boss's arrest ordeal

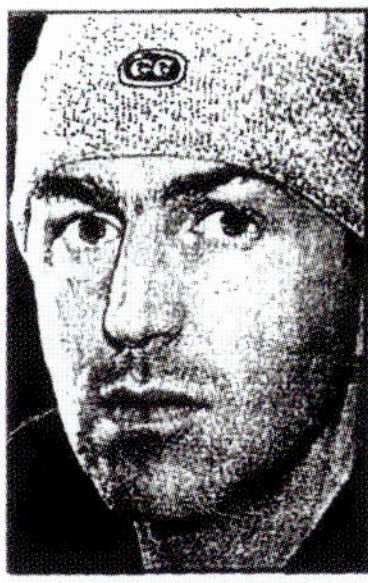

ANGRY ... Donnelly

By Paul Taylor

MANCHESTER fashion entrepreneur Christopher Donnelly told today of his seven-week ordeal accused of a serious drugs offence.

Prosecution lawyers told city magistrates they were dropping their case against Mr Donnelly, who had been accused of conspiracy to supply heroin.

He spoke angrily of how he had been arrested at gunpoint and how the charge had cast a cloud over the Gio Goi fashion empire, where he is one of the bosses.

Mr Donnelly, 26, was arrested last month at his home in Kingsway, Didsbury — one of several held after an undercover police operation.

"The police kicked down the door at 6:00am when I was in bed," he said. "They had me handcuffed in the street, face down with a gun at my head.

"They told my neighbours I was a drug dealer. Now the charges have been dropped — and I don't suppose they will tell my neighbours that."

Mr Donnelly was released from custody 36 hours later, after a court appearance at which he was bailed on £10,000 surety.

Mr Donnelly had to check in with police daily as part of bail conditions, which hindered his work.

His fashion firm has been described as Wythenshawe's answer to Dior and Yves St Laurent.

Mr Donnelly and his 29-year old brother Anthony founded their firm in the late-80s, finding support from celebrity friends from bands like the Happy Mondays and Stone Roses.

Now Gio Goi's brand of upmarket casual gear is in demand as far afield as Japan.

The *Manchester Evening News* report on the aftermath of Chris's arrest by armed police.

The Gio-Goi shop opened in Covent Garden while Anthony was on remand in Strangeways as a Category A prisoner.

June, Arthur and an officer from HMP Full Sutton. Arthur was allowed out on day release to attend his mum's funeral.

Arthur and Tracey at the yard.

were notorious as people. There was rarely any trouble – most of the doormen at The Hacienda, they'd be on door and then you'd see them later on the dance floor. The Hacienda had great doormen – Jimmy, Fred, Donald – who really looked after the people and you'd respect them like they'd respect you. There was no gangster vibe in the club at the time – we were as rough as it got. I'd be shouting to the doorman in the queue, 'Have you got our names on there? Tonight it's Anthony Donnelly plus twenty.' It was the most friendly place in the world at that time.

Christopher: We could do what we wanted in The Hacienda. It was our club. I had my own guest list. People would come up to The Hacienda and say, 'I'm on Chris Donnelly's guest list.' Anthony had his own guest list. That's not because we were running the door; that's because we were nice. We were not enforcing any power on anybody. We were there to have a night out. We were part of this whole thing, at the forefront – pioneers of the Acid House period. When Anthony says we own The Hacienda, he makes it sound gangster. It wasn't like that. We were welcome – we'd go to the front of the queue and get waved in – not because we were being thugs but because we were at the forefront of this explosion. Don't get me wrong, we were still in there with the lads who are from our area and you had other crowds in there, but at that time there wasn't any trouble between any of the firms.

At Stuffed Olives there was an eclectic mix of music but at The Hacienda it was pure dance music. Once the dance thing kicked in I was full on into dance music. Only the DJs knew the names of the tracks, though. I was constantly saying to Mike Pickering, 'Play Swan Lake, play Swan Lake.' He'd say, 'I've just played it for you.' I'd be thinking, 'I've not heard it.' I learned six months later it was 'Voodoo Ray' [*key Acid House track by Manchester's A Guy Called Gerald*].

Anthony: I watched my mate, the chef, in the queue at The Hacienda. That amazed me. I watched the queue, before the doors opened, being served. He was going along the queue and shouting, 'Ecstasy,' and people were waving £20 notes waiting to be served. There were hundreds of people in the queue. It was amazing. The police wasn't on it with the tablets at the start.

Christopher: The first time Anthony and me went to the Kitchen [*an infamous Acid House era illegal after club hours meeting place that consisted of a couple of squatted flats in Hulme with a hole crudely knocked through the adjoining wall*], Kermit from the Ruthless Rap Assassins and Black Grape was on the decks. We walked straight into the main room and started dancing – Anthony, me and a couple of lads from our estate. All these black geezers burst into the room and were staring: 'Who are these skinny white kids who've just come into our gaff?' Kermit was playing Public Enemy's 'Don't Believe the Hype' and we were losing the plot to it – they couldn't work out what it was. They were freaked out.

At the time the Kitchen was a shebeen, a smokers'-type place. Within the space of a week, two weeks, it turned into an Acid House thing and the place was bouncing. I came out of The Hacienda one night and saw our cousin. I walked up the road to the Kitchen with him and he was saying, 'This is just what Manchester needs.' Our cousin was the last person you'd expect to get into the dance vibe. You'd see him as the person who was always the first one to steam into a fight, now he's on the dance floor getting down with me. It was a real buzz.

Anthony: We went to London for the launch of the Happy Mondays' second album, *Bummed*, at Spectrum [*September 1988, in London, a Monday club night, with DJ Paul Oakenfold, where Acid House began to be popularised in the capital*] – just for a night out. I had this Page 3 girl in tow. I love what Noel Gallagher says about Liam when they used to go to the zoo when they were kids and the chimps would go get their kids to come out and look at Liam. It felt like we belonged in a zoo. We went to the club and everyone from London was like. 'There they are – that's what we're hearing about in Manchester.' The amount of drugs being consumed was unbelievable. The London E scene was much bigger for the raves but nowhere near as out of it as Manchester – it became a religion up here.

At Spectrum this kid came out of the toilet and flicked water all over me. All he wanted was a hug. Before E I would have kicked off. I didn't give him a hug but I certainly didn't attack him.

In Manchester I'd see all the hard-core football hooligans going to games and there was no violence. There were a lot of people at Old Trafford and Maine Road E'd up. The knives were put down. The football hooligans ended up going to the away games and, instead of fighting, meeting up and going out clubbing. That's where the link came with all the other towns. The main crews, the kids that were always at the forefront of football and fashion, they was now embracing each other and they were buying Es and getting on the dance floor together. It was a revolution. Mobile phones started kicking in. You could get things and do things. We were communicating with people. The lack of Ecstasy actually brought people together. We were Ecstasy takers and suspected of being Ecstasy suppliers. It truly changed my outlook on the life that I knew. As people, Christopher and I were transformed. We come from such a volatile background and now it was like we were being moulded into something else.

Christopher: I was going to Liverpool for a night out whereas before the Acid House explosion I would never have gone to

Liverpool – not with a Manc accent. Manchester and Liverpool was not cool because of the football, but Acid House broke all those barriers down. Violence became non-existent. The main football heads were on the dance floor and not just hooligans but proper geezers – I called them dancing gangsters. We were partying with all the main heads in Liverpool, we were treated like royalty over there and they were treated the same when they were in Manchester.

We loved the scene that much we decided to do Manchester's first illegal 'warehouse' party. It was seize the day. The Hacienda closed at 2 a.m. and we wanted to party all night. We called the party 'Sweat It Out' and on the flyer we used an image of a lad who used to go to Stuffed Olives – he was a black geezer who wore these big, weird goggles on the dance floor. We were promoting the party for about a month.

It was advertised as Store Street. We were going to do it there but the warehouse was that bad we couldn't put it on there – but the flyers had already gone out. So what we did was we sprayed a smiley face and sign at that venue saying, 'Wait here at 11 p.m.' Everybody waited, hundreds of smiley faces, and then they were transported to somewhere else – there'd just been a whole load of railway arches done up by the council. We'd built a stage out of scaffolding, used our dad's wagon to transport it, bolt-cropped the railway arch doors, drove the wagon in and we built it all in there.

We had Mike Pickering and Jon DaSilva DJing. It really kicked off. We had five or six strobe lights; never stopped once, right though until ten in the morning. It went off with a boom, not a bang. The police turned up in the morning and they didn't have a clue what was going on. All they could find was water and juice and probably a hundred bottles of Bollinger champagne for the little VIP area we had in there for Tony Wilson and friends. The police couldn't get their head round putting on a big party and there wasn't any beer. They were confused. They didn't know what to do. Bottles of water everywhere. Wilson really liked what we were doing. He was into the punk thing and this scene was the only other thing that moved him. Anything we did, a rave or warehouse party, Tony would be there.

Anthony: Sweat It Out was 8 October 1988. There were about 1,500 people there. It was a great success. Tony Wilson, Rob Gretton [*New Order's manager, Factory Records' partner and co-founder of The Hacienda*], New Order and Noel Gallagher were all there. At one point my neighbour passed out and looked dead. I spent half an hour worrying about trying to get rid of his body. We carried him out of the building. 'Don't let him die in here.' He soon came round as we carried him to the car. Me, Shaun [*Ryder*] and Tony Wilson were in a backroom and I pulled out a big twelve-inch blade. Wilson looks up and goes, 'What the fuck are you doing?' Shaun was laughing. Then I pulled out a bag of powder and put the knife in and then Wilson was laughing. I was snorting the powder off the blade. Someone was filming us. We didn't care nor did we know when to stop.

Christopher: We ran out of drinks at one point. I had a Fiat Uno and all the drinks were in the back of my car. We lifted up the shutters of the warehouse and it was thick with smoke, there was people dropping with exhaustion because we had the strobe lights on. I put the hazard lights on the Uno on and slowly drove it into the crowd. It was like *E.T.*, everyone was staring at the car, waving their hands in the air. It was definitely about putting the thing on rather than making money – the doormen charged three quid to get in but it was twenty-five quid for a pill off the guys who were serving in there. Ecstasy was getting to be big business for the dealers.

Tracey: I was put in charge of all the promotions at Factory, so I arranged all the T-shirts, photography and all that. If Anthony and Christopher were doing [*bootleg*] T-shirts anyway, I'd want them to be involved. It was a way of getting them into it. I think they did an early Hacienda T-shirt. It was Sweat It Out though that changed things.

I invited Tony Wilson, he came down and they'd made a little VIP area for him. Don't forget the last thing he had heard of them two is the big fight on the door at The Hacienda. But he was blown away and he became their biggest fan from that moment – he noted their ambition and talent.

Mike Pickering: I loved Anthony and Chris. Sweat It Out was brilliant. At another party of theirs the coppers arrived in the morning and me and Chris were sweeping up all these water bottles and Fanta cans. We said, 'Look, as you can see, it was a really sober event. Tony Wilson from *Granada Reports* was here.' There was nothing they could say to that so we managed to get away with it. Brilliant night.

That was right at the beginning of the revolution. At that time, if you were in that movement, it was like being in a secret society; no one knew about it. The first eighteen months was the whole beauty of it. It was only really when *News at Ten* and *The Sun* got hold of it that our cover was blown. We could do anything and go anywhere and the police didn't have a clue, all they could see was people that used to cause trouble not causing trouble anymore and no one drinking. They didn't realise that there was Ecstasy or anything like that at the time.

Anthony and Chris organised another rave in a warehouse just behind the Mancunian Way. To get in you got on this flatbed lift which took you right up into the middle of the rave. When the police came we left the lift at the bottom so they couldn't get up. They were stood at the bottom, going, 'Get this lift up!' We were at the top looking down, going, 'No sorry, we can't. It's broken.' Anthony laughed at the thought of a dozen policemen negotiating on his terms – we weren't coming out until we were finished.

Anthony: As things progressed we got on great with all Tracey's crowd. When it came to the Acid House era The Hacienda was taken over by the lads. As soon as we decided it was going to be ours it was ours and not hers. As soon as the E pill dropped it was our thing and all her crowd suddenly wanted to come to our parties.

The next warehouse party we did was 'Sweat It Out 2' on New Year's Day 1989. We did it in a bed factory in Ardwick, on the fourth floor. The police turned up, but the only way up to the warehouse was by the lift and we locked them out by pushing the lift up a floor. They were arguing with us all night through the lift shaft. The police turned up at all of our events but whether they got in, that's a different story. With Sweat It Out 2 we picked the worst night possible; we must have been mad. We'd been out all night at The Hacienda on New Year's Eve and then decided to do a party the night after – we thought everyone would want to continue the party. The hard-core was there but it didn't achieve what we set out to do. It turned out to be more of family party . . . the immediate 200 or 300 E-heads who always turned up.

The next morning the police were happy to let people go home but they wanted to come in and see who was left. They found me running about with Mike Pickering – as always the last to leave.

Our relationship with Factory had really started to strengthen. One night I was summoned to the roof of The Hacienda to meet Rob [*Gretton*] and Tony [*Wilson*]. I was on the dance floor and someone tapped me on the shoulder and said, 'They want you upstairs.' I'd never been on The Hacienda roof before. I got up there and we were smoking weed and discussing what can be done with the club. It was beautiful. I was young and it's a very attractive, shiny business, the music business, or that's how it appears on the surface. We were being sucked into all this. We're starting to build all these connections and the main men wanted to talk to me. I felt like I was in charge.

We were invited to go to Box studios in Bath where New Order were recording the album *Technique* for an Acid party. Box was part of Peter Gabriel's recording studio, Real World Studios. It was all filmed. Tony [*Wilson*] filmed it. No one's ever found the footage. We got the coach down and I was sitting with Pickering. I put a little parcel of E in Rizla papers, everyone was eating them; we were calling them 'E bombs'. I was off my barnet dancing with Tracey. Stephen and Gillian [*Morris and Gilbert, of New Order*] were saying to Tracey, 'Who is he? Is he mithering you?' Bernard [*Sumner*] knew me already.

It was around the time of the big importations coming into the North-West, so there was good charlie starting to creep into the scene as well. We were up all night and Peter Gabriel was coming back, so they had to try and get us all off the land – fifty-two Ecstasy-crazed Mancs with eyes like fifty pence pieces, no one knows what day it is. This was the A-Team of the E heads from The Hacienda, hand chosen. It was a New Order party for the crème of the crop. When we were leaving the coach got stuck and there were six or seven of us thinking we had the strength to push it out of the mud.

Christopher: They might have been there recording six weeks and they were missing the Acid House vibe so they booked a coach that left from The Hacienda. We all drove up, had a full-on night, and then got on the coach in the morning to come back. On numerous occasions I recall being on the dance floor with Bernard and his missus, Sarah. When New Order released

Technique [*January 1989*] they asked us to organise a rave in The Hacienda basement. It was strange the way they did it – like a VIP party that went on all night. By now the scene was getting recognition in the mainstream.

I came back from Ibiza and I put *Top of the Pops* on and 'Big Fun' [*by Inner City, released late 1988*] was on. It was a great tune but in the video they all had smiley face T-shirts on and everyone was dancing in this uniform way. It had gone to the masses. It was our thing and all of a sudden the vibe changed. We still loved it. We still believed in it. But it wasn't as pure. It was our beautiful thing and then everybody woke up. It was getting bigger and I wanted to keep it for us, just the original Acid House corner. Like anything cool it becomes a trend. We were already starting to look for other things to do.

Anthony: Rob [*Gretton*] loved how we operated. We were asked to organise the rave for New Order in the basement of The Hacienda but we had our own plans by now. We couldn't vouch for anything that went on inside. We didn't want any responsibility. And these people were now our mentors. All we did for that party was provided a service – we supplied the doormen and we didn't take wages. I couldn't work out why they had a buffet? Why they wanted food in a rave? Anyway, they were very appreciative and the doormen we supplied were really grateful because they got paid well.

The Hacienda then did a joint party with The Roxy club in Amsterdam [*May 1989, The Hacienda's seventh birthday party*]. The Mondays went over on a coach and I flew there. [*New Order bassist*] Peter Hook didn't go, so I stayed in his room. I was with Bez. We saw a bird onstage – a transvestite – with a hat on, naked, ramming a chocolate cake up her fanny. We left the club and there was this other girl we'd been with and she started talking like the devil on the pavement. That freaked me out. Six in the morning, dusk meeting dawn, that nice happy, medium light, and she's rolling about speaking like Lucifer. We were all on acid. But Amsterdam wasn't ready for us – they were so far behind. They had some beautiful drugs but the scene was really raw. Once again, the circus had been and gone and left its mark.

Christopher: The party that goes down in folklore – anyone who was there will tell you – was my twenty-first birthday [*May 1989*]. It was held at my mum and dad's farm in Stockport. Graeme Park, Mike Pickering and Jon DaSilva were DJing. I whitewashed the whole barn. Every warehouse party we did, we painted the warehouse first, whitewashed it, because we wanted it to be clean. Then I sprayed all weird symbols and pictures on the wall of the barn.

The Roses were there, the Mondays, New Order were supposed to be bringing Quincy Jones – why I don't know. Anybody who was anybody, my grandma, my mother-in-law, some of my aunties, thousands of my pals from all over the country. It went on all day and night and into the next day. I've got all the footage. It was complete cross-section of people. It felt like we were all in the mix together – the wrong 'uns from Wythenshawe were together with pop stars. The police said we'd thrown this party under the guise of being a twenty-first but really it was a rave. In the end they said if we filtered everyone out slowly they wouldn't make any arrests.

Mike Pickering: I used to play everything for them. I was like their family DJ. Chris's twenty-first birthday party was amazing. I'd been asked to DJ later because they'd got a kid in to do the early slot; he was used to family weddings, etc. I remember there being all kinds of goings on outside. The police had walked up and down the road, smashing a load of windscreens – it was the obvious standoff. It got to about eleven and this DJ went, 'Right,

I'm off.' Anthony asked him, very politely, to stay on for a bit but he wasn't having any of it. He picked up his records and went to walk out. Next thing, I heard June say, 'Oh, Anthony,' and he had the lad by his neck and lifted him back across the dance floor. I said to the DJ, 'I think you should stay, mate.' It was a mad party. I recall stumbling into a barn full of telephone boxes that Arthur had picked up from somewhere at one point.

Anthony: We were now going to Ibiza and [*the club*] Amnesia, when it had no roof, with DJ Alfredo – the legendary DJ. We were having it with people like him, we were putting our own nights on, we were still doing the tickets [*touting*] and basically it was really taking off. We are now known as key players on the Acid House scene and people are saying, 'They're going to smash it, those two brothers!' And now the thing we detest most, the farm, because it's so far from the estate, has become a valuable asset because everyone wants a venue to put an illegal rave on. At some point we thought someone should put E in the reservoirs to get the message across to the people of this country about how great Ecstasy was, that's how insane we had become.

Christopher: The farm became somewhere we could use. We'd have bonfire nights and barbeques there . . . there were a hundred of us and it was proper military. Now we were a 'team'. That was it, full on. We'd be at the farm clay pigeon shooting and that was how we rolled – the farm became a retreat for us. Our old firm still look after each other and it still exists to a certain extent today, but obviously a lot of them are dead. I mean a hell of a lot of them. If we could we'd go to every party in the country.

There was a firm from Blackpool used come to Manchester every week. They became friends of ours. We went up there for a period of time to a club called Oz on the pier run by Magoo – nothing like The Hacienda; it was an old-fashioned club. After the club had finished, you'd get to a service station and all the boots would be open on the cars. People would be dancing at the side of the cars with the tunes going. All that was going on. That's not a myth – all that used to happen. We wouldn't be involved in that shit, but some pals of ours were charging people to go on the service station and these fuckers were happy paying to get on.

The first year of Acid House passed largely under the radar of the authorities and the mainstream media. Then, in July 1989, sixteen-year-old Claire Leighton died after taking a £15 E at The Hacienda. A moral panic ensued as Acid House was explicitly linked to this relatively unknown new drug. The Sun *ran an infamous 'Evil of Ecstasy' front cover. In 1988, the Greater Manchester Police had not arrested one person for the supply of Ecstasy. Now they were beginning to take a real interest. James Anderton, head of Greater Manchester Police, was particularly eager to crack down on warehouse parties in the city. As a consequence, the nearby Lancashire town of Blackburn would become a focus for an explosion of warehouse parties in the summer of 1989. There was talk of the Blackburn firm ram-raiding a shop window to acquire a generator and police patrol cars set alight outside their parties that attracted up to 10,000 people.*

The Government also began to act. Home Secretary Douglas Hurd ordered an enquiry into unlicensed parties. The BBC banned Jolly Roger's 'Acid Man' track. One thousand police, with dogs and tactical aid, busted an Energy party. The Pay Party Unit was formed with 200 intelligence officers to police raves. They began monitoring names, vehicles and telephone calls. In this climate, The Donnelly Brothers were planning their most audacious rave yet: Joy in August 1989.

Anthony: Now we were going for the monster raves with our cousin Tony. A friend chose to do it at Stand Lees Farm, Ashworth Valley in Rochdale. The farm owner was related in some way to a member of the Donnelly family. I hated the land because it was on a slope. Between Sweat It Out 2 and Joy there were no raves – we just went very intense, setting up a big operation. This is when we were forging links with people in Essex and London, people in Leeds, Liverpool, the main firm from Blackburn. We were working with someone from London on Joy – we were affiliated with someone, one way or another. Joy was a north/south coming together, the only one done illegally.

If we were doing a party the last thing we would want would be a load of other people doing parties on the same night. So we went to Liverpool, to the Underground, where James Barton [*now the celebrated owner of Cream*] was putting a night on. James was like us in a lot of ways, he used to sell tickets like us. We'd say, 'Listen, we're putting a party on we don't want you to have your night, so we can get all your crowd to our party.' We'd go and speak to all these people in different towns to ask them not to put on their event on the same night. It was all friendly, and maybe they would end up doing the tickets in Liverpool or Blackburn or wherever. Together [*rave organisers*] Genesis, Sunrise and Energy had done events down south that attracted up to 20,000 people. It's not about warehouses any more; it's about these massive events with lasers, fairground rides, and huge sound systems. That's what we were aiming at.

Christopher: A warehouse was already built. You broke in or rented it, put in a smoke machine and strobes. Joy was a major challenge. We had to build a humongous stage, hire fairgrounds, generators, lighting rigs – we were putting on an outdoor event. The police were flying around in helicopters looking for marquees going up. They were actively out trying to stop these events. The police have got light aircraft on the look out.

Anthony: Inspector X was in charge of licensing. He was the Acid House squad, and he would try and follow us. If you were into raves, you were into pills – that was his logic. But putting raves on doesn't mean you were a drug dealer. These things cost a considerable amount of money to put on and the finger of suspicion was always on us: that we were involved in the illegal supply of Ecstasy to fund the event. I categorically deny that. Our backers raised the money through sponsorship with drinks companies. Rumour has it that certain celebrities also financed it. But, also, you can't go and put something substantial on in a town that's twinned with Chicago without being affiliated in some way, it just doesn't happen unless you're connected.

For two weeks we had scaffolders on site, the production, the marquees and the fun fair – these things can't be dropped on site on the day. That's why they, the police, were in the air looking for things like this being built. It was a really expensive production –£5,000 on fireworks, etc. Grooverider, Sasha, Paul Oakenfold, Mike Pickering, Laurent Garnier, Graeme Park and Frankie Knuckles were all booked to DJ.

Cyril Smith was the MP for the area where the farm was in Rochdale. He started to put a case together to oppose the party – this was played out in the *Manchester Evening News*. Then some bright spark told Cyril to get on a plane to the Houses of Parliament so he could drum up some support to get an injunction signed. They had to hire three seats for the fat bastard on the plane. In Parliament, he called us, Christopher and me, 'menaces to society' and 'the main organisers behind this revolution they call Acid House'. The injunction was passed – it was actually hand-written because they didn't have time to type it before he got back on the plane. The next morning on the front page of the *Manchester Evening News*, the headline was, 'It's Off'.

Christopher: The police were on the top of the hill filming us setting this big rave up: two carloads with suits and binoculars. It was like *Life on Mars*, they're up there and they've got the broad ties on and silly blazers and we've got the All Stars on, tie-dyed T-shirts. They couldn't stop it. The feedback that came to us was: are they going to have 10,000 kids on drugs all whizzing round these mountains looking for this party and the police telling them to go home, or is it easier to just let them go into this field and fill their boots? Contain it all and then fuck everyone off home when they've had enough.

Anthony: They served Mike Pickering with the injunction. They couldn't find anyone to serve it on except for Pickering. He was named on the flyer. Pickering had to evidence the fact that he wasn't in the area at the time of the rave. [*Tony*] Wilson videoed Pickering holding up the front page of the paper, stood under a clock . . . on the front page of the paper it said, 'Party Goes Ahead'.

Mike Pickering: I couldn't play Joy. I had a flat above the Arndale at the time; on the Friday morning the police kicked my door in, dragged me out of bed and said I had to be in court by 10 a.m. the same day. They were saying there was an injunction being placed on me by Rochdale council because I was planning to DJ an illegal rave. I rang Tony Wilson and Anthony and they were all sat in the public gallery. I managed to get a lawyer at the last minute. They put an order out saying I couldn't go within a fifteen-mile radius of Rochdale for the whole weekend. It was unheard of, but that's the effect these raves were having.

Anthony: Twenty thousand people turned up. We built a stage that was 200ft long, like Glastonbury. We had a big wheel and dodgems. We marketed T-shirts. This was an illegal rave but it had an official T-shirt and a programme. It had everything. We had a World War Two searchlight and I was sat on the light because you had to sit on it to move it. I was out of my head. I kept swinging the thing onto the people trying to sneak in and they would freeze like rabbits. We called them E bunnies. You could see these E freaks coming over the hill, groups of ten, trying to sneak in without paying their fifteen quid. One kid got sectioned because he reckoned an angel came down and visited him. It was the light. He was on acid.

Christopher: Our mum and dad were there. They weren't taking drugs or anything, just watching events unfold. In 1988, on New Year's Eve, my mum and dad were in The Hacienda with us. They saw midnight in and went off to do their own thing while we carried on partying all night.

[*My wife*] Natalie's dad, Jack, was at Joy. He was the most chilled out nice fella, a painter and decorator. He was in the tent where the money was and he was there all night trying to keep an eye on things for us. Money was going missing on the night because it was all cash and everyone wanted paying in cash. You can't account for how many have come to the event unless you get your tickets back. We were open to snides [*fake tickets*]. It was a difficult thing to control. Hard work. There was no ultraviolet or hologram on the tickets, and even if there had been we were in a field surrounded by mountains in the pitch black. How ironic – the ticket touts are being touted. Funny.

Anthony: It was happening everywhere: people were forging tickets for raves. You just want to smoke pot at that age, get up late and go to a club. So, who's dealing with the holograms, who's dealing with the people taking the phone calls, who's distributing tickets, who's going to collect the money? I just wanted to dance all night. I was one of the last to leave.

Joy was a big success but no one got paid. We didn't get paid. I went to collect some money from Spin-Inn Records in town and there was a bird I didn't even know collecting the ticket money. It was a free-for-all. There was money everywhere and a lot of suspicion about who had the majority of it. People were just grabbing what they could. Ultimately, there was no back end and everybody lost money.

It caused a few complications. People who had not been paid needed paying. It got a bit heated. I had people coming to see me and basically they were very upset about not being paid. I had to explain that I'd not been paid. It culminated in me and some other people from London going to see somebody who'd been paid handsomely for the event. It ended up in a bit of a fallout, resulting in a car ending up looking like Swiss cheese. It was intense – the trouble over the non-payment – so I went to Amsterdam to chill out.

I went with all my guys on a stag do. I was sat in my hotel room smoking a joint, waiting to go out with the boys and watching Sky News. And it came on the news that two kids have been decapitated in Manchester. I was working with these kids and they'd been bought a motorbike by somebody to do whatever they were doing. These two kids got high on amphetamines, left a club, drove into a lamppost and both lost their heads. I was on the phone to the UK, saying, 'Is that right, the two kids we were working with have both lost their heads?' My mate came to knock on my room. He had been downstairs in the bar scoring some weed and someone had walked in and shot another fella in the head and killed him. It was never fucking ending – a constant river of shit.

We never made a penny from the parties. We were losing money. There was a major investigation into Joy by the police. And it was like, 'Was it the farm owner? Was it the Donnellys? Was it the production company? Was it a promoter? Who was making the money?' Nobody would admit to it. You can only imagine what the police were thinking: with parties come the drugs. If you're at a rave and there are 10,000 people there, for this to work there needs to be 10,000 trips or 10,000 tablets. It was getting too much, all of it.

Christopher: Joy was a nightmare afterwards. We were always about putting the best possible show on for the people coming to the parties, and we still are. So we never made any real money out of any of the events we were involved in. As long as our reputation was intact for putting the best party on, that's what we were about. It was about making money when we were putting them on, but it never panned out like that. We would always over spend. We'd want it to be the bollocks – that's the way we are. So it doesn't matter, it's not about the money – if it was our name it had to be the best it could be. You could have fitted 30,000 people on that field at Joy.

Everyone from Oakenfold to Adamski, all the best DJs of the time, were there. The kid who put the light show on had done Biology and Sunrise. I went to Blackpool on the bus to sort the geezer to bring his laser show to the party and I had to use a bandana to cover my face. You couldn't let the geezer see your face because if he got nicked he'd have stuck you in as the organisers. It was just: here's the address, here's the paperwork, see you then. That's how it was done.

With Inspector X, it was like a comedy. Everywhere we were, he'd turn up ten minutes after we'd left. He interviewed Anthony and me at my mother-in-law's over Joy. He was three or four parties behind us. They were like, 'Bastards, they've just left' – so we became a kind of urban myth to him.

Anthony: I have read that we did Live the Dream [*a huge outdoor mega-rave that took place in Blackburn, September 1989*]. Not true. We were not involved in any shape or form in promoting it, just affiliated with the people putting it on. I went down there and people were swimming in a lake. It was complete madness. At another night in Blackburn it was out and out war with the police. We were still up for parties but not the big raves with the mother ship lasers and all the monster stuff. All that was important now was the sound system and getting the thing off the ground. Everyone went back to grassroots – a generator and a sound system. We put a party on in Cheshire. You take security and you put a perimeter fence up round the marquee and funnel people in – security will monitor the perimeter of the marquee. We had booked Frankie Knuckles to DJ. We were laughing because a prison was so close the prisoners would have been able to hear the music. We were aiming for 5,000 people, a marquee in a field, a generator and lights.

Christopher: We were in the field all ready to go. Instead of putting up the marquee we left it flat until the last minute and then the idea was 'bang', up it goes. Once the people are in there, the police can't do fuck all. It was down a country lane and we'd told everyone to keep the wagon lights off. But one of the drivers of the wagons drove down with his lights on full beam and the farmer saw it. He rang the police because somebody had been nicking the farm machinery. When the police came, somebody had nicked a manhole cover and a copper fell down and broke both of his legs. And then a wagon was flying up and it nearly took his head off. It was one of the wettest and windiest nights as well. It was carnage, all the party people arriving and the police blocking the road off. The security was there – fifty men – and they all wanted paying. It was not their fault the event didn't go ahead. The marquee man had got his tent halfway up . . . it was just chaos.

We had a van full of booze and soft drinks and Anthony, me, and John the Duck drove to Blackburn looking for a party there. We took an E each and spent the night driving around. I can't remember if we went to a party we were that off our heads. Then the next day you wake up and you've lost loads of money and the security still want paying. You have got to go and front all this security – big geezers. I was twenty-two, about nine stone wet through and the bouncers back then had no licences. So you hoped you could come to an amicable agreement.

Anthony: What did you achieve in your life? That's the question you got to ask yourself. If we did have some money spare we would have a go. Every other fucker was too tight to make that attempt and that's where we got our respect. We would at least try. We had the balls because of our upbringing to challenge the authorities and that's what we did.

5
BLAGS TO RICHES (MADCHESTER)

In November 1989, the Happy Mondays played their biggest gig to date at the Free Trade Hall in Manchester. The same night fellow Manchester band The Stone Roses played their biggest gig to date at Alexandra Palace in London. Days later both bands appeared on the same edition of Top of the Pops. *The Roses played their single 'Fools Gold' and the Mondays played 'Hallelujah' from their* Madchester – Rave On *EP. It was a watershed moment for both bands and precipitated an avalanche of media interest in all things Manchester. The city was declared the 'Rave' capital of the UK and 'Madchester' was born. The* NME *would run fifteen Manchester-related cover stories in 1990. The success stories were to be found elsewhere as hungry record labels snapped up every available Manchester band. It was a new gold rush. Some said the cloth was mightier than the chord, as Madchester quickly became as much about the look as the music. Bands' T-shirt sales were a massive money-spinner. Eric Barker, for instance, was now making a lot of money handling 808 State's merchandising. The Inspiral Carpets were said to sell more T-shirts than records. Leo Stanley, who owned the Identity shop in Afflecks Palace, hit pay dirt with a T-shirt that read ' . . . AND ON THE SIXTH DAY, GOD CREATED MANchester.'*

Christopher: We'd known the Mondays for years. I first met Bez when I was sat in Swing having my hair cut. He'd just robbed a fruit machine. He was off his head mid-afternoon. We went to the Mondays' gig at Corbieres in 1985. So although we were from Wythenshawe and they were from Salford we were pally with Shaun and Bez – through our Tracey. When Shaun was arrested in Jersey for cocaine possession, Tracey was the one that went to get him out of custody; she had clearly learnt from us about bail situations. She pretty much looked after the Happy Mondays at Factory and she was there from the beginning. We'd always be at the same sort of places as the Mondays, and they were just lads like us but they were in a band. We just became pals.

Anthony: Tracey was the bridge. She said, 'You'll like them and they'll like you.' This 'Madchester' scene that everybody was going on about, it was thirty people. We were asked to do the Happy Mondays T-shirts. Tony [*Wilson*] gave Tracey the artwork for 'W.F.L.' [*the twelve-inch remix of 'Wrote For Luck' by Vince Clarke and Paul Oakenfold, released September 1989*] and she'd sent it to us – we were supposed to do the official T-shirts. The artwork was by Matt and Pat Carroll [*of the acclaimed and notorious Central Station Design, who did all the Happy Mondays covers*]. We drove round with the artwork for a week and we did nothing with it. In the end we just sent it back. We were too busy bootlegging other bands and it seemed too corporate a thing for us to do. We stuck to doing it outside. But what we did for the Mondays was the party after the Free Trade Hall gig.

Christopher: We did it on the fifth floor of this broken down warehouse. I had to get the generator, the lights, the sound system, off the back of the wagon and into the lift. You're driving on someone else's property at night, looking out for security guards in a seven and half tonne wagon. I set up and met Natalie at the Free Trade Hall gig. She'd been to Afflecks and bought me new jogging bottoms and a top. I had oil all over my hands. I was standing on the side of the stage watching the Mondays and Nathan [*McGough, Mondays' manager*] came on stage at the end and said, 'If you all want to go to a party, come off at this junction off the motorway, third exit off the roundabout, there's a warehouse.' We had booked Sasha to DJ.

Anthony: We always call this one the 'Manchester Siege'. It looked like a break-in but wasn't. A man who had three months to live orchestrated it. He had the key and wanted some money off the ticket sales on the door but there was a siege. The police turned up. The kids that helped put on the party were off our estate and they were bricking the police. They were on the roof throwing slates at the police. The *NME* was there and there was a load of Dutch media. The journalists all thought this was great – a raid. We had started to get a lot of heat off the police for the parties, so we thought it wise to start to tap into other things.

Christopher: The first parties the police came to they just let everyone go, they let the DJs go and let the equipment go. Now they had the bright idea to start confiscating decks and stuff so someone had to put their hand up and say, 'Can I have my decks back, please?' Then it was, 'Well, who put the party on? Who booked you?' That was when Inspector X started becoming a bit of a pain in the arse. At that party we were running with the decks. Sasha had a deck and I had a deck. We got bored of the police shutting us down and losing money. You're losing money, so you put another one on, you lose a bit more, so you put on another, thinking this is going to be the one. You can only take so many knocks. We were getting kicked in the balls off the authorities shutting everything down, making it hard work.

So we decided to open an office in Imex House [*office complex on Princess Street in Manchester city centre*]. You could just go in and say, 'I need an office for a few months' and they'd say, 'Right, it's £50 a week.' There was no leases or anything. It was quite posh. They had a receptionist and our office was all glass. We had no reason to open the office whatsoever. We put two desks in and turned up on the Monday and went, 'Right, now what?' It was a case of if you build it they will come – and people did start to come. James Barton and Andy Carroll used to come down once a week. Dave Hardy came in with World of Twist [*upcoming Madchester-era band*] and they were asking us to do bits of merchandise. Then two fellas who needed finance for some video projects approached us. They were called Dat2Dat and they'd filmed the Happy Mondays gig at the Free Trade Hall but didn't have the money to do anything with it. Factory [*Records*] couldn't take it on so we did it as a bootleg but with Factory's permission. We formed a company called D2D and we sold it to HMV as a legal bootleg. We called it 'Madchester'.

Anthony: We always wanted to go into business. It was easy. Because there were no leases, you had a lot of people coming through Imex House. We had our own office and then when we were doing D2D we had another office in there full of editing equipment. In our office we had record decks. During that time people used to come into the office and we'd sit there and make it up as we went along. Then the Mondays did a tour at the end of 1989 [*the Rave On tour, November/December*] and they wanted us to do the end-of-tour party. We booked a place called Hamiltons and called the party 'Madchester'. At that time, nobody wanted the Happy Mondays or us, and that was the only club we could hire – some backward cowshed. It ended up kicking right off. The police shut it down and threw everyone out at midnight.

That was the first party we did with these two Jewish geezers from London. They had been on Esther Rantzen [*That's Life!*] every week for putting on these big car boot sale things, where it was a pound to get in. They open up in a town and take £100,000 out of the town and leave. They were experiencing problems and were looking for something else. We were also looking to legitimise things. They were in £2 million mansions in Wood Hill in London, very flamboyant. They financed the 'Madchester' party and although it got shut down we made money. I think we laid out £10,000 and made £18,000. Then we booked Silver Bullet, Orbital, Mike Pickering and Sasha for a big party in Trentham Gardens in Stoke on Trent. It was a legal party. We approached the authorities and made the necessary applications. We booked strobes, lasers, pyrotechnics, 50,000 watts of sound and video screens. The idea was we were going to do the best in legal house parties, a series of events all around the country catering for between 3,000 to 25,000.

Christopher: We did it legally with these two Jewish kids and the police shut it down. The police were on everyone's case so you had to do legal parties but we got stamped on. It was all legit, but it was the never-ending stigma of the name Donnelly . . . that's what the undercurrent was.

Anthony: The police went down to Trentham Gardens and said, 'This is a load of gangsters from Manchester.' They said, 'If you put it on, we'll be here and we will stop it.' We also booked Blackpool Winter Gardens. We called ourselves Pulse, 'with our finger on the pulse of a nation'. We also had a limited company called Movement Productions. The venues were interested in putting the events on but the police were telling them, 'You're linked up to an illegal Acid House thing here. You're a corporate business and you're going to have every E head in the country turning up at your place.' That's how it was then. If you said you liked to dance, you were literally guilty of being a drug addict. We'd done them illegal and been closed down; now we were trying to do them legal but we couldn't even get through the door.

With the Blackpool one, I was with a girl at the time. I didn't know but her dad was a senior policeman. She went home and told him she was seeing this fella from Manchester and he was doing a rave at the Winter Gardens. He did a police records check on us and it got into the local paper – 'We don't want the Donnellys here' – and it got stopped. She confessed to me. I thought it was an informant as we were in the background on this. I was sat there smoking dope in her house when she told me, then I noticed a photo of her dad with the Queen on the mantelpiece. She then showed me his uniform and hat. I banged her all round the flat with his uniform on. It was great feeling of revenge.

Rave organisers all over the country were losing their battles with police. On New Year's Eve 1989, a Sunrise party for 10,000 was called off when the venue received an injunction. The Sun front page read: 'Ecstasy! The Party's Over'. The Donnelly Brothers were friendly with Sunrise boss Tony Colsten-Hayter. He had hired Paul Staines as a PR man as he fought back against the authorities, launching the Freedom To Party campaign. Staines was a political aide to right-wing maverick and advisor to Margaret Thatcher, David Hart. Today Staines runs the influential Guido Fawkes political blog.

The Freedom To Party campaign was a loose alliance of all the main rave organisers: Sunrise, Energy, Biology and the Donnelly Brothers. They pointed out that in Europe clubbers could legally dance all night. In the UK Graham Bright's Entertainments (Increased Penalties) Bill proposed to raise fines for organising an unlicensed party from £2,000 to £20,000 and six months in prison. Parliament was also implementing the 1988 Criminal Justice Act that allowed for confiscation of 'criminal proceeds' from illegal parties. Ten- and six-year sentences were handed out to organisers of a Thames boat party rave under the Misuse of Drugs Act. Freedom To Party protests in Trafalgar Square and Hyde Park attracted thousands.

Christopher: Paul Staines came up and stayed at my mum and dad's farm. They were in the process of bringing a law out that said if you were in your living room with more than eight people it was considered as a rave. So we said we'd set a protest up in Manchester. The one in London attracted about 20,000 people so we did one outside the Town Hall in Albert Square [*February 1990*]. Three thousand people turned up. I took the generator on the back of my dad's wagon and rigged the DJ up. I did an interview for Granada TV. They asked me what it was all about and I said, 'All we wanna do is dance.'

Anthony: I was a revolutionary. I was part of something. The country was tipped upside down and shook by Acid House. Look at what punk did, and that was a gang of thousands. With Acid House you're talking hundreds of thousands of people closing towns down, no wonder they wanted to stop it. The same night as Freedom To Party in Albert Square there was a warehouse party in Haslingden, Rossendale, near Blackburn. We did an amalgamation with the Blackburn firm – we had become good friends with them. They came to the office. Tony Wilson did a thing about illegal raves [*on Granada TV*]. We were asked to appear on that programme but we declined. The Blackburn firm did it instead. We always wanted to sit in the background.

Christopher: We were all about putting an amazing light show on . . . the Blackburn firm were quite militant, do anything to get their party off but they didn't go to much expense – just get into a warehouse, put the system up and not really have many lights as such. But they were getting huge crowds, and on a weekly basis. To drive over there and just see car after car after car was pretty phenomenal. It was an industrial town; Thatcher had destroyed it, empty warehouses everywhere. What better place to start a party? They were nice kids all of them, the whole Blackburn firm.

Anthony: The party in Haslingden got raided – there was a police helicopter hovering overhead. Even though you wanted to advertise the party you didn't want to advertise anything else and it seemed to be nine times out of ten that the promoters of these events were normally suspected to be linked to other 'business', do you understand me? That's why people tended to want to be in the background. The Blackburn firm got nicked with thousands of trips. Everybody was guilty by association.

The Freedom To Party campaign was a key start in the push for the liberalisation of licensing laws, but a second reading of the Entertainments (Increased Penalties) Bill took place in March 1990 and it would become law in July. At a Love Decade rave in Leeds the police arrested 836 people. The Broadcasting Act closed down pirate radio stations. It was the end of an era. Almost. The final hurrah came courtesy of the Stone Roses. The band's April 1990 epochal gig on Spike Island, a man-made island in Widnes, attracted in excess of 30,000 – the largest rave in the country.

Anthony: We were approached by Tim Mulryan on behalf of the Stone Roses to do the merchandising for Spike Island. We get Securicor to come to the office because we'd got delusions of grandeur and thought we were going to make a fortune. We said, 'Right, we want De La Rue machines. We're doing this gig and it's going to take hundreds of thousands of pounds on merchandise.' So we were putting a plan in place. Tim was the manager for Steve Coogan, another one of our happy Ecstasy friends who'd drop in to the office. He put us together with the Roses management.

So we go to meet Gareth [*Evans, the Roses' notorious manager*] in Knutsford. Apparently this Gareth is a bit weird. So Gareth was told that the Donnellys are waiting for him to do the meeting on the merchandising. We were sat in the car and I could see Tim arguing with Gareth in the street, obviously there was a problem. Gareth was throwing his hands in the air. I got out of the car and approached him. He was shitting his pants. Then what can only be described as a Benny Hill chase ensued – we were only there to do the merchandise and this geezer won't even speak to us. Spike Island is upon us and we've got to get it ready. We ended up chasing Gareth through Boots, throwing soap at him.

We spent that much time messing about trying to do it, before we knew it the gig was upon us and we missed it. I think when Spike Island came around we just went to watch the gig. Then after the gig I sat and drank a bottle of Wild Turkey with Ian [*Brown*] having a laugh at the after-show party at Genevieves.

Christopher: We were now looking for something to get into as a proper business. Had we not had so many bad experiences with putting events on we would have ended up in the music industry. The police were all over us like a rash even when we tried to do the legal things. Manchester was also at war. You now had people from the outside looking in, thinking there's good money to be made here, as opposed to people doing it for the love of it.

Organised crime firms in the city were leaving behind risky activities such as armed robbery and entering the rave scene. The amount of Ecstasy coming into Britain multiplied by 4,000 per cent between 1990 and 1995. One Wythenshawe gang reputedly smuggled £5 million worth of Ecstasy from Amsterdam to Manchester in a few months. Criminal gangs could turn a vast profit from importing drugs; running clubs, operating rave security and taking protection money from clubs. There were reports of shotguns in mouths at raves. In Manchester, the Thunderdome club closed down after a drive-by shooting of a bouncer. Other clubs were burned down. The GMP began to focus their attention on The Hacienda – the city's beacon of Acid House/Rave culture.

Anthony: We were still going out into town and we were still strong as a family, so none of that shit affected us but there was definitely a rise in the gang side. Around that time we just strengthened ourselves in numbers, took a back seat and got on with our own thing. We were just going into town, drinking in the [*new Factory-owned*] Dry bar and not going to The Hacienda as often, concentrating more on bands, music and festivals. We did Glastonbury 1990. [*The year of the notorious battle of Glastonbury that resulted in the festival being cancelled the following year. Ecstasy usage and tent crime were rife, pitched battles broke out between travellers and security teams that ended in 235 arrests and £50,000 worth of damage. Many blamed the increased presence of organised crime gangs.*] The Happy Mondays were playing and when we received our VIP passes they were just yellow Rank Xerox carbon paper in plastic laminate. We just looked at this thing and somebody went, 'Oh my God, we can print this round the corner.' So we get to Glastonbury with my mate, who printed copies of this ticket. That's what caused the trouble – all the people with backstage passes. There was full-on running battles between security, police, crusties and all the ticket touts. The next time they had the festival the wall went up – because of us, allegedly.

Christopher: We would go to The Hacienda from time to time but now there were different factions in the club. We were just another firm in there. We were still doing the merchandising in Europe. Just before the Mondays played G-Mex [*for two nights in the 10,000 capacity Manchester venue, 16/17 March*] Bez came with me to do the swag for Pink Floyd and Simple Minds in Denmark and Sweden. Why? I have no idea; he was doing well with the Mondays. Guess it was just for fun. He was part of our firm driving about. Bez was pretty recognisable and the Mondays were famous then. We got on a boat crossing from Rotterdam, and it was a cheesy disco boat with a cheesy DJ with a load of truck drivers and stuff. We took an E each and there was me, Bez and a couple of other kids on the dance floor in the club lounge dancing away to Acid House hits on this car ferry.

Anthony: At this point we're thinking, 'Fuck it, we're going to do something else.' We were burned out with it. But it doesn't matter what goes on now because we get tarred with everything. We were becoming more withdrawn. We thought the rave scene was over by the time it had hit the mainstream. We loved it but it wasn't for us. We were beyond that now. We'd done it. Time to move on. We just didn't want to be associated with all that shit, but then three years later when our friends were doing fortunes every week with Cream, of course you were thinking we should have stuck with it because we were at the top of the game doing the parties – we were the best.

Christopher: I'd already had the idea of clothing. When the Acid House thing happened, I knew that I wanted to do something that didn't involved nine to five. Ideally I would have gone into music. Mike [*Pickering*] was kicking it, 808 State were kicking, but I couldn't play anything. I used to play guitar but I was never one to sit at home strumming my guitar waiting for someone to knock on my door. We were out grafting. The clothing thing seemed more achievable and I've always loved clothes anyway so it seemed more natural too. And all the other people in the clothing game at the time were capitalising on the vibe and weren't what it was about. So I thought we should do the real version, instead of the outside looking in, do it from the inside outwards.

Then I started taking to Matt and Pat [*Carroll at Central Station Design*]. I'd become good friends with them. They were talking about putting art onto people's backs – that's how we spoke about it at the time. It wasn't about putting a graphic onto a T-shirt. I had a couple of meetings with them and it became a focus. We were working with Central Station on different things like the [*Happy Mondays'*] merchandise and they were our pals. If we were doing anything, flyers for parties and stuff, Central Station would do it. They'd actually done the invite for my twenty-first birthday; it was a pink banana on a trippy background.

Anthony: We're starting to build all these connections but we weren't going to become a band, so the next best thing was to become was a rock 'n' roll brand. There were companies out there cashing in on the commerciality of our scene, so that was a factor in us deciding to do clothes. You know what, it's not about bucket hats and Kickers and Wallabees, it's a real scene for the people who know and that was a catalyst for us – to right a wrong.

There were people dropping out, the original people, the pioneers were dropping out and it was going mainstream. People were walking round with skullcaps on, bucket hats and long-sleeve T-shirts. Originally Eric [*Barker*] used to wear one of those hats and that was like Eric's thing, but when people started making them and selling that look in the shops as 'this is the thing', it was over. The 'look' became a long-sleeved white T-shirt, a pair of flares and a pair of Kickers, and that was a million, million miles away from what it really was. All these people were saying, 'It's like this,' and it was for us to say, 'No it's not like that, it's like this.' We turned our back on the Acid House thing and moved more into the clothes to right the wrongs. We drifted into clothes but we were known for parties.

In the summer of 1990 New Order took their World Cup song, 'E for England' to the top of the charts and 'Madchester' made it to the cover of Newsweek, *dubbed 'Britain's Feel-Good Music Movement'. Local clothing company Joe Bloggs had been the main financial benefactor of the Madchester fashion boom – reputedly turning over £60 million selling baggy or flared jeans and heavily logo'd hooded tops. The Happy Mondays, New Order, Inspiral Carpets and The Charlatans had all appeared in a number of music press articles, and on TV, sporting Bloggs – and for many it appeared Bloggs had invented the 'baggy' rave look. The Mondays, in fact, did not really like Bloggs but had been led to the company by Tony Wilson for a segment in a Madchester documentary being made by Granada TV. Bloggs told the Mondays to help themselves, and their whole crew turned up and walked out with a vanful of the clobber.*

Anthony: When the Mondays watched that [*Granada documentary – Celebration: Madchester – Sound of the North, broadcast 1990*] they went mental. They were not happy. Bloggs had cleverly said, 'Let's get the Mondays in and get them in all the Madchester gear to endorse our product.' Power to them – if we were as switched on, business-wise, as they were, watching loads of kids create something, and we had the power to rinse it . . . I'm not saying we would do it, but if they made millions of pounds from it, fair play. But we were the scene – Bloggs was just following the scene. [*Joe Bloggs founder*] Shami Ahmed was saying he was at the forefront of fashion with the Acid House scene and he was linked to 'Madchester'. We knew 'Madchester' didn't exist and we knew he was full of shit because the gear he was producing was absolutely nothing like the lads would wear! I'd met this fella clubbing who worked for a large clothing brand. He started talking about setting up a clothing label with us. He worked in marketing. We suggested that he acquire the database of shops that the brand he worked for supplied. He did and there were about 8,000 shops on it. Now we're talking with this lad about how we can structure this new thing. How do we get it to work? Well, out friends at Central Station make art, but we need a designer . . . we start to bring in all the different aspects. We were learning. The database was no good – it was just people that sold lower-end clothes. We needed a better class of stores that sold mid-range product to sit next to ours.

Then Chris said to me, 'I've just got some space in one of my dad's mate's buildings if we want to take it,' some place that made knitwear. That was the first sign that we were going to do it. We had meetings at Imex House but when we were there we looked more like gangsters with just an office as a front and we had no control over the door, who came in – it had become a meeting place for a gallery of rogues. We were not getting any work done.

So we go over and take the space in my dad's mate's building. The place is free, we can monitor the cameras, we can vet who comes to see us. We were starting to take it a little more seriously and the whole rollercoaster started.

Christopher: I was having meetings with manufactures and people in the clothing game. I met a geezer called Billy who was using manufacturers in different countries. Me, Matt and Pat [*from Central Station Design*] went and said, 'This is the idea, this is what we want to do, put art on people's backs.' That was one of the initial conversations. He seemed quite up for it and we tried to do some stuff but never got off the ground and we ended up setting up on our own in that building. That was when Anthony got with the idea.

The whole building belonged to these brothers who had a knitwear manufacturing company in there. They'd been doing it for years. My dad knew them. The building was close to his scrapyard. They had this shitty building and they tried to make it tricky by putting these massive big glass windows in. The building was on a road with all these other knitwear manufacturers and you had their building that looked quite trendy. They were a wealthy family. They had expensive knitting machines. They were on the top floor and we moved into the basement where there were no windows. We had a punch bag up and one desk . . . that was it. I loved clothes but I'd had no training in clothes design.

Anthony: We thought we were now in the fashion industry. If they were producing a piece of knitwear, we thought automatically that they could make socks or jeans or T-shirts. We thought they could make everything for us. Simple. But it doesn't work like that. We'd invested a certain amount of money in orchestrating this business and we'd set up an office. It was the kid from the large wholesalers who had the knowledge that was going to kick it all off but he didn't deliver. He moved from his job onto another company and then just went off the radar. He was a sales rep. We'd given him a car to run about in, and he fucking smashed the car up. It was parked up at our office all banged up. It took us a few weeks to find him but we found him. He ended up getting a slap and then we moved on. That was that one dealt with.

Christopher: He was the man we were looking towards to put everything in place. He was in the fashion business. We did some TV shows (as guests) and his label tried to send us clothes to wear. That's how I got to know the kid and he came on board bringing all the sales knowledge. He brought his mate in, a man on the ground selling the gear. We had Matt and Pat to do graphics. The kid from the wholesalers introduced us to a designer, a kid called Jelly Universe who'd been at St Martin's [*College of Arts and Design*]. He was the first designer. He'd been at St Martin's with a designer called John O'Garr, who had made all the clothes for the video for Adamski's 'Killer' [*featuring Seal, a UK No.1 hit in May 1990*]. He made Adamski this jacket and a pair of trousers with square cubes coming off them and he made a baseball cap that was twice the normal height with a towelling lining [*Adamski wore a distinctive over-sized O'Garr Donald Duck baseball hat on the cover of* NME]. Jelly got John involved with us. John moved back from London to Manchester to work with us. He was originally from Macclesfield. He'd been through the Acid House experience down south. He was a white Rasta, long blonde dreads, who only wanted to be smoking dope on a beach on Bali. So now you had us, known for the Acid House raves, these two proper designers, plus Matt and Pat who did amazing artwork and a couple of people who were going to be the sales side, the lad from the wholesalers and his mate – it looked like a great team. We were trying to build a co-operative so that everyone would get something out of the project. We were looking at the kid we had set all this up with, saying, 'Now what? We've got all these people in this office, now what?' And he just disappeared and we were left holding the baby.

Anthony: So we've moved our office and we are going to start producing clothes. We need to come up with a name. I found the name. O'Garr went to a bookstore in Chinatown, a little trinket shop, and he bought a Vietnamese dictionary. He brought it back and he randomly put a pin in and it said 'Gio.' I said, 'That's good.' He said, 'And underneath it says Goi.' I said, 'It sounds like Giorgio Armani, why don't we just have it as Gio-Goi?' We didn't want to pass it off but if you put the word Gio-Goi it was kind of instantly familiar but its own word. That's when we went to Matt and Pat and told them the name. They objected and wanted to call the brand 'Shit Clothes'.

Christopher: We've told a dozen different magazines a dozen different things about the name Gio-Goi. I told someone recently that it was named after a snake in the Andes and this snake shed its skin while it was still moving. I said, 'That's what the company's like, we keep evolving.' That's true but that story was just a load of bullshit. I told someone else we'd met these two Portuguese lads named Nuno Gio and Eduardo Goi when we went on holiday as kids and named it after them. We were looking for inspiration from different things and it just so happened O'Garr had been to Vietnam, he was into American soldiers, the GI's and the Vietcong. We had a Zippo lighter from Vietnam that featured the famous Vietnam War quote: 'Though I walk through the Valley of Death, I shall fear no evil, for I am the evilest son of a bitch in the valley.' We also liked that. It seemed to sum things up.

6

DODGIN' THE RAIN 'N' BULLETS

Christopher: Matt and Pat did a design based on an Aztec bird – the eagle, with Gio-Goi at the side of it. That's the design that launched us – an Aztec bird with a red bull's eye in the middle. That was the initial piece of artwork. We decided to use that on the labels with 'Manchester, Paris, LA, Tokyo' as an alternative to New York, Paris, London. Matt and Pat did a lot of designs for us – there was one with fishes on, the very first Gio-Goi garments had fishes on which they took from the 'W.F.L.' cover. We had them in weird placements – the swordfish tail would be up and over the shoulder so the front of the fish would go down the back.

John [*O'Garr*] went to Lahore, Pakistan, to put our first full range together. The knitwear brothers had contacts over there. It was all jersey material based – sweatshirts, joggers and long-sleeve T-shirts. The T-shirts had an unusual neckline shape and the pocket shapes were an unusual shape on the joggers. While John was doing that, we decided we needed to get some T-shirts out there on the streets and in the stores.

We got 200 Screen Stars T-shirts in Grey Marl and we printed the Aztec and the Gio-Goi on the front. Then we started giving them out to friends of ours – the Ruthless Rap Assassins, the Roses, Mondays, New Order. There was festival on in Manchester, a Granada festival, and we went down to give some T-shirts out.

We gave them to a couple of kids who were in band called the New Fast Automatic Daffodils. The festival was on television and the lead singer was wearing an Aztec. That was the first bit of PR we ever got, they were the first people to wear our clothing as product placement. If they read this book, I'd like to say, 'Nice one.' It was a moment that will always stay with me.

We also did 200 T-shirts that said, 'Dedicated to Those Dodgin' the Rain 'n' Bullets'. That was the company slogan. It was on our letterhead. It was always pissing down in Manchester and there were now lots of bullets flying about. We also did 200 'Gibraltar' T-shirts because everyone was smoking rock [*crack*]. No one got it. It was an insider joke that we thought was funny. But why would you want a T-shirt with just Gibraltar on it? Some of things went down like a lead balloon but it made us laugh.

What were a success – huge success – were the warm-up jackets we made in Leicester in fabric called Tactel. We only had that one design for a year and we'd just change the fabrics, the colours, keep the block the same. It was based on the jacket American baseball teams wore when they came out to play, a very simple jacket – two welt-pockets, a fold-over collar and press studs down the front. The knitwear brothers had their factory make a knitwear piece for the neck, so it had a nice little touch on the inside of the collar. We must have ended up selling tens of thousands of those jackets. Everybody wanted the warm-up jacket. We did it in four colours: green, blue, red and black and then we expanded it into colours like peach and indigo.

Anthony: There was also a journalist from *The Sun* chasing us called Charles Yates. He'd been calling us because of the raves and we'd tip him off, send him in the wrong direction, 'Yeah, we're doing one in Stockport Saturday night, have your journalist there.' It was so he could get shots of all those 'Ecstasy monsters'.

He wanted the pictures of the illegal Acid House scene. Charles got wind that we were setting up this fashion label and interviewed us. On the morning of the Gulf War, *The Sun* [*2 August 1990*] had the front page, 'Iraq Invaded' and we had a full page on page five. The headline was: 'Acid House Kings become Fashion Kings'.

Manchester was booming; The Hacienda was huge news. We were going to take over the world with this brand. Next Hooky [*Peter Hook*] appears on the front cover of the *NME* in one of the T-shirts [*4 August 1990*]. We started a vibe. People were saying, 'What is this thing? Who is it?' Then the samples come back from Lahore, and we booked MAB [*Men and Boys Wear show in Earls Court Exhibition Centre, London, for September*]. It's an annual event, we just did the one – we were banned.

Christopher: For the show, we built a stand in a church where they used to do *Top of the Pops* in the '60s. I was dropping off beers and some smoke. I walked in and Matt had a clear plastic bin bag over his head and a cig through the plastic. Pat threw paint all over the bag and Matt lay on the floor. He was painting the stand with Matt. Matt was the brush. It was a weird and wonderful time.

Anthony: We left a kid, Dave, in the church overnight finishing the stand. I got a phone call the next morning, 'He's freaked out!' He was taking whizz and smoking dope to stay up all night to finish the stand in preparation for the show. He had to be taken to hospital. The stand was shipped to Earls Court where we caused mayhem. Our friends had a flat on Portland Street and they let us use that while the exhibition was on for three days. There were thousands of people from the fashion industry walking round, looking at stands and buying clothes and all of a sudden this spaceship landed in the middle of it. A bongo flew out and all these kids were wearing multi-coloured stuff. Security came over:

'Turn the music off.' All the beer was drunk – I'd hired some fridges, the shelves were taken out and Chris was padlocked inside the glass fridge. In the background you had one or two straight people with us. We said, 'Please, tomorrow will be different,' and it was no different. The smell of cannabis coming off the stand was overpowering. We had Adamski playing live. Nigel Benn came on the stand. They threatened to close us down. Happy Mondays were in London, in the recording studio [*finishing* Pills 'n' Thrills and Bellyaches, *released November 1990 and widely regarded as album of the year*]. Matt and Pat are Shaun's cousins and obviously the band are friends of ours and friends of our Tracey, so they came to the show. It was absolute carnage.

Christopher: We weren't really that familiar with Nigel Benn, he just got on the vibe of the stand. He just put himself about. But a year or two later we ended up working more closely with him. Adamski was wearing the clobber, or at that point he was wearing the samples. He was interested in doing something with us. At the show someone asked, 'What's your minimum order on these?' I said 200 and he only wanted to order fifteen T-shirts. I had no concept of the business, absolutely no idea how the business ran.

When the show finished we took the stand down and sent it across London to a photographic studio. I built the stand myself with fucking hammer and nails so that the Happy Mondays could do a photo shoot with the stand. There are pictures of Shaun and Bez laid out on the stand in these Gio-Goi warm-up jackets – it might have been *Smash Hits*.

Anthony: We created a massive stir at the show. Top Shop came and said, 'We want to buy all your denim and spend three million quid with you.' And we said, 'Nah.' We were young and didn't give a fuck and we didn't want to be in Top Shop. We ended up taking £500,000 worth of orders at the show and we only had twelve samples. We couldn't fulfil the orders but that worked to our advantage because every time somebody came down we told them we'd sold out. The more you get told you can't have something, the more you want it.

Christopher: After the show we looked at the orders and we needed to deliver all this stuff. It was going to cost x amount to produce, in the region of £250,000 to bring the stuff in from Lahore. We didn't have the money to do that. Everyone was ringing up for their orders and we only had the samples on a rail. So I went and got loads and loads of long-sleeve T-shirts, different colours, relabelled them and took them to a place in Plymouth Grove, Longsight, an embroidery place called Hothouse. We embroidered Gio-Goi on the front of the chest but instead of putting the placement on the left, I put it in the middle of the chest, and instead of just having Gio-Goi once I had it repeated three times. We carried on buying T-shirts in, labelling them and embroidering them right through until the stock started arriving.

At the same time I went with John [*O'Garr*] and Jelly to Leicester and we had some proper long-sleeve T-shirts and sweatshirts made to our specifications with the Aztec print embossed on. We could go and buy 500 pieces of each. We now had our own little production line. In the basement someone was pressing all these T-shirts, folding them and putting them into bags. We were delivering them to Identity and Arc in Afflecks. There was shop in town called Bozo we wanted to get in but it was getting close to Christmas and they said they were fully stocked. We said, 'Just take fifty on sale or return, to see how you get on.' They said, 'We've not really got the space but we'll take them.' Within two hours they rang and said, 'We sold them all and we want another 200.' Bozo was a new shop in the Royal Exchange. It was small but it did amazing business. It just started rolling and rolling and rolling. Bozo must have spent a million pound a year with us.

Anthony: We did the video for 'Unbelievable' by EMF [*September 1990*], and the [*reissue of*] The La's' 'There She Goes' [*October 1990*]. We did the product placement for those videos and we might have been contributing to the funding of the videos, I can't remember. We were systematic, we were bang at it, we product placed, we dressed them for those videos. Manchester was the centre of the universe at that time. Leo was doing '. . . AND ON THE SIXTH DAY, GOD CREATED MANchester' T-shirts. Madonna and Jean Paul Gaultier were wearing those. Everyone wanted to be a part of this thing. We were right in the thick of it and we were the only people making credible clothes – we weren't corporate. We were making clothes for the lads by lads. It was real. Everyone wanted a piece of the Mondays and Roses. They were our pals and wearing our gear. Everyone was wearing Gio – New Order, Inspiral Carpets, 808 State, Charlatans, Northside, Adamski, a black kid called Ricky [*Ricardo Da Force*] who did stuff with KLF, The Fall – we'd pretty much cornered the market. At the same time we started doing merchandise for the Ruthless Rap Assassins. So we're doing Gio-Goi and the merchandising for their tour – all in the basement. We had the Gio-Goi stock on the floor in boxes. There were boxes and boxes of stock. People could come down like a cash and carry. What we were doing is going round the corner, getting 5,000 T-shirts and printing them in the same place – we were doing cash business and we became an in-season brand.

Christopher: We didn't do seasons. We just made stuff constantly, brought it in and put it on the floor. The shops loved us because they could come down and, as fast as they could buy it, they were selling it. They'd be down the next day for more gear. There were buckets of money and we were off our nut. Looking back now, we went through that whole Madchester period and never recognised what we had. The whole world was looking at us and we just thought we were going on a night out. We had all this going on around us, which was us, but we were totally oblivious. Customers were going, 'Wow, I've been down there. You want to see it!' That was what made it what it was. If we all had our heads screwed on straight, we wouldn't be sat here now talking about it. It wasn't just the product, the whole thing about the company was the anarchy – the lads off a council estate going out and doing this stuff and employing their mates for a buzz.

Anthony: It was Christmas Eve 1990 and everyone had gone home. There was me, a punch bag, a bit of stock in the basement, a case of Red Stripe and a bag of weed. David Evans, who went on to own Hooch and Bench, walked in. I'm smashed out of my mind and he had to write his own order out. He sat with a calculator and left with a massive box. Leo Stanley came in and did the same thing. They had to serve themselves and stuff a note on the table to tell us what they took.

Christopher: From the profit we made from the T-shirts, we managed to buy the full range from Pakistan and started distributing that to the shops – Gio-Goi's first proper range. It was all really well designed stuff, but the quality was horrendous. The striped T-shirts were printed stripes, not woven, and when you put them in the wash they came out plain. They hadn't colour-fasted the stripes. But we could send anything out and they would sell it. It was ridiculous. The consumer wasn't what they are today.

The range had a signature 'kangaroo' pocket; a big looping, rounded pocket that ran from the shoulder to the side seam. We did it on the joggers as well. The joggers were purple, bright red, proper mental colours. The T-shirts were sky blue with yellow stripes. It seemed like a vast amount of gear. We had 1,000 per style, so 5,000 pairs of joggers in five different colours. At the same time we were still doing T-shirts and jackets in Leicester. We forward sold, but the beauty of the business was you could come down every day to the office and spend £200 or £2,000. We were fresh, stuff was changing constantly: as well as your main range, a kid could go into the store every two or three weeks and buy a new T-shirt. The big companies churn out seasonal ranges and we were doing new stuff weekly.

Anthony: It was a lump of shite the first collection but there was so much hype behind the brand it was a success. The marketing, the interviews on television and the radio stations were rock 'n' roll. All of a sudden we were the coolest things since sliced bread. We created a huge hype.

Christopher: The business was evolving and we started to get deadlines. Matt and Pat were just too wayward and couldn't keep to the deadlines, pure rock 'n' roll. Plus, they had all the Factory Records stuff to do. We were moving at a rate where we needed stuff off them daily and they were more into creating art. We needed graphics to keep the stock fresh – that wasn't their vibe. They wanted to spend two weeks creating a piece of art to put on someone's back. They did some iconic T-shirts for us – 'Hold On To Your Hats' stands out for me. They also did some amazing cartoon graphics. They even did the 'Gio-Goi All Stars', which was cartoons of Matt and Pat, me, Anthony, John and Jelly. And, remember, in the middle of all this there was a lot of rock 'n' roll going on. It was just the way Manchester was at the time.

Anthony: Every time I went over to pick up the designs, I'd get off my napper with them – booze and chemicals in this little cubbyhole studio they had. It was great. Even though they'd do the artwork they wouldn't work at the speed we needed – their art was art. We wanted to do prints; we wanted to do ten prints a week. They were used to having six weeks designing a Happy Mondays sleeve. It was never going to work but it was fun whilst it lasted with them.

Christopher: I started using the knitwear brothers' factory in our building for Gio-Goi. I started to produce short-sleeve knitwear. We did some with fully-fashioned collars and a zip-up front. We sold bundles of it. Knitwear was really big for us at one point. We were doing the knitwear as if they were T-shirts, so they were really bright and multi-coloured – tangerine and yellow. Relations with the knitwear brothers were great. They've gone from making tat for the markets, doing cash and carry, making stuff to sell at £2 a garment, to making stuff for us and probably getting £6 a garment. They can't make it as fast as we can sell. Their factory was working non-stop. They'd bring a thousand pieces in every morning and it was gone in an hour. We could not make the gear fast enough.

There was an article in *Vogue* and we'd never even spoke to *Vogue* – no one had done an interview. It was a half a page with headline: 'Manchester United'.

I went to Dubai to do the next range. We were used to doing £2,000 a week. I went away for two weeks and when I came back, Anthony said, 'We've taken £80,000 this week.' It just went ballistic. We took this big order from a shop in the South West. The owner of the shop had a Ferrari and we wondered how he'd got it. We were slowly finding out there was a lot of money to be made in fashion and he'd obviously just treated himself. But at the time our default setting was we presumed everyone with money was a criminal.

I think we had the front cover of the *NME* – it featured at least one Gio-Goi piece – for six or seven weeks on the spin at one point in 1991 with 808 State, New Order, Happy Mondays, The Charlatans, Stone Roses, MC Tunes and Electronic.

With Gio-Goi expanding rapidly, the company moved out of the windowless basement and took over the stunning top floor that had huge windows. They kept the basement as a storeroom and the top floor became a showroom/office where the full range could be displayed, as well as furniture especially made for trade exhibitions. Matt and Pat Carroll had moved on of their own accord. O'Garr and Jelly Universe were the only real professionals amongst a staff that was largely made up of old friends such as Jeff Oughton and Donny, who worked in the warehouse. The sales reps, who went on the road and sold the clothes to shops, included Harry Franco, who the brothers had met doing swag; Joycey, who was a friend of Anthony's; Nico; Wack; and Rob Rushy, a DJ now called Rob Tissera. Chris's wife Natalie worked it the office, as did the brothers' sister, Tracey, who had left Factory. Harry Franco's girlfriend, Susy Franco, also worked in the office. She spoke five languages and was handling the international orders.

Anthony: We had a staff of twenty and nobody over the age of twenty-five. Harry was the funny one. He'd come back with these mad tales of his trips to the shops. He got involved in a threesome with the shop owner and his wife in Glasgow and he was talking about hoovers being involved. He was very boisterous. Harry the Handbag we called him. He had been one of the official bootleggers, one of the main players from Wilmslow. I met him in a bar in Oslo on one trip bootlegging abroad and saw a beautiful woman walk up to him and get it on with him – I mean really beautiful. I saw him the next day he said, 'She wants me to go live with her and raise reindeer with her in Lapland.'

Nico was Tracey's friend, so we said bring him down. We had to give him a makeover so he would fit in. Wack was another bootlegger. The people we did the Mondays' Free Trade Hall video with introduced Rob Tissera to us. He got mugged on his first appointment. He went out with his sales range to Norfolk and got mugged off four turkeys. Joycey had been in LA taking Es. He flew back and bumped into me in my local pub, The Firbank, and he just looked the part. He'd met bands, he'd met villains and he was a good networker for the brand. He was given a car. We bought them all cars.

Christopher: We hired my brother-in-law to be a sales rep. We bought him a brand new BMW so he could go round the country. But people kept saying to me, 'I saw him the other day in Didsbury.' I was like, 'Nah, he's in London.' He was supposed to be in London all week but he's with some bird round the corner. He'd come in on a Friday and just write a load of bogus orders and we'd send all the gear out. Because the gear was flying out, the boxes would just turn up and people would go, 'Er, right okay,' and put it out and sell it. He did that for months and months and months until his luck ran out.

Jeff, who did the warehouse, was stood at a bus stop in Wythenshawe in the rain looking bedraggled. I pulled up and asked what he was doing? He was on the dole, so I said, 'Right, do you want a job?' I took him into Gio, gave him a job, paid for him to take his driving test. He was a top addition to the team. We looked after them all. We took them all to Paris for a trade show [*SEHM, February 1991*]. There was no reason to take a warehouse man to Paris but he's my pal and we're a team. We gave twenty friends £200 for spends and had a ball.

At the trade show, you had the international part of the hall and then upstairs would be where all the British brands were – little booths with grey walls to put your range up in. Us being the way we were, we said, 'Fuck that, we're not going up there. We're going downstairs next to Chipie and Chevignon.' We built this massive stand and we had cactuses made – the new range we had made in Dubai featured cactuses on the chenille badges – don't know why. We put in a stone floor, big metal, wavy wall – we had it all built bespoke. We took it to Paris on a container and then put all our clothes out downstairs with the big boys.

In Paris we went to a restaurant and ordered steak tartare. When it came out we were like, 'What the fuck is this? Raw meat and a raw egg?' I quite like it now.

Anthony: This was the honeymoon period. We were having parties in Paris to see who could drink the most champagne. I think forty-eight bottles got drank one night in Paris. We flew all the lads to Paris on a private jet for a party. They brought sheets of trips. On one night out, we had 150 people all given free acid and tripping off their nuts – the bar staff were giving free drinks away. Daniel Poole, the barrister who set a clothing label up, was with us. The next day his staff turned up at the Paris clothes exhibition doing a Grand National over people's stands, totally out of their heads. They barred him from the show. I was dropping £2,000 on restaurant bills, as opposed to a fiver in the local chippy.

Harry the Handbag had all the shops for Scotland. He had five shops. Their first order in Paris was ten grand. He was delighted. All the sales reps worked on commission. I said, 'Nice one!' And then these Scottish geezers went, 'Yeah, but Harry, you've got to times it by five – a £10,000 order for each shop.' Harry's legs nearly went – he had a fifty grand order. He was on commission and had made £5,000 in the blink of an eye. That set the day off. We took over seven hundred thousand pounds worth of orders on the first day.

Christopher: We were taking massive orders but we just didn't have the stock. We couldn't keep up with it. It was a cash flow thing. We couldn't manufacture that much. We did some jeans that had a leather patch with the Aztec eagle on. We made them with washing instructions that said, 'Mum, please wash my jeans.' The knitwear factory put a nightshift on to cope with the demand. The gear was selling that much that in the warehouse we had to start splitting the stock between the reps. They were fighting over it. Say we had 1,000 pieces of knitwear come in; it would be 250 for Harry, 250 for Nico, 250 for Joycey and 250 for Wack. Any one of them could have sold the full amount that day. Then they'd be screaming they had no stock. Jeff started taking backhanders in the warehouse. They would then give the factory backhanders, 'Make me an extra 200 pieces!'

Harry Franco [aka Harry the Handbag]: Because we had so little stock, there was always big competition between the reps. One of my orders from one account in Glasgow was £36,000. As I was taking that order I was thinking they were never going to get £36,000 worth of gear. I think I managed to get about £12,000 worth of stock to them. They wanted so much more. Anthony knew that and he'd wind everyone up, 'I know where Nico's got a load of jeans hid.' Then they'd put the stock into the warehouse, open the doors at one end and Anthony would stand at the steps watching us literally fighting over a pair of jeans.

My areas were Scotland and the South West. I'd get the red carpet treatment in those areas. I was going in to clubs in the evenings with the shops guys and being given free drugs, free beers, on the guest list. You were 'the guy that worked for Gio-Goi'.

It was a strange dynamic between Chris and Anthony. Chris was the quiet, mellow one and Anthony was the completely mad, manic one. If Anthony was in the room it was as if you had a wasp in your ear. It seemed at the time that if there wasn't any trouble in his life, he'd go and find somebody else's trouble to get involved in. Chris was bang into his clothes. Anthony just liked the kudos. The clothes didn't really matter – it was just the status. Anthony loved all that, whereas Chris loved the clothes. Chris really wanted to learn about the industry and he got really into fabrics and designs. They knew everyone on the Manchester music scene. They managed to fire directly into every band. I was sent down to Northwich to find The Charlatans with a box of clothes, or I'd go round to Johnny Marr's house and knock on the door and say, 'There you go, Johnny. Here's a box of clobber.'

Christopher: We've always known the importance of marketing and product placement. [*Actor*] Max Beesley came to the office – he was playing the bongos in the title sequence of [*new Ch4 youth TV show*] *The Word* at the time. He became a big friend of ours. He was in a band called Incognito. Max was also going out with [*soul singer*] Mica Paris and working with the Young Disciples, so we'd send them clobber. He'd also get the clothes to Jamiroqui, The Brand New Heavies and Paul Weller.

Because of John O'Garr's connection in London we were dressing Galliano. We had this really cool thing going on. We had our pals in the gear, the Mondays, Stone Roses, 808 State, K-Klass, A Guy Called Gerald . . . we had it boxed off. We dressed Take That for a tour. Max was playing percussion for them. Every week, whoever was playing *The Word*, we'd send a parcel of gear down. It wasn't just the northern bands wearing Gio; we were rocking London also.

Jeff Oughton: I went from warehouse man to warehouse manager to Jeff 'friend of the stars' – that's what they called me. We used to have a book and any band that came in – Happy Mondays, Stone Roses, all the Madchester scene – if they took anything, they had to sign for it. Anthony used to write letters to

The Rolling Stones and slip it in their box and the next thing he'd say, 'I'm sure that's one of our jackets Keith's got on.' He was unbelievable at promoting it.

When Barney [*Bernard Sumner*] and Johnny Marr were doing Electronic, Barney came down to the warehouse. I don't know if he was a bit off his tits at the time but he picked up these sample jumpers and they had codes on them. He thought that was part of the design. It was just a code for the knitwear. I said, 'Yeah, that looks sound on you that, Barney.' He took the gear and wore that jumper on *Top of the Pops* and in the video. It had Gio-Goi written round the neck – you couldn't miss it. I was like that, 'Get in!'

Anthony: We never had a general manger or a PR or anything like that. Magazines would just ring up asking if they could send someone down. Then we'd poison them with booze and drugs, get them off their head. But you'd realise they were as mental as you and they certainly didn't need to be force-fed anything – certainly at *i-D* magazine. It was in *i-D* that Vivienne Westwood described us as 'ambassadors for a generation'. [*'Anthony and Christopher Donnelly are at the forefront of fashion and music, ambassadors for a generation.'*] We were appearing all over the press.

Christopher: We were doing business in Europe, Japan and America. Someone went to New York and came back and told us the staff in the Stussy shop in Greenwich Village were head to toe in Gio. Union in New York stocked our stuff. We had 200 shops worldwide stocking us. We had a cult following all over the world. We had the Japanese coming over, buying the stock and then they would send us pictures of the biggest Japanese bands all head to toe in Gio. All the doormen at Peter Gatien's Limelight club in New York wore the gear.

Anthony: The first year that we traded, we didn't have an accountant or anything, we just had a tin box in the office. And there was quite a lot of money being taken. We got a guy in – a little Jewish guy called Jack Dunkirk, 'Jack the Hat.' He got a desk in the corner of the office and he wanted to go through the first year's trading to get everything in order. I think we'd turned over about a million pounds and there was a tiny cash box with about 87p in it and a couple of receipts for some bizarre things. That cash box got smashed so many times. I used to come in and ask Jack for the keys and he'd go, 'No, you're taking fortunes and it's being run very unprofessionally.' I'd smash it open, take the cash and just fuck off. Quite a few people said, 'You can't behave like this.' We thought turnover was profit.

Christopher: Jack did a great job and soon had the company on the straight and narrow. He was about sixty. He used to go ballroom dancing and he ended up with the maddest firm in the world. He sat through all sorts of people coming in. We would often have difficulty with cash flow; there was one particular supplier owed a lot of money, and I mean a lot of money. They were saying they were not going to supply us anymore. Jack had words with them and guaranteed that they would get so much each month, to bring the bill down, and they continued supplying us. It was lucky because they supplied all the labels and badges. Jack was worth his weight in gold and extremely honest. The suppliers thought we were mad but they would listen to a respectable geezer like Jack.

We were getting the stuff made out of Portugal, a bit closer to home because of the long lead times in China, Hong Kong and Pakistan, and the quality was not right. That's when John [*O'Garr*] started doing the cola bottles and cow heads on T-shirts. We had one T-shirt that had this weird shape with Gio-Goi in the middle of it. I'm driving down the motorway one day and I saw the logo on the side of a van. It was for Seeley beds. He'd just taken their shape. I was like, 'Fucking hell, he's just taken that badge for a bed company and banged Gio in the middle of it.'

While John was doing that I was making our own designs. I did a 'Drug Free' T-shirt that was an insider joke – you'd see kids on the dance floor all over the country all off their heads in a 'Drug Free' T-shirt. Was it, 'I'm on drugs and free'? Or was it, 'I'm drugs free, I don't take drugs'? And we did 'Narcotics Officer' – which Anthony had seen on a girl he fancied at the time. All the doormen wanted 'Narcotics Officer' embroidered on the warm-up jackets. They looked official – black Gio-Goi jackets with 'Narcotics Officer' on the back. The police were not happy about those jackets. We put stuff on T-shirts that nobody else would do. We didn't care. That was the beauty of it, that's what made the business what it is.

Anthony: We were dressing the doormen at The Hacienda. We changed the style of the doormen; we put them in black bobby hats and black warm-up coats that had more of an effect. They moved from that white shirt and dickie-bow look. We made it a bit more menacing and badged them up with the brand. It was when Manchester was going haywire. We stopped going to The Hacienda then. We were international fashion bods now. Manchester was like a pie and it was being carved up.

Christopher: When the dark stuff started coming into play as the Ecstasy thing started to become really, really commercial, we pretty much stopped going to The Hacienda. When The Hacienda was being shut down with guns [*closed in January 1991, reopened in May with metal detectors on the door*], we weren't going in there, we'd moved on. We were into our business. We'd been at the cutting edge of Acid House when it was a revolution, at the beginning of it, and we were instrumental in making it happen. When it became commercial you had all these people coming to do the doors. We'd already moved on by the time they were taking over and it went from 'Madchester' to 'Gunchester'. We were on with doing big business in fashion.

Harry Franco: There was an estate in Newcastle and the kids had got into robbing cars off it and stuffing them through shop windows of either nice clothes shops or electrical stores. They coined the phrase 'ram raiding' to describe what they were doing. [*Newcastle-Upon-Tyne uprising of September 1991 – the biggest citywide rebellion since Liverpool in 1981.*] Anthony came in the next morning and he was on his mobile screaming at John O'Garr. 'Fill your bag full of our gear and get up to Newcastle and get that guy that you know – your mate from *i-D* magazine – get him on a train, get him up to Newcastle, find out who's doing that and get them wearing Gio-Goi today.'

O'Garr and the photographer went up to Newcastle and he said it took them about two minutes. They got out of a cab at the shops on this estate and the kids were all over them. Next thing they were all in Gio-Goi. The kids were like bang into it, they'd been on the news the night before, then this Manchester clothing firm had come down and given them free stuff. They took O'Garr and this photographer out to a club that night, this dodgy club in Newcastle, and one of the kids got a bit carried away. He pulled out a .45 and all hell broke loose. The police were everywhere. The next day it was in the national papers. We got a page in *The Sun*. There was a picture of Anthony and Chris and an interview.

Christopher: The kids all had baseball bats and stuff outside the club. The police turned up and thought it was a riot. We had all the pictures of the kids being arrested with baseball bats in the magazine. At the time Gio-Goi was very drug orientated. There was no MD, there was no one running the company. It was just everyone doing what they wanted to do. John O'Garr went out to Portugal to make a new range and the next thing we were getting things he liked but weren't really viable. He did a load of sweatshirt jersey jackets but with short sleeves in two different colours. We had 6,000 jackets with short sleeves – weird shit. John decided he was into boating shoes when no one else was wearing them. He made thousands of pairs in Nubuck – green, red and sky blue. They were slick but there just wasn't a market for Nubuck boating pumps at the time. John also did a range called 'International'. The badges were horrible, a picture of plane on it in yellow and black stripes. It was supposed to be a diffusion thing, you had main Gio-Goi and International, but people just didn't get on it.

So I started designing and making stuff myself and bringing that in, like the shirts – stuff that was a bit more sellable. I started choosing the fabrics and the buttons and having the stuff made in the UK because there was still quite a lot of factories about then. I was working out of a factory in Sheffield because the lead times from abroad, and the minimum order numbers, were a pain in the arse. We were still doing a hell of a lot of knitwear and I was doing that too. I might see a tie or a pair of socks with a stripe I liked and then I'd give the socks to the lads in the knitwear place and they'd develop the stripe.

Harry Franco: John [*O'Garr*] went away to Portugal and sourced a load of fabric and a range came in, which was really nice and very hardwearing, but it was really expensive. It was over-the-top expensive – we'd have to put sweatshirts out at like seventy, eighty quid, which was about twenty, thirty pound more than you wanted to sell a Gio-Goi sweatshirt at.

Chris started to do more of the designing but he didn't do it in an overpowering way. There was a reason for it. Chris would research things a lot more, he'd want to know what was selling and why it was selling, then how he could make that better. That was really how he thought of it. Anthony would just be flying around. He'd come up with the ideas that were just gold, like the Newcastle thing.

Christopher: John and Jelly would come in every day, get stoned and leave. You'd be like, 'What have they done today?' You'd have people coming in to sit down to talk business and they were both stoned. Or you'd find out that John had bought a load of fabric from Portugal and the bill had come in for £60,000 and then he's decided he doesn't like it and he's doing something else over here. It was like, 'What the fuck are you doing?' So it got to point where in the end I just went like that, 'I've had enough.'

Anthony: They didn't deliver on their end of the bargain. The last thing I heard was one had slept with the other's girl and they were fighting like animals in the street and one of them knocked the other's teeth out . . .

Christopher: They had a massive fight in the office over a girl. We were at a party and John had tried to have a bash at a girl Jelly had a crush on. On Monday morning they were kicking the fuck out of each other. Jelly left. He said he couldn't work with John. I've never seen Jelly again from that day to this. John was head designer but he was getting stoned and he wasn't doing any work. I was doing more and more of it, and in the end we said it's not really working out. We said to him, 'You need to bail,' and he left. We were turning over millions of pounds. We were quite a way down the line and it was becoming a business. We were growing up, saying get with the programme or jog on. It was a shame it ended like that but that's rock 'n' roll. They were both nice kids and should be proud of being a part of something special.

Anthony: There was a bloke in the background who had a fashion business and anybody who left our place, he'd sign them up. If he'd have managed us, he would have taken us somewhere other than the out of control rock 'n' roll road we was going down. He was working up the road, importing shoes for us. When John left, he went and set up business with this fella. He gave John 1 per cent or 2 per cent out of the brand that became Hooch, which was around for a good few years. I gave John O'Garr the name for Hooch.

Christopher: It was probably worth the money we spent, the money we lost, with John for the photo shoots we got off it. We did a shoot for *i-D* [*April 1992 issue, headline: 'Blags To Riches'*] with photographer Grant Fear, a friend of John's who became a friend of ours. We didn't want to use proper models so we used our friends, people like Stephen [*Yates*]. We did it down our local shops in Wythenshawe, outside Flanny's, with Stephen and a few kids off the estate, Boz Eye, Gilly and Dale.

John [*O'Garr*] had made some samples: silk shirts, silk waistcoats and striped cords. He spent a fortune on the sampling. It all looked so incongruous on these estate kids. Those shots ended up in a museum in New York; they became iconic. Things like that gave us kudos. But those clothes never got produced, the designs were never going to get made – they were just not what people were wearing in the street at the time. No one was watching John. The things we were selling were the stuff I was designing . . . knitwear, T-shirts, jackets, shirts, and all the stuff we were making in the UK.

John was tripping off going to China making the craziest shit you can imagine. He was a great designer but we should have kept hold of his ankles and kept him on the ground. Saying that, he went on to do some really cool stuff and set up on his own.

Harry Franco: When John left, we had grown up a little bit business-wise – Anthony mainly. The way that John left was handled quite well. He still got slagged off and stuff like that but no one blew his car up.

Anthony: We had another kid join us, Steve, a pattern cutter. We were told we needed a pattern cutter. You could have told us we needed a pink horse with yellow spots and we would have hired it, we didn't know our arse from our elbow. As was often the case, he was a friend of the person who told us we needed one. He wasn't with us long and he left to set up a brand called Mas-if – which, funnily enough, we ended up owning. He was basically trying to replicate our model. Then we found out his dad was the head of the Dog Unit for GMP. Nobody had told us when we gainfully employed him. Allegedly our family is linked to organised crime and his dad was a bogey, so the two don't sit very well.

He was in bed on the sixth floor and apparently his car passed him at 60mph going up in the air. Someone had blown it up. We fell under suspicion. One newspaper report said, 'We contacted Anthony at Gio-Goi and he remained tight-lipped. He said, "I have no knowledge of the car being blown up but I would have loved to have been there to see it."'

The Face ran a piece about how we had blown up this rival fashion brand's car. We rang the kid from *The Face* and said, 'What the fuck are you doing, writing shit like that when you don't know the ins and outs of it? It's fuck all to do with us, we never burnt his car out.' And then the kid wrote an article a month later in *The Face* about the phone call. He said that he'd received his first death threat! We couldn't win.

7
F*CKED UP

Harry Franco: The sales reps were really hungry for stuff all the time and we were all waiting for jeans to come in. Everybody wanted jeans. Everyone's account was screaming for jeans. Then they arrived. They'd been dyed really dark blue and stone-washed but they'd been over-stone-washed, really battered about so all the edges, on the tops of the pockets and stuff, had already gone – frayed too much. The jeans had gone beyond looking worn and actually had holes. We all looked at them and thought, 'Well, we might just get away with it.' They were a great colour and they were a good cut. I blew about 200 pairs out to my accounts as fast as I could.

A day later the phone rang. It was one of my accounts in Glasgow. 'Yeah, we got the stock but it's a bit fucked up.' Chris picked up the phone and said, 'Yeah, that's right, that's right. It's fucked up, it's fucked up. It's part of the new range.'

Christopher: So the F*cked Up range was born. It was a total blag but it meant we could produce any shit we wanted. Suddenly those T-shirts where the stripes came off were selling. We ordered 'F*cked Up' labels from the company who made our labels but when they were delivered they were just a big blue badge with the word 'Range' on them. The geezer who owned the company said, 'I've not put it on because I'm a Christian.' We had 10,000 badges with just the word 'Range' on them. Anyway, we got that sorted and this F*cked Up range took off. We did sweatshirts, a baseball jacket – you could make something, then screw it in a ball and say it was part of the F*cked Up range. You had kids buying the stuff and their mum taking the clothes back to the shops and complaining. The amount of complaints we got was great. It created a big stir. We were selling millions of pounds' worth of clothes internationally – we were doing really well in places like Japan and Holland.

Anthony: There were complaints all over the country about the F*cked Up range, people saying, 'What's the world coming to?' Then [*snooker legend*] Alex Higgins got involved. Higgins had turned up at the funeral of a friend of the family, Mike Pollit. That's when I started palling about with Alex. He came to the office and started just being round us. We didn't mind him being there, Alex was okay.

Christopher: Alex became a pal. I went to give him a load of clothes at a hotel in Liverpool while he was doing interviews. He was sat there in his skinny undies. He went on *Wogan* [*Terry Wogan's BBC1 prime-time chat show*] with a Gio-Goi 'Get Fresh' baseball cap on and a F*cked Up baseball jacket. He stuck the baseball cap on Wogan's head and opened his jacket to show the F*cked Up label live on TV. Alex then went away and when he came back he called me from the airport. He wanted me to pick him up. Alex had got it in his head that he was our figurehead – what a lovely man, he was crazy so it was a good fit.

Anthony: It wasn't unusual to have a lot of press and a lot of TV but *Wogan* was the most shocking. It was peak time, 7 p.m. Wogan was at his height. The phone rang a dozen times, 'Terry Wogan's got your hat on.' Alex took it off his own head and put it on Terry. After that Alex thought he was on the payroll. He kicked off at the snooker World Championships at Preston Guildhall. It was big news; he had a row with a ref and Steve Davis or Stephen Hendry and then held a press conference. He was wearing a F*cked Up jacket – you could see the label – and he told the press, 'You're all fucked up.' The press conference descended into chaos.

I was in bed one night having a joint watching Alex being interviewed by James Whale on TV [*The James Whale Radio Show, shown late-night ITV*] and Alex started talking to me down the camera: 'Anthony, this gear's mega.' Then the next minute Whale goes, 'Anthony, is there any chance you can get me some as well?' I'm not talking back to the telly but they are talking to me.

Higgins also introduced me to Ronnie Wood. We just kept sending clothes out to Ireland for Ronnie, to County Kildare, where Ronnie had his pub built at the bottom of the garden.

It caused murders that F*cked Up Range; people were writing to *The Guardian* and *The Times*. The national press were saying the last thing that was openly sold on the high street that was as bad was the Sex Pistols album, *Never Mind the Bollocks*. It appeared in all the red tops; how dare these people put F*cked Up advertising boards in their shop windows. It was great for us. It drove sales. We did a F*cked Up car sticker that went viral . . . remember, this is before the Internet. How do you make a country talk to each other before the Internet?

Christopher: Everyone had the F*cked Up sticker in their car. We used to do a lot of stuff like that. One of our mates had something wrong with his pecker after having sex. It was swollen. We were going to do a car sticker with the word 'Cheese' on. Somebody came up with 'Cheesy Helmet'. Then I said, 'Very Helmet'. We did an orange car sticker, 'Very Helmet', named after my mate's knob. We'd be interested to see where they'd turn up. 'Who's driving that car with that Gio-Goi sticker in the back window that says "Very Helmet"?' If it made us laugh that was it.

Anthony: There was no real organisation. It was just a gang of lunatics. We were on the cover of *i-D* [*with the F*cked Up jacket*] and we went to do a club night in Stoke with the magazine. We had a Gio-Goi stand with all the F*cked Up range and we sold everything. We'd also smuggled loads of brandy in with the clothes and by the end of the night everyone was smashing the stand up, off their heads.

Amidst all this mayhem, Chris was slowly falling into it. He was messing with fabrics, cutting cloth; he wanted to be a good designer. It went from the back of the fag packet to developing ranges.

Christopher: We did a pair of jeans with a skeleton on, skeleton bones. Random people would turn up at the office with ideas and we'd just say, 'Cool, let's have a go.' This kid said he could do paintings on garments but he needed an airbrush machine. So I went out and bought this machine that cost £500. We designed the jeans with the bones on, did a few, and I never saw him or the machine again – but who cares?

The skeleton jeans became part of a fashion show we did at Manchester Town Hall. There were other labels at the show but the way we approached it was different. We had girls in white denim suits and we painted the suits down the front with the words, 'Lick', 'Rock' and 'Fast'. We gave all the lads replica guns and they were also on Ecstasy, so they came out dancing to the music waving guns. We saw ourselves as different from every other clothing brand that was around. In the programme there was space to describe the brand and everyone had put things like, 'The silhouette for our range, the colour for this season.' I put a poem about Jesus carrying this bloke when he's at his lowest ebb [*'Footprints in the Sand'*]. The bloke was walking with Jesus on a beach. There were two sets of footprints but when the bloke was at his lowest there was only one set of footprints, so he asked Jesus, 'When I was at my lowest, why did you leave me?' Jesus said, 'I didn't leave you, I was carrying you.'

Anthony: The skeleton jeans were just for the fashion show but we were now selling thousands of pairs of jeans a week. On the back pocket it had 'Gio-Goi' and 'Dedicated' together in the shape of an eye. We'd keep the same shape of jean and we'd change the colour of the embroidery on the pocket every month, green and red or blue and purple.

The jeans were being made by a fella from Preston. He had a factory and his dad had one that did Marks & Spencer. Unfortunately, he started to back door our jeans. Someone tipped us off that our jeans were turning up on market stalls in Cumbria. Wack and me went up, bought a few pairs and traced it back. We asked this lad to come for a meeting. He came in to the office laughing and joking with his fluffy moustache and he went home in tears, devastated. We needed compensating. We could have taken his factory off him if we'd wanted to. That's the law of the street. Steal off me. I'll steal off you. We brought the street mentality into our business.

It was my responsibility to make sure the product didn't appear on the grey market. What he was doing was not bootlegging but over-production. I'd order 10,000 pairs of jeans and he'd serve me at £18.99 with a V.A.T. receipt but he'd make 15,000 pairs, a bigger run, and charge £15 cash for the over production to whoever. Once I picked up my garments the back door of this factory was open. They had 40,000 of our labels in stock, so they stole 5,000 and put them on these jeans and sold them out the back door for cash. He was using our rivets and our zips but on cheaper denim and selling them on market stalls. That was a one-off situation.

Other brands were virtually ruined by bootleggers. Gio-Goi was never ever bootlegged. We were the bootleggers! We were the biggest pirates in town. Why would anybody bootleg Gio-Goi when every bootlegger in town, in London and Leicester, knows us? If someone came in and said, 'I want to print up 10,000 Gio-Goi,' they'd just ring us up. You go anywhere and every brand is getting battered but people won't bootleg Gio-Goi – not in this country, not if we are involved.

In May 1992 The Hacienda celebrated its tenth anniversary with a fashion show called TEN: THE FASHION, *featuring Michiko Koshino, Vivienne Westwood, John Richmond and Body Map. Gio-Goi was one of the most talked about fashion labels in the country but they were not invited to the show. They took it as a snub.*

Anthony: The organisers of that fashion show hadn't recognised us as a brand. We were deeply offended. We knew much more than a bunch of pretentious people with their underpants stuck up their arse. We knew what sold.

Christopher: We gave 100 of our guys a white T-shirt each with a black sheep on it and the words 'Gio-Goi – Black Sheep of the Fashion Industry'. They walked around this fashion show in these T-shirts. It was fashion terrorism. I think they had balaclavas on with their hoods up. It didn't go down very well at this show. I think it intimidated everybody. It completely freaked out all the arty people, so it had the desired effect.

That was a set-up but Gio-Goi was very real. All our pals who we'd go out with on a weekend in pubs or clubs were all fully kitted out with Gio. We were also dressing a lot of long-term prisoners, so we did kind of ask for it [*the label's reputation*] a little bit as well. Someone's in jail, or coming out, they've got no readies and someone asks, 'Can you send my pal some T-shirts?' Yeah, course we can. Then a parcel would go to Durham prison and we would be spoken about. 'It's off that Manchester firm, the Donnellys.' The same was happening in Nottingham, Brixton . . . all over.

Anthony: We had Barry Grant [*actor Paul Usher*] wearing the gear on *Brookside* when he was [*involved in a storyline about*] blowing up shops – he was the bad boy at the time on *Brookside*. He had a big Gio-Goi badge on the arse of his jeans and they were panning in on the badge to make it look like he's associated with some bad guys. He's burning down these shops because he's got those jeans on.

Harry Franco: We did a 'Bank Robber' range as well. The coat had an inside pocket on it that was about two inches wide and about two foot long – a perfect fit for a sawn-off, apparently. There was some really nice clobber coming in. Half the range was really nice and half the range was padded out with absolute crap, with absolute shit knitwear. It was really hard to flog a full range. The shops really wanted it but we couldn't meet demand. That was still the main problem. We had big international accounts but we didn't have the stock. It needed a huge injection of cash.

The next step up was instead of manufacturing in thousands, it needed manufacturing in tens of thousands and that was a huge big step. There were people certainly sniffing round interested in investing, but Anthony wanted to keep complete control.

Anthony: The knitwear brothers were doing thousands of pieces of knitwear for us and you'd get slight seconds. They'd be pulled off the conveyer and put in bags – 150 in one bag, 1,000 in another, an amount was building up over a period of six months. One day

I went looking for more space in the building and I came across this stuff and I sold it all for cash. The knitwear brothers found out and were not happy. The communication with the knitwear brothers was breaking down anyway. They were being pushed to one side.

The 'Bank Robber' range was a wax range – like Barbour but lighter. We did wax jeans, wax shirts and wax three-quarter-length coats with the concealed pocket. We would do anything we weren't supposed to do. Our friends were bank robbers and they requested coats they could put weapons in. We made sure you could easily access the pocket on the inside. We gave [*Alex*] Higgins coat number 147 from that range. Then the next range was the 'Prison' range. All the stuff had mock prison labels and 'Gio-Goi State Pen' and stuff written on them.

Christopher: It was full range of over-dyed garments made out of cotton canvas. The badge had my date of birth as the prison number: 240568 and underneath 'Manchester State Pen'. We did jeans, three or four jackets and shirts. They ended up in *GQ* [*magazine*]. The reason it was all cotton canvas was because we could buy bulk fabric and then over-dye it. It was also easy to handle, even the swing tickets on the range were canvas. We were not working with any factories in Portugal or Dubai anymore. We were using the factory in Sheffield and others in the UK. We were back in fast turnaround mode just trying to get stock on the floor.

Gang-related gun crime in Manchester had continued to escalate throughout 1991 and was now attracting mainstream media attention. A spate of shootings involving young men and reports of teenagers carrying handguns as 'fashion accessories' led to Manchester being dubbed 'the Bronx of Britain'. Mac-10 automatic machine guns were reportedly spotted as attempts to control the doors of the city's clubs grew more intense. The Manchester Evening News *declared this was the 'Menace of Gunchester' as recorded crime in the city rose to be 57 per cent higher than national average.*

Anthony: Everyone was getting blasted in Manchester so we started to do a line of bulletproof vests. There were a couple of incidents where gang members came and test-fired our bulletproofs. Somebody put one on and somebody shot him and it worked perfectly. The vests were surplus stock from the army, green Kevlar army issue. Someone fired one bullet in the warehouse, a .45, and it went through a box of baseball caps. The caps got sold for more money 'cause they had an entry and exit hole. We were doing a roaring trade in bulletproof vests but then everybody started getting shot in the head. Once the headshots started, people stopped buying the vest. We sold about 800 of them in Manchester alone.

Christopher: We were taking the covers off them and embroidering them up with the Gio-Goi logo and 'Dedicated To Those Dodgin' the Rain 'n' Bullets.' We did one for [*TV presenter*] Normski when he used to do that [*TV*] show [*BBC2, Def II*]. We sold them for £200 each.

Unless a shop requested the vests we were quite happy to sell them from the office. There might have been a few quid in it, there might have been a necessity for certain people to use them, but for us it was a marketing tool. It didn't matter whether the press was good or bad. There was not another company that'd sell bulletproof vests at that time – or any time.

Anthony: We were a multi-million pound clothing company but there was also a massive suggestion that we were heading up a gang and we were heavily involved in the drug market. We were suspected of being involved in the importation of Ecstasy. The police misinterpreted the Gio-Goi label as being colours. If you wearing Gio-Goi, you were with us. If someone was caught robbing a post office in Gio-Goi, they were part of the 'firm'. The reputation of the brand, the undercurrent, became the Quality Street thing. Then one day we came to work and a whole row of trees and had been cut down so there was a clear view from the building opposite into our office. So now we were under observation. The police were taking photos; they were about 150 yards away. It was blatant. So I used to walk in to the office in the morning and I'd tell all the staff, 'Wave to the police.' The police would then start coming in over this and that. It didn't make any difference to us because it was what we were brought up with. The police thought we were very, very serious. There were all kinds of other activities going on around us. Manchester, at the time, was mental.

Christopher: If we were in the pub with one of our gang of friends on the Sunday and they've gone off on a Monday and committed a crime, why was that automatically linked to us? Because we were tearaways when we were growing up, even though we have now got into legitimate business, the police would always assume that there's got to be more to it because of our associations. They thought you couldn't be successful from Benchill and in legit business. Whatever we did they always assumed there was more going on. They used to bust our office on a regular basis for different reasons but never found what they were looking for.

Harry Franco: John Collin from Glasgow was one of my accounts. He was sat in the office and the Serious Crime Squad arrived to turn the place over. The word went round from John, 'It's real. Them guys down there, it's the real thing. This isn't like some middle-class designers sat in some nice little office instigating all this in a Malcolm McLaren style. This is proper.'

The night shift in the factory caught a sneak thief in the office one night, down in the warehouse. It was a pal of Chris and Anthony's. When they arrived, because it was an old friend, they didn't know what to do with him as he was pleading he didn't know it was their warehouse. They allegedly stripped him, put him in the boot of the car and took him to the Bench [*pub*]. When Anthony opened the boot everyone from the pub started bombarding the kid with pots. Then they let him run off naked. I think the kid probably shit himself but he got away lightly with that one. No one attempted to rob the warehouse again after that.

Christopher: We thought we were getting professional – we got loads of Gio-Goi tape to put around the delivery boxes. It was at a time when we were getting boxes of clothes stolen by the delivery drivers. So we decided to set up a bogus delivery and follow it. We were all sat having a chippy [*fish & chip shop*] dinner that day and we got our chip papers and threw them in the box and any shit that was hanging round the office, old tins of paint, were put in as well. We gave the box a value of four grand and sent it out. Anyway, it didn't get nicked and it went to the shop. This box has turned up and it was cash on delivery – so the geezer handed £4,000 over and opened the box. It was a laugh for us and then the story would go round the industry. He'd just paid four G for a load of shit from Gio-Goi.

Harry Franco: There was a band from London called Flowered Up, they were like the London version of the Mondays and they were just as fucking mad. They might have the edge on the Mondays actually, because even their management was loopy. Anthony had known them for a while and we were supplying them clothes for the 'Weekender' video. I went to meet them to give them a box of clothes. They were playing in Warrington at Legends. I think I nearly had a heart attack that night. These lines of coke were like the M1. I thought they must have been doing speed. It was cocaine and it nearly killed me. I drove back in my car, all hunched over, driving with one hand clutching my chest, thinking, 'I'm dying, I'm fucking dying.'

I had half an ounce of powder hidden in the steering wheel of the Peugeot. I was knocking a bit out because we were in between seasonal ranges. I got this stuff and then someone showed me how to rock it up. This was just completely insane – drug dealing and selling Gio-Goi clothing seemed to go hand in hand at one time – let's sell some drugs to keep it going. I watched someone throw an ounce of powder into a pot of boiling water and then the bicarb [*bicarbonate of soda*]. I'm thinking, 'This is mad.' You knew yourself that it was totally insane, that you were now a dealer as well as moving your clothes around.

I smashed my car up, actually. I was coming back from somewhere and I was holding a parcel – it could have been prison for a long time. I was right out in the country and I hit a tree. It was the only thing that stopped me going down a huge drop. There was a big bag of the stuff, a fucking snowstorm going on inside the car.

Anthony: Around that time we got heavily involved with quite a heavy team from Loughton, Essex. They had a breaker's yard and other business. We had an on-going interest with them in the secondary car market. They gifted me with a BMW convertible and sent Chris an Astra GTE. There were lots of other things going on. Our horizons were expanding: there's nowhere we can't go, nothing we can't do.

Christopher: The business is booming but we've got all this stuff going on outside of the business. We then decided to put our money into a club with our cousins Tony and Dominic. It was part of the Apollo Theatre [*in Ardwick*]. It must have been an old ballroom because the dance floor was still there. It was all set up but it was disgusting, no one had been in there for fifteen years, maybe longer. So we started to refurbish it. At that time it was birth of the superclub [*Miss Moneypennys, Cream, Renaissance,Ministry*] so it made business sense. The PA system cost £100,000. We bought a £16,000 light for the roof and had to get permission from Manchester Airport to use it.

Anthony: We thought that we'd have a club. We wanted a nightclub. We looked after an awful lot of people. People we were hiring to work on the club were our friends. The police were watching us more intensely now, unbeknown to us. What we'd do is one day a week we'd close the office and our friends would come down and sit in the office and smoke and drink and play music. We heard that people we know were getting taxed from people outside our estate. That was how it was moving in town. One particular person wanted to speak to me around this time and I had to go and confront the situation because I thought it was a direct challenge. It was exactly what I was trying to avoid. I didn't need this shit.

The meeting was arranged in a quiet location on the edge of my council estate. Manchester was a dangerous place. I had no choice. As it turned out it was not a problem, more a case of finding out where we actually stood with certain people. We have always acted independently – we do our own thing, mind our own business and do what we need to do. So we were both relieved that we didn't have a problem but there was clearly still a situation brewing. Our friends were doing their own things and we were doing ours. We had no idea of half of the shit that was happening on the estate, so it was no surprise when something bad happened.

Six days before the Donnelly Brothers planned to open their club Parliament, in late November 1992, Christopher's best friend, who he had know since nursery school, Stephen Yates, age twenty-five, was brutally murdered in Wythenshawe.

Christopher: Stephen was my best friend and I loved him with all my heart, but he was getting friendly with firms from all over and I thought immediately it would end in tears. He was bringing different people to the office. One Friday night I was sat watching *The Word*, waiting to see which band was wearing our clothes, and Stephen burst through the door, shouting, 'Get me a gun, get me a gun.' He was stood there crying he was that frustrated. He was going mental. He was having trouble with these kids like I knew he would. I sent him on his way, told him I couldn't get him a gun and to get his head down. The next I heard was Stephen saw them in a car, chased them and shot at them about five or six times. Stephen knew there would be repercussions.

On another night Stephen had a fight in a pub. I said, 'You can't keep doing that shit, you'll end up getting done in.' He said, 'It was all right afterwards.' But Stephen recognised there was going to be trouble and he was in the process of moving house off the estate. I'd just moved another pal off the estate to Didsbury, near where I was living, and Stephen was going to move house to get himself away from the trouble. He had his bin bags with his stuff in and was on his doorstep leaving to get away from it all. That was when he got killed. He knew it was on top. He was saying, 'I've had enough of this shit,' but it was too late.

Harry Franco: After Yatesy had been shot Anthony and Chris went missing and I got a call to come and pick them up from a pub in Wythenshawe at half ten in the morning. You could tell the landlord had the 'wasp' in the room with Anthony. He'd been there for about two days and this landlord was all on edge, at the end of his bar shaking. Anthony claimed that the inside of his head had caved in and he couldn't feel the roof of his mouth. He'd been taking cocaine for about five days non-stop. He kept trying to show me, saying, 'Look, look, there's nothing. My head's hollow.'

Tracey: Stephen was like a brother to them. Chris locked himself in his house, wouldn't let [*his wife*] Natalie in there or anyone. He started drinking heavily. Stephen didn't get buried for about two months, because of the investigation [*into the murder*]. That was an awful time. I always remember Chris and Anthony telling me not to go to the opening of their club because I may get hurt. They said the mood was too hostile and there were too many guns on the premises.

8
IT'S COMIN' ON TOP

Anthony: How can you enjoy the opening night of your club when your pal has just been blasted to death? But we'd signed leases and we had to get the place open because it was costing us all money. Everyone from the music and fashion industry turned up for the launch but also every gangster in the town was in there as well. It was a blinding club, Parliament. We all spent a lot of money on it but we put no thought into what we were doing because the clothes were that successful. It was in the wrong area of town. Ardwick was not a nice area. The light on the roof was supposed to attract every top clubber in Manchester but it brought the wrong crowd. On the opening night all the villains were stood around the edge of the club looking at each other – it just wasn't a very relaxing vibe. We used to wear bulletproof vests on a regular basis to get in and out of the club. It came with the territory, really. Everybody carried guns around that time. Manchester was a very, very violent place. If the club had been in the heart of the city centre it would have been successful but it was in a dark, desolate out of town spot. It was destined for failure.

Christopher: We tried to make it into a really nice vibe. We booked all the best DJs of the time, people like Justin Robertson. Tracey was trying to book credible things but it just didn't pan out to be a cool place. In fact, it was fucking crackers. Stephen was my best mate from the age of three, so opening the club a week after he died, I didn't know whether I was coming or going. In Parliament you felt completely on offer. You just didn't know where it was going to come from next because of the shit that went on in there every fucking night. We were constantly fighting with different people for a variety of reasons. I turned up one day and the builder said, 'Two blokes have been asking after you.' You just didn't know if someone was going to run out of an alley and put one in your head. If it wasn't the door politics, it was something else. It was just one big headache that club. I was caning the booze and drugs to null the pain I was in.

Harry Franco: The slogan for Parliament, on the posters and everything, advertising the opening, was, 'No Guns, No Drugs, No Paranoia'. Out of all the clubs I've been to in my life, Parliament was the one that was most full of drugs, guns and paranoia. The atmosphere was just nasty. It was on the edge of kicking off all the time. Everybody knew who Anthony and Chris were and they'd know that most of their pals would be in there, so that could attract people from all over Manchester. People would want to get in amongst it. It was high profile, all of it.

All the Gio-Goi staff were made to go to the club for certain events and it was like, 'Ah fuck, got to go to Parliament. One night I'm going to lose me life in there.' There was a platform above a bar and a little door round to it so you sat in there with your girlfriend. They built a cage round it so you got a drink and then went and sat in this cage with your girlfriend to watch the madness.

One of my accounts came down from Scotland and I took them to The Hacienda. At about half one they started saying, 'We want to go to this Gio-Goi club.' So we left The Hacienda and drove over there. These four guys from Glasgow went off wandering around. They came back after no longer than ten minutes and one of them had been threatened with a broken bottle. They said, 'Just get us out of here.' So we went out and, sure enough, all their coats had been nicked and the motor had been done outside as well.

Anthony: It was the biggest mistake we ever made. We spent fortunes on the refurbishment with Tony and Dominic. The sound system was a Peavey and it was brought in from America – state of the art. We were the first people with a paramedic for people in the nightclub. But I pulled up one night and there was a kid leaning out of the window firing a gun. It was like the Wild West. We were trying to do something nice, we'd spent a fortune, but it just attracted violence.

One night I was hosting a big player from London and someone fell out of the ceiling in between us – head to toe in black soot. He'd taken loads of Es and crawled through the ducting. On a couple of occasions I flushed ears and bits of bodies down the toilet. The paramedics were for saving kids on E, but being able to stitch noses and ears back on was another thing. Guns were fired in the ceiling regularly. We built the cage above the bar where we locked our birds and then sent in the champagne. They banged on the window when they wanted the toilet.

The women were actually so violent that we got a psychologist to come down to identify what was happening. The women were kicking fuck out of each other. The psychologist said, 'The root of your problem starts with your toilets, so let's go and have a look.' When we walked in they said, 'Your colours are a bit anti-social and you've got no whale music.' We employed this firm to come in, paint the doors pastel colours, put flowers in, new sinks, paint the walls, put mirrors up and put this ambient tranquil music on so they can chill out. We thought it was going to be great, the women were going to be really mellow. We opened the club doors; the women smashed the mirrors, kicked the doors off, broke the tape cassette and ate the fucking flowers. It was known as the most violent club in town – and still is. Even though it's closed down its reputation lives on.

Christopher: Some nights you'd have five or six different firms in there. The politics of that situation were just a stress. It was a situation where they don't like them and we're mates with them. We were dealing with all that and still grieving for Stephen. The clothing business had been going from strength to strength but now we don't feel like going in to work and we've been boozing all night. The business suffered and started to take a bit of a nosedive. Gio had been taking £100,000 a week and we owned a club and things were about to kick on further. It wasn't the business that nosedived, it was us – our personal lives. Now we were going to our own club in our own bulletproof vests that we were selling three months before to other people. I used to put a vest on coming out of my front door with Natalie in the morning and took it off when I got to the office. Then I'd put it back on when I finished work to go home in.

Anthony: We had this nightclub but the police wouldn't leave us alone. The licensee, Richard Singleton, was registered from Gio-Goi's office and the police were trying to close the club. They sent faxes to Richard saying, 'Anthony Donnelly walked in, Donnelly was joined by other males known to the police.' The police were obviously sending undercover in there to watch us. Basically the faxes said, 'Donnelly's the promoter in that place, how can we allow this man to run that club.' That was like sending us a postcard saying, 'It's on you.' That was another reason to get away. It felt like the film *Scarface* in that club.

Christopher: The police were investigating us. We met our Tony and Dominic in the club for dinner one day and told them, 'Listen, it's not for us. We're going to continue with our clothing company and we just want out of the club.' It was too much aggravation.

All through this the only thing that kept me going was running. I was running marathons. I ran into the office every day eight miles, sometimes in the bulletproof vest. I ran home. That kept me sane. Then on a Sunday morning Natalie would drive me out thirty miles and I'd run back. I'd been done drink driving so I was banned from driving.

Anthony: We left Parliament after about eight weeks. We put a piece in the *Manchester Evening News* saying, 'We've had enough, we're going to concentrate on our clothes and we're opening a fish restaurant in Cornwall.' Funnily enough, they printed it in the *Manchester Evening News* and that was that, we were out of there.

Christopher: We started taking some extra-long holidays in Tenerife because we had friends there. They were from Nottingham and London. They were out in Tenerife running the timeshares with the Italian Mafia but one of them had decided to open a shop in Las Americas and we just kept sending the [*Gio-Goi*] product out there. They were also looking after Nigel Benn when he was out there training for a fight. Nigel's daughter and Anthony's daughter had a joint birthday party out there. Daryll was five and Nigel's daughter was a similar age. We went for a nice meal with both families. Then Nigel started wearing Gio-Goi baseball caps in his press conferences before his big fights with Eubank.

Anthony: We were looking after our families – after Stephen's death we were trying to disassociate ourselves from a lot of shit.

Trying to put a gap between all the trouble and us. We were about to clinch the rich title. We could see the Bentleys, we could see the mansions and we were mixing with people who were giving us million pound orders. If we could fulfil them we would be very rich. If we had any kind of management we would have made it. But people were afraid to get involved with us.

Christopher: If we had some decent management the business would have gone from strength to strength no matter what. But you know what? No one could have managed us in that period anyway – we were unmanageable. So it was always going to be a car crash. When we were in Tenerife I told Anthony I'd had enough. It felt like we were fighting with every fucker. I said, 'I'm going home and if anyone gets in my way, any fucker, anybody at all gives me any fucking hassle, I won't be responsible.' If anyone had approached me in a couple of months' period after leaving Parliament, I don't know what I would have done. I was about to combust. I started to go a bit demented with grief and frustration.

Then on top of everything else that was going on, when we came back from Tenerife we found out the knitwear brothers were trying to nick the brand. They had removed our names from the paperwork, allegedly forged our signatures, and put themselves as sole company directors. It was made to look as if we had resigned and handed over our shares. They must have seen we were vulnerable and thought, 'We'll have this for ourselves.' They had made more money with us than they'd ever made in their lives. The factory was on twenty-four hours a day, they couldn't keep making the stuff fast enough. They didn't think we would understand what they were trying to do.

Anthony: They could see we weren't spending any time on the business and were trying to take it over. So that was something else we had to deal with. We needed some information from Companies House and we found out what they were up to.

Christopher: The atmosphere in our building was not great. To get into our office you walked through the loading bay, up a set of stairs, and then through a bit of their factory – and their office had all glass windows. So none of us are talking and we'd have to walk past their office to get in to ours. It made life uncomfortable knowing what they were trying to do. They were saying, 'We are this business.' I said, 'No you're not. You make fucking jumpers.' We decided to up sticks and take the office, all the staff, the stock and the desks. We got a forty-footer and emptied the lot in a day, left this massive big empty space.

The knitwear brothers were shouting, 'You can't do that!'

'Who's going to stop us?'

We refurbished the stables at my mum and dad's place and we moved the business to the sticks. It was the only place we could take it.

Harry Franco: It all retreated to the barn and Chris was just keeping it going with some shirts and stuff. We released a girl's range called, 'Gio-Goi Jus'. Everybody wanted it but there was no stock. The hunger for it was still there but a lot of the really good accounts were abandoning us because of not getting their orders, not because the gear wasn't selling in their shops – they just couldn't get the gear, and so they'd lost faith in putting orders in, really.

Christopher: We didn't have a Gio-Goi Jus collection as such. I made 2,000 T-shirts to take to the Clothes Show [*Live, trade show at the NEC, in Birmingham*]. We just had a load of fabric – pink, red, green – and I got a long-sleeve women's T-shirt made up and mixed up the sleeves. You'd get a T-shirt with a green body, one pink sleeve, and one red sleeve with Gio-Goi Jus on. I sold out in day. It was a different business model. If we knew we could make £50,000 at the Clothes Show we would make the clothes just for that. I bought a load of check miniskirts, £8 each, put the Gio-Goi name on them and put them out for £15 at the Clothes Show.

Two of the reps, Nico and Joycey, opened a showroom in the building where Factory Too was [*Factory Records had collapsed in 1992 and now Tony Wilson was attempting to revive the label*]. They were all reps exclusive to Gio-Goi – they got a wage, we paid for their car, petrol and they got commission. If you were an agent you got no wage, you used your own car and you got a higher commission. We'd sacked everyone as reps so we didn't have the overheads and they'd all become agents. Nico and Joycey were selling Gio and whatever other brands they could get their hands on. At that point they didn't want us anywhere near their office! They thought they could go it alone, I guess.

Anthony: We'd disappeared to do the label from somewhere more tranquil and peaceful. We just wanted to be left alone. It was a very violent time; we could only trust our immediate crew. We did a photo shoot with some pals from Moss Side and one turned up with a bullet in his leg. Our models were turning up with snapped knives in them and bullet wounds. We were blagging it, saying we were proper businessmen, but we had not made that complete transition.

Christopher: We then found out the knitwear brothers had attempted to register the brand name Gio-Goi to themselves solely. It was coming from every angle.

Anthony: It was full-on, non-stop shit. The knitwear brothers thought they had a claim on the label. It was a business arrangement that they'd misinterpreted. We felt it was ours and they felt it was theirs. We were ready to prove it beyond any doubt, but we weren't ready for the fact statements had been made saying we'd coerced and threatened the label out of them.

Christopher: Anthony and I had a meeting with some acquaintances on top of the Arndale Centre car park. Both sides decided it would be best left alone at that point. It was agreed to let the legal dispute be settled by lawyers.

Anthony: Around this time, Chris went to see a psychologist because of the way his head was. He lay down on the shrink's sofa and the shrink got all geared up and ready with his pen and paper. He told Chris to close his eyes: 'I'm going to help you.' Chris put his head down and started to rattle off what was going on in his life and when he woke up the shrink's hair was on fire. He turned round to Chris and said, 'There's nothing at all I can do for you, son, but could you do us a favour? Can you come back when it's all finished and tell us what happened?'

Christopher: We had legal bills coming out of our ears. We were living hand to mouth regarding the business. It was getting harder and harder to make stuff. We had taken our eye off the ball. The product wasn't great. We couldn't concentrate with all the other stuff going on. We were trying to run a business, but one minute I was picking buttons the next I was in a dark alleyway having a meeting with a load of lunatics carrying guns. The whole thing was chaos.

While we were out at the barn, we tried to inject new blood into the company. We took staff on. A kid left Bozo, one of our stockists, to work for us. He got pally with Anthony but he had a nervous breakdown. Anthony ran him into the ground. We took another kid on, a friend of a friend. He said he was a black belt at karate but he was a compulsive liar. He was packing boxes for us. Soon after all our clothes were turning up on the street around Manchester and we couldn't figure it out. It was this kid. I put it on him; I didn't hit him, just shouted at him. He pissed his pants in front of everyone. It was in his trainers and he squelched as he walked out. He'd been robbing us for months. He'd had about £5,000 of gear. He repaid us.

Anthony: It was a struggle to keep things going at the barn. So much was going on that our concentration waned – the candle was burning out. We were in the barn around six months and then we decided we should move back to town. We met a third party who found us a building. They didn't know exactly what was going on and they got the story same as everybody else: everything is fine. So we agreed to buy this building for the business. It was at the top of Princess Parkway near Castlefield. It was an easy location to do business from. Business was suffering from a barn in the country. It made more sense to move back to town.

Christopher: All our stock was in the barn at my mum's house! It doesn't look very good. So we moved in to this new building. We wanted to get Gio-Goi back to where it belonged. It had gone through a very sticky patch. We were getting fabrics from where we could, whoever would give us credit – so they were not necessarily the fabrics we wanted to use. We were trying to put a range together but we still had these problems with the litigation over Gio-Goi. We found a shirt manufacturer in Manchester. We made some nice shirts but there was no real vibe behind the label anymore, there was no energy or rawness. I found this peach check fabric and made thousands of beach trousers, basic chino shape, pockets and drawstring. We sold loads of them. I made these gold and silver parka-style coats, 500 of each, and we could not give them away. They were the statement pieces. A year later everyone was doing gold and silver coats. I did some press and was talking about using natural fabrics: wools, sheepskin, leather. Blur started to wear the stuff. The PR kept the brand alive.

We were trying to rebuild our lives. A friend of our cousins, Perry Hughes, was helping out. He had got involved with Parliament during the licensing problems. Perry was good at dealing with the legal side of things regarding the ownership of the brand. He now took over the legals, allowing Anthony and me to concentrate on Gio-Goi. A friend of ours came in to do the sales called Bobby. Our pal John [*Faulkner*] turned up and was with us. I trust him with my life. He's a great lad, a grafter. He wasn't really working for Gio-Goi, but he came in the office every day to help out. It was a bit of a difficult situation because we were still in litigation and we might lose the label. We were just trying to push things forward.

For some strange reason we also decided that we would open a shop in London, in Covent Garden. We took a lease and started working on the refurbishment of the shop. We also took a flat in London. The shop soaked up a hell of a lot of money.

Anthony: The London flat was above Issey Miyake in Knightsbridge overlooking Daphne's restaurant. It was not cheap. The litigation with Gio-Goi came to a head in February 1994. I was running through town with a barrister to overturn a judgement that the knitwear brothers had got to say that they'd won. The barrister was putting his wig on as he was running through town. We overturned the judgement. One of the knitwear brothers took his Gio-Goi shirt off in court and spat on it.

Christopher: He was shouting at our representative, 'Go on, you might as well take the shirt off my back.' We were fifteen minutes away from losing the label. It was one of those where it was going to get stamped at 4 p.m. We ended up getting the brand back fully. We were the ones doing all this work, trying to keep the brand going anyway, so it was justified. Gio-Goi was ours and is in our bones.

Anthony: So finally there was some good news. But what we didn't know was at the same time there was now a serious police investigation that had been put on us. The police called it Operation Bluebell. It was just a progression of the observations they were making when we were at the building where the trees had gone missing earlier. Twenty-five of us went over to Puerto Banus [*on the Costa del Crime*] for our Tony's stag do. The hotel had a casino; after twenty-four hours the casino couldn't take any more bets because we'd bought all the pesetas in the place. We were young, talented men but there were all kinds of rumours circulating about us and our associates still.

The police had been looking to break this thing [*Quality Street Gang*] for years but they couldn't infiltrate. Now they had new powers and new technology, this right to infiltrate gangs, introducing informants to people. The informant who was put on to us went on that stag do without anyone really knowing him after befriending my dad. My dad was none the wiser – it was a piss up, so it didn't matter. We just thought he was my dad's mate. He was called Neil Thompson and he was from Warrington; he was reporting back to the police. He was an active criminal, a paid informer. That whole stag do must have been under observation. The twenty-five people on the table, a mixture of fresh and older faces from Spain, London, Liverpool and Manchester. It must have looked like an empire, a big organisation, when in reality it was just a family stag do, not the meeting of the five families.

Thompson got in to my dad first. They did a fifteen-month

surveillance on my dad, maybe only six months on Chris and me. We started getting wind that Thompson was trying to do things that my dad wasn't normally involved in – he was asking my dad to get him things, especially drugs. So we didn't like him around our dad and we tried to lead him away. We did that good of a job at pulling him away from my dad that we got all the attention on us. They were not getting anywhere with my dad, we were much more interesting – it was the Ecstasy scene they were after.

Thompson had introduced himself as being on the run and was hiding in Newquay. He said he was going to open a clothes shop. We were having trouble on so many fronts that our guard was down. Thompson then introduced us to what we now know to be an undercover police officer, Quinny, who said he was from Newquay as well and wanted to buy Gio-Goi clothes off us. He kept coming to the office, saying, 'Your clothes are great and, by the way, can you get me some drugs?' He'd been vouched for by Thompson and at the time we thought he was a reliable source because of my dad. We had no idea he was an informer. I kept saying, 'You give me some orders and I'll get you anything.'

Thompson and Quinny spent the next six months asking us – on the pretext they were going to buy clothes – 'Can you buy us drugs?' That was all the time. We gave them fuck all.

Christopher: They were saying to me, 'We want to spend £100,000 for our shops.' So we're saying to them, 'Sweet, give us your orders.' They were saying can you get me this and can you get me that? We said, 'Yeah we can get you whatever you like. We'll get you the Eiffel Tower if you want it, but spend your money with the company first.' They were mugs but we just wanted the money for the company. The rent in London was a grand a week just for the flat; we had a quarter of a million pound investment in the shop refit in London. This was all still going on. We just wanted the clothes order.

Anthony: I gave Quinny a nervous breakdown. Everything he asked for I asked for the same back. I made his job impossible. He'd say, 'Here, can you get me twenty stolen cars?'

'Yeah, you can have them, fucking give us £100,000 for the clothing order.'

He'd ring me on a Spanish number, so I'd ring this Spanish number back, and he'd be in a police station but on a Spanish divert. He'd go, 'Are my drugs ready yet?' I'd go, 'Have you got the order for my clothes?'

They got fucking nowhere. That's why they introduced another officer, Scouse Paul. We'd turn up at work and see his silver Saab that we later found out had got all the secret recording equipment in it . . . and we'd think, 'What the fuck is he doing here again?' You'd think you'd just got rid of them. 'Have you put your order in, Paul?' He'd say, 'No. Listen, can I have a word? I'd like 30,000 pills.' It was just bullshit.

He was after tonnes of pot as well. I'd talk to him because he was a potential customer for the clothes. I was being polite. Then when he leaves I'm saying, 'He's a fucking loon; he keeps asking for tablets and smoke.' I was just giving him a load of waffle. We wanted his money for the clobber.

Christopher: Then they'd come to me and try the same thing and get nowhere. Then they'd go to our pal John Faulkner. They offered us the Saab at a fraction of the book price – the one with all the secret recording equipment in it. They were turning up every other day with car boots full of crates of whiskey. We were buying it off them for three or four quid a bottle. They were buying it from the wine shop round the corner for £15 a bottle. It was just to make themselves look right and to try and impress us.

Anthony: They were confusing everybody and confusion is a great method. They were actively concentrating on how to manipulate us and then monitoring phone calls. You'd be ringing each other and saying, 'Do you know about this bloke?' Everybody didn't know what everybody else was talking about but everybody was just talking. They get you into a state of confusion. It was a well thought out process. The police had thousands of pounds' worth of expenses to spend on us, just to impress us, to get us to do business with them.

We had businesses. You could come and ring our bell or go to my dad's yard. So it was a great platform for them to start the investigation from, as you could just walk into the yard unannounced. Although they tried to embroil everybody, nobody wanted to speak to them. My dad was allegedly threatening to blow heads off and all kinds of mad shit around this time. He was behaving totally out of character. He was the most difficult person in the world to deal with. You couldn't have a conversation without him wanting to kill you because of the shit that was going on with these fuckers mithering him. It's a tight family and it's a well-oiled machine but our dad will help anybody and that was his downfall with this shit [*undercover investigation*] that was going on – talking to Thompson the grass was affecting his personality. He was like a different person, all caused by these fucking undercover officers badgering him for drugs, and I mean constantly.

They never had the opportunity to do anything before so now that they had the technology, new toys, they were going to do their utmost to get our dad and us. We were the number one targets. This new 'squad' had the powers to bug, video, but what they didn't say was entrap, ensnare. My dad's never been involved in drugs in his life. My dad's notorious but he's old school, he's not a drug dealer.

We were heavily suspected of being involved in the importation of Ecstasy because of the success of Gio-Goi and the illegal raves.

We were not whiter than white . . . but we had no involvement in what they were asking for. Little did we know that this investigation by the undercover police and the paid informant was going to bring our business and lives crashing down, leaving us almost on the edge of being totally broke.

9
WAR IS OVER

Anthony: It was a Saturday night in Manchester and 808 State were playing at a live venue. I was in the dressing room and four or five doormen came in and approached me. I turned around and I said, 'I don't want any problems.' It was part of some old shit that had not fully been resolved around the Parliament days. I just gave them the body language that I wasn't up for a fight. One of them wasn't having it and the situation was looking very dangerous. So I suddenly pushed my way past them and grabbed the door. Someone pulled out a blade and was trying to chop me. I was surrounded. I fought my way through the door and it led out to the stage. In the struggle, my coat got pulled off with my car keys in the pocket. I was going under the stage like a monkey on the scaffolding while 808 were playing live. The doormen were chasing me. I popped out in the pit, dived over the barrier into the crowd and then ran through the club and out the front door, leaving my jacket and keys behind.

I wanted my keys and my jacket back. So I went to another club and asked my mate for help. Within thirty minutes I was back at the venue. I went in the club and someone with me sprayed CS gas in the reception. I couldn't find the kid in the club who started the trouble, so I came back outside and he was stood there with his firm and all their men. It went right off. It was a vicious fight that went into the main road. Someone got stabbed.

People were trying to diffuse the situation. I got bust in the face with a Maglite [*torch*], lost a couple of teeth. I got my car keys back, etc., I then went out and went to a rave in the woods with a big gash in my face and partied all night.

Christopher: On the Monday morning I was in the office with the staff and this firm turns up and wants to know where Anthony is. I've ended up having a bit of a row. There weren't a lot of them in there, three or four. I've gone, 'Get out of the fucking office. There's normal working people in here; you're in a fucking work place.' I had a pair of stepladders and I was trying to push them out with these stepladders but ended up fighting with them. They overpowered me. I ended up with the stepladders pinned against me chest and they stabbed me a couple of times as I fought them. It was only a brief struggle and was over as quick as it started.

Anthony: Then it just went off. There were others parked up the road but we had not noticed them. My car windows got put through and there were fights breaking out all over the car park. Then the police turned up and both groups were allowed on their way.

Christopher: We were under surveillance at the time, weren't we? We still hadn't clocked what was going on with the undercover investigation. But apparently they were watching from a flat across the road but that actual situation wasn't recorded, we found out later, as the observation camera had run out of tape and they missed it all. The surveillance crew radioed through that there was fighting and gunshots at the scene of the observation. The police turned up and found a gun in the car park; a 15-shot Beretta, fully loaded. The police were like, 'All right you lot, don't do it again,' and they left. We've gone, 'That's not right,' because nothing came of it. Alarm bells started ringing in my head. None of it made any sense.

Anthony: The next day Quinny and Scouse Paul came to the office asking for tablets again. We were already wondering who they were and we decided we needed to get rid of them. There was enough shit going on without these pricks driving us mad. I actually rang my pal and said, 'Do you want to serve these mugs? Do what you want to rob them, they're mugs.' And he said, 'Yeah, I'll rip them off.' So I sent them to pick up the supposed drugs. They were nuisances, so the best thing to do was fuck them and they'd go away. They were sent to a house in Wythenshawe and they came back to town after being served with the tablets. They went straight to my dad's yard. Something clicked. I knew the minute I sent them to get served that it was a wrong move. The way they'd been behaving, there was only one thing they could be. It all clicked into place but it was too late. I said to Chris, 'They're police' and we drove to my dad's yard to tell him what we thought. I'll never forget when I looked at Scouse Paul in the yard. He knew that I knew he was an undercover. He left sharpish and I said to my dad, 'You've been dealing with the police. What have you been doing?'

Christopher: We twigged that they were old bill and they twigged that we knew exactly at the same time. They would have liked to take the investigation on another year but we'd got on it and they knew. That night, about five in the morning, I was in bed and my door came off. I jumped up and it was the old bill. The police had these big lights on the house, shouting, 'Come out with your hands up.' The old lady next door came out with her nightdress on with her hands in the air. The police were shouting, 'Not you, love, you go back in.' The Armed Response Team had me on my knees with a gun at my head. They'd blocked the whole of Kingsway off. They put me in a van with a dog because I wouldn't shut up and left me sat in pyjamas handcuffed. They took ten of us down all at the same time in different parts of Manchester. It was 5 October 1994.

Arthur Donnelly: They blocked my road off. I opened the window and I said, 'I'm coming down, don't be fucking smashing anything.' Anyway, smash, smash, smash, wrecked my house. They grabbed me by the hair, slung me on the floor. I was only wearing underpants. The back door was wide open: I was lay on the floor freezing, shaking and every time they walked past they stood on my back.

Anthony: They had no regard and no respect. They actually fired a shot on the farm. That was the first shot ever fired by the GMP. The copper tripped up with his shotgun and nearly blew his daft mate's head off.

June Donnelly: The place was crawling. They were armed. I knew what was coming because I'd had it at Benchill. Before you had time to turn round, they were in. They smashed the entrance – they'd obviously done all the pre-planning. We had big red dots on our heads from the laser sights on their guns. They ripped the carpets up, they were in the loft, everywhere. They came at five in the morning and didn't leave until about dinner time – different teams kept coming in with metal detectors and God knows what. There was nothing to find. And then we couldn't find out where they'd taken Arthur. I didn't even know what this was for. When they took him off, I thought he'd go in court and be out in a couple of days, whatever it is. And then I found out they had Chris and they had Anthony. I thought, 'Same thing again: they'll be straight out.' When they let Arthur make a phone call, he told me what it was for. He said, 'I can't even bring myself to say it.'

Tracey Donnelly: Getting nicked was like an everyday thing – they go off and they come back. And then they didn't come home that night and the next day you read the papers and you're like, 'Shit!' This was totally different. It was a shock to everyone. I lived across the road from Chris. I was due that day to have [*my son*] Milo. Our dad would have been working away and the only reason he was in Manchester is because I'm due. My mum was like, 'Don't come here, don't come near here,' but I went up and the house was smashed to bits. Because my dad had always worked away they tried to make out that he was working away transporting drugs. Unfortunately my dad was the fall guy in this instance. That was the start of the end then. I went ill about five months after the arrests. It was the shame.

Anthony: Eight addresses and the [*Gio-Goi*] warehouse were done. There were eighty police raiding the warehouse with the Armed Response. One hundred and twenty officers it took, all told. They were on me, Chris, my dad, John Faulkner, anyone who was around us at that time. The front page in the paper said, 'Fashion Brothers Arrested in Drugs Raid'. Allegedly we were key players.

Christopher: These geezers had come to the office, pulled me around the corner and said, 'Can I have a quick word with you. Can you give this to your dad?' They put two grand in my hand and said, 'It's for something I'm doing with your dad. Do you know about it?' I said, 'I don't know fuck all.' And when it came down – the police nicked me for laundering money. They gave me the money and then charged me with conspiracy to launder money as well as conspiracy to supply drugs.

Arthur: They wanted the firm. He [*informant Neil Thompson*] came here buying engines and got into my confidence and blah,

blah, blah. The police got hold of him, nicked him selling drugs; he'd stuck people in before and was working for the police. He mentioned the name Donnelly, so they'd asked him to infiltrate the family. Really, though, they got fuck all. Got nothing. In the end, I got eight years for it. I've never dealt in drugs in my life. No matter what you believe – I was set up. I was entrapped selling drugs. I did what I did. And then my sons – they said that it was all drug money that they started Gio-Goi off with. They were after the QSG. They were after Gio-Goi as well. I was on remand for seventeen month. I thought I'd get out. I was going nowhere.

Anthony: In the police car on the way to the Central Detention Centre [*CDC, above the Manchester Magistrates*] my brain was in overdrive thinking about how this had happened. The first thing I said to my lawyer on arrival at the CDC was, 'Are tapes allowed in court?' I knew that I'd been talking to the police on tape.

I knew it had to be taped by Scouse Paul and Quinny. How else could I be being arrested when I hadn't served them? When I got to the CDC, Chris was there. So was my dad – he'd been there three hours and got everything boxed off already.

Chris got released after two days and I got taken to Salford Crescent. I went there because Strangeways was overcrowded. There was a police officer, a little woman, and she had a brown envelope and it said 'Major Incident' right across it. They read the charge and that was it. I was aware that I was being watched in Salford Precinct. I was locked up for twenty-three hours a day and I was there three weeks. We'd just made Gio-Goi footballs, so I kept getting balls sent in for the one-hour exercise. I kept on kicking them back over the roof.

They charged me with conspiracy to import 32,000 pills. I was charged with four conspiracies. What they tried to do was charge us all with the same thing, making out we were all in it together. We weren't. That was the first thing to do, to try and separate

Pete Doherty in Gio-Goi white label.

John Faulkner in Lyon dropping off clobber for the Arctic Monkeys.

Arctic Monkeys wearing Gio-Goi in Lyon.

Robbie's a Goi boy

HE JOINS PETE TO MODEL CLOTHES

ROBBIE WILLIAMS has always had an eye-opening dress sense – from leather jump suits to his black briefs with a lion's head on the crotch for the Rock DJ video.

But now he has become a proper fashionista by signing up with Gio-Goi – one of the coolest clothes labels in the country.

A source said: "Robbie has always taken a real interest in his image. Even as far back as Take That, he dabbled with different styles – the skinhead and the Britpop indie look.

"Since going solo, he has taken it further – wearing leathers, make-up, tattoos and piercing. Gio-Goi think he is perfect. He's a Northern lad and definitely a trend setter."

The Manchester based firm have dressed some of the best bands in rock history, such as the Rolling Stones, Happy Mondays, Oasis, New Order and Primal Scream. Gio-Goi even provided last week's singles chart-toppers Arctic Monkeys with their outfits for their Top Of The Pops debut performance. Now Rob, whose album Intensive Care went straight to No1 yesterday, has agreed a mega-bucks deal to be kitted out as a Goi boy and be the face for their next big range.

[redacted]

"Having the Gio-Goi name on your chest gives you confidence, especially when you're on the streets."

Robbie also follows in the footsteps of **PETE DOHERTY**. The Babyshambles frontman befriended the brothers behind the label – Anthony and Christopher Donnelly – during the band's tour earlier this year. They ended up spending hours together on the tour bus and came up with a range specially for Pete.

I've managed to get hold of the first pictures of Pete modelling a jacket, *left*, bearing the trendy Gio-Goi logo.

Wouldn't Kate be proud.

Piece in *The Sun* stating Robbie was the face of Gio-Goi, which wasn't the case. The story went global, causing a problem with his management.

Dear max [illegible]

We are sorry for the piece in todays sun I am sending a copy of what was sent to the press as the feature was a[illegible] gio-goi where they have got that story from God only knows we go back a long way with you guys and have been to hell and back this morning over this shit we will be having a very seriouse word with the two people involved (a very seriouse word!!) We want you to know we would never do anything to harm our relationship and we are truly sorry for any upset caused. were embarresed

Anthony Christopher

The letter of apology.

Amy Winehouse in
Gio-Goi. RIP.

Pete and Kate Moss backstage with Anthony and Chris at Glastonbury doing an impromptu photoshoot. Photos by Chris.

Chris backstage waiting for Peter to arrive. Two hours late already.

Babyshambles backstage.

Pete Doherty modelling the Rudolph Dassler vintage coat that Chris ruined for the shot.

Ben Drew and Chris at Café de Paris in London for the launch of Ben's *The Defamation of Strickland Banks* album.

Peter, Chris and Mario Testino doing a photoshoot with Gio-Goi and Christian Dior for the front cover of *Vogue Hommes* (this copy personalised by Peter).

Calvin Harris loving Gio-Goi.

Liam Gallagher, Rhys Ifans, Tom Meighan: *The Sun* ran a full page.

Lily Allen, Fred – the original Hacienda doorman, Fergie from the Black Eyed Peas and Kid Rock all in Gio-Goi.

Ian Brown and Arthur on the Stelify video shoot
in the rain.

Keith Allen and Anthony at Glastonbury.

Arthur, Noel and June at the opening of Chris and Anthony's pub, The Prince of Wales, in Camden.

Chris at the opening of the pub in Camden with Brian Duffy and the pub manager, Mark.

Noel, Daryll and Mani at The Prince of Wales opening.

Peter and Carl reunited for the first time since the split of The Libertines at The Prince of Wales.

The main characters from the award-winning Chase & Status video 'Blind Faith'.

Saul and Will (Chase & Status) at the 'Blind Faith' video shoot in Manchester 2010. The video was based on Chris's 21st.

Rihanna modelling Gio-Goi.

Carlie, Rihanna, Paris and Daryll at Anthony's local pub.

Gio-Goi photoshoot. Anthony's daughter Daryll (in pink) far left and Paris, Tracey's daughter, in the centre (in gold). Burning car in the background.

Rihanna in Gio-Goi.

Tracey's son, Milo, with Chris in Ibiza.

The inspiration behind everything we do: Grandma
Julia Frances rides again with Chris.

the charges so we didn't all appear together in the dock looking like one of these Italian Mafia family trials.

Christopher: In the paper it had 'drugs, guns, cash'. The cash was probably a couple of grand and they might have found a quarter of weed in someone's house. They blew it all out of proportion. I was only there two days – I got [*£10,000*] bail and then [*after seven weeks during which he had to report to a police station in Chelsea twice a day as part of bail*] they dropped the charges against me. They didn't have anything to charge me on. The *Manchester Evening News* had done a massive front-page piece on us getting arrested, but when my charges got dropped I got them to do a retraction, an apology. They put it in [*20 November*] but tiny. [*In the apology, Chris is quoted as saying, 'The police kicked down the door at 6.30 a.m. when I was in bed. They had me handcuffed in the street, face down with a gun at my head. They told my neighbours I was a drug dealer. Now the charges have been dropped I don't suppose they will tell my neighbour that.'*] There was a picture of me with the caption, 'Angry'. So in jail my dad had the picture up and everyone started to call me 'Angry Donnelly'.

I had the business; the shop in London was about to open. It was hard, hard work. The story had made the front cover of the nationals, so any customers, or suppliers of fabric, they didn't want to supply us. I'd ask why. They said, 'Well, you could refuse to pay us and there's nothing we can do – don't take it the wrong way.' The bank shut us down; the police froze all our assets. The Financial Investigation Unit was doing a drug trafficking order against the family. The bank took my house. It was put up as collateral for the company. They took the cars, everything – we lost everything. And we'd borrowed money against the deeds for my dad's scrapyard, £50,000, so we had to try and raise that. I was on a pushbike. I'd gone from a millionaire to riding a bike. We couldn't move because of the police. They were all over us. They'd got what they'd been trying to do for years. They ruined us. The only thing they didn't ruin was our spirits.

But we had to open the shop. We'd spent so much refurbishing it. Anthony was in jail. The only person who came to the launch was my mum. I had to get clothes off different brands; we didn't have enough of our own Gio stock because everyone was shutting doors in my face. I was pulling in favours. I'd buy cheap garments for cash and send them down to London. The lads in the shop didn't know and they'd put it out. It was anything I could get my hands on to feed the shop. We had three staff in the shop and they all went on to be names in fashion: Fraser Moss started YMC with Jimmy Collins. Steve Davies partnered Eddie Prendergast from Duffer and they started the Present shop in Shoreditch. Robert Excell is head of sales for Moschino. I did two T-shirts at that time: 'Don't Believe The Hype' and 'Framed'. I went out and bought Screen Stars T-shirts and sweatshirts and printed on them. I don't know what I was trying to achieve. No one gave a fuck.

Anthony: Chris was sending me pictures of the shop in jail. We'd spent £250,000 refurbishing the shop. Celebrities were coming in there, all the pop stars of the day, but it was not making enough sales. I was sent to Strangeways. I was on induction there for seven days on twenty-three hour a day bang up. On induction they explain the rules and you're evaluated, you find out what you're to be categorised as, what level of threat you are to yourself and to others. I spent a week in there. I was quite happy. My pal John Faulkner was with me. The next thing my door goes and three screws with a dog enter the cell and tell me, 'You're going to a special place.'

At that point I knew I was being labelled the serious person that they thought I was. I could see a book with a red letter 'A' on it. They said, 'Come on, you're going to see your dad in Category A.' I'd gone from smoking pot for a week in a prison cell with Faulkner, laughing like kids about the whole situation, to now I'd got to ride this thing that had just got a whole lot more serious.

My QC told me that I was getting twenty-two years. Ecstasy was poison at that time. Every 10,000 pills equates to a kilo, so if you weigh 32,000 pills which I was charged with conspiracy to import, that's three and half kilos. They were talking about drug smuggling, gunrunning, murder. It said on the top of my paper work: 'Gang-affiliated, means to escape, access to fire arms and aircraft.' To visit me you had to put an application in that took three months to vet. Any visitor's house could be raided at any given time.

They sent me to the G wing – home to the dangerous of the dangerous. I walked into the wing and my dad walked toward me and held his arms out and said, 'Look who's here,' as if it was great to see everybody – all my pals, some armed robbers who used to frequent Parliament were there. It was the last place I wanted to be. Everyone was going to jail for twenty to thirty years. It was a high-risk unit; everyone had their own cell. It was a segregation unit – where there should be 200 men on a wing, we had twenty-five. I got to my cell and two people were sat on my bed waiting for me, people affiliated with my dad, and they told me whatever I needed, whatever I wanted, was available to me – should I need anything to speak to them if my dad was not there. Within forty-eight hours I was having my own way in there. There was nothing I didn't want for. I had booze and sleeping tablets – plus I always had a great supply of weed. I met good people on the Cat A section but at times I just thought, 'This is it, it's over.'

Another pal from Wythenshawe was in with me. He'd been charged with smuggling millions' worth of drugs. I was there when he came back from the Crown Court. The night before court he gave me a spliff and was laughing. When he came back he was almost unrecognisable. He looked dazed. He'd been handed a twenty-five-year sentence.

I made some very good friends on that high-risk section from all parts of the country. People were coming to my cell for a booze-up. My dad had it boxed off. He had the orange juice, Vimto, Pot Noodles, mackerel, Old Holborn, phone cards – he had everything. There was always a queue outside his pad. It was like a corner shop.

Arthur: The screws called my cell the 'Off-licence'. At the time there was a thing in the paper about the 'Golden Polo' mint. So I got a Polo and painted it gold and put it back in the packet. I opened it up in front a screw and he shouted, 'Whoooaaaa . . . The Golden Polo, a million pound!' I said, 'What? What are you talking about?' They took the golden polo and put it under guard in Strangeways and someone fucking nicked it! It was in the papers after that, somebody handed it in and that was when they found out it was a wind up.

Christopher: While Anthony was in Strangeways the thing with the rival gang got put to bed. I was at the meeting before the meeting. It was agreed that they wouldn't interfere with anything we were doing and we wouldn't interfere with anything they were doing and we would all live happily ever after. It was all talked out but it was still messy. Then most of the charges were dropped against Anthony and Faulkner and they were released on bail just in time for Christmas [*23 December 1994*]. We picked Anthony up in a limousine. Someone had given us a limo and I picked up a hearse at the same time. I thought it'd be funny to deliver our clothes in a hearse. It was bit of fun.

Anthony: We still had a good sense of humour when we were going through all this shit, but once those things had been in the newspapers no one in their right mind would work with us. We had all our bank accounts frozen so it cut us off completely.

They took me home to my new flat and then on to my kids, who were playing in the avenue. We pulled up at the house and the kids got in the back of the limousine. I was hiding under a pile of coats. Their dad was back. The next day I landed in the Gio-Goi car park and the business was dire. Even though the fighting was supposedly over, there were still tremors from the gang war. We changed our lifestyle. We weren't going out in town as much.

The documentary programme *Forty Minutes* wanted to make a film on us. There was interest from overseas TV companies, magazines, TV in the UK, but we really didn't have the stomach for it. It was such a bad time, the answer was no to everything. We just wanted peace and quiet.

Christopher: We decided to fold Gio-Goi – that old saying 'Gone fishing.' We kept the name and sank the company. We lost the deposit we put on the new building in Castlefield because we failed to complete on it. People were still coming to the office that we didn't want around us. The staff were a constant worry and needed paying. I didn't need the stress but at this point we still had the shop and the flat in London. We'd not paid the rent on the flat and the landlord was keeping all our gear until we paid him. We got a van, drove to London after all the shops had shut: Anthony, me and a guy called Bobby. We went to the shop first and emptied it – robbed our own shop – then went to our flat in Kensington and took all our stuff out and went back to Manchester – another headache gone.

Anthony: We'd been reduced to nothing. We had no credit facilities. You go to London and there's £1,000 in the till – why wouldn't you take it if you had to feed your family? This is where the disappointment came with us. I reckon we had given away a million pounds' worth of stock and money to friends. We employed all our friends and now we were experiencing all this shit, no one was helping. We were dumped high and dry by everyone. It was just a mess. Our family really suffered and there didn't seem to be any help coming from any of the other quarters, including from our own camp. We had a problem and we were left under no illusion that it was our problem and we had to deal with it.

The stress took its toll on my relationship with Annette. Things hadn't been good at home for some time and she'd asked me to leave before the arrest. I already had my own place in Salford Quays and was seeing a new girlfriend, Rhianwen, who I had met at Parliament.

Christopher: After we closed the business we were concentrating on exposing the informant, Neil Thompson, in the case. The idea was to help my dad. I went to see people all over the country, other people he had set up. That's what we spent our time doing, driving around prisons visiting people. I found out where he lived in Warrington; I followed him to find out his routine. We employed a private investigator. We wanted our dad back home.

Anthony: We wanted to prove Thompson was a registered police informant and he got paid for setting people up. Why is there no mention of Thompson passing my dad the drugs to pass to the police? You have to go out and collect the information. Nobody else had ever put the time and effort into looking at Thompson and he was still walking around acting like he was a bad guy. We went to a jail in Cornwall on a visit and spoke to a pal from Manchester who he had set up in Newquay; we found a kid in a Staffordshire jail from Warrington doing seven years he had set up. We gathered all the information on Thompson. It became a personal crusade to get my dad out of jail and expose Thompson for setting us up – and to destroy him and to warn others against him.

After twelve months of our own investigation we produced 35,000 books and deposited them all over his town, Warrington, in bars, pubs and clubs. We distributed them around Manchester and the north-west and gave them to all the relevant gangs. We put his face on the front cover with his home address. The book included the transcripts and witness statements from other trials he had made.

The books were too much for him. We went on a meeting with him. We went to Warrington and met him in a club car park; again it was arranged that no harm would come to him on this occasion because we wanted him to testify on behalf of our dad. I said to him, 'You set me and my dad up.' He denied it. We wanted my dad out of jail so we wanted him to stand up and tell the truth – that he set us up – he said he would help where he could. After that he just went missing but we had done enough to destroy him at that point anyway, we thought. He ended up in prison. He'd battered someone because, as well as being a grass he was a bully, and he'd been sentenced to three months. He was in a jail in Cumbria. We had him subpoenaed through his jail to Manchester Crown Court. On the morning of my dad being sentenced he wouldn't come upstairs to give evidence for my dad because he said, 'If I come out of my cell I'll get killed.'

Christopher: My dad went guilty [*February 1996*]. They said he was getting fifteen years if he went not guilty and run a trial and he'd get three if he went guilty. He went guilty and he got eight. We got it down to six and half in the Court of Appeal. Next it was Anthony's trial.

Anthony: That's still a long stretch my dad got. We destroyed

Thompson as best we could but he didn't give a fuck, he still carried on setting other people up. What's ironic is that he died of throat cancer – probably through talking too much.

My case and Faulkner's ended up falling apart. We'd sold them legal Ecstasy tablets, legal ones! They had all kinds of charges for everybody leading up to the court case but it all got reduced to nothing in the end. Neil Thompson was an active criminal and the police decided not to use him for that reason. Thompson was a loose cannon and we think while he was undercover investigating us he was doing stuff without the police knowing, stuff they hadn't condoned – being a bit too devious. All they had in the end was I served these pills through a third party and they turned out to be legal highs. I actually got a nine-month sentence. Faulkner got six months after it all panned out, and as we both had already done time on remand, we had months to serve.

Chris was there in court. I burst out laughing in the dock as I got sentenced, for supply of a class C drug, namely diazepam. There was a grain of diazepam in the tablets. The rest was just shit herbal high. I had gone from a big sentence to a shit and a shave.

I served my sentence in Strangeways but this time in the normal part as a Cat C prisoner. As it happened, the other firm we had been fighting with on the outside were in there running the jail. We were supposed to be all good with this other firm, but it was a very volatile situation still. I was pretty concerned that I was on my own in prison. Faulkner went to Risley. I knew they went to the gym every day and so the following morning I put my name down for gym. I met the main man who we had been fighting with over the years and he said, 'What you doing here, Tricky?' I said, 'I'm doing my sentence.' He said, 'Well you better watch you don't get a bar on your head.' I said, 'You better watch you don't get a bar on your head.' With that the ice was broken. I said, 'What about them machines in there, can we get on them and have a private chat?' Next minute, he's on one, I'm on one, and unbelievably having a good laugh about how things had turned out and the shit we had all been through. We shook hands and remained on friendly terms. The war was officially over.

The time spent finishing my sentence was bliss, as much weed as I could smoke and three square meals a day. It sounds daft but that sentence after that meeting was great, but I couldn't wait to hit the streets again. All the trouble was over, it really was over – I thought, 'Let's get back to what we're good at, making money.'

10
GONE FISHING

Anthony: I'd been home for a while and I was trying to get back out there. Finally, we were starting to live again. We were back out there wining and dining people, faking it, making it look like we had a million quid when we had nothing. I got involved with some financial people from overseas and they decided to put a few quid behind Chris and me to get Gio-Goi going again.

Christopher: Anthony came to see me and said he had someone who wanted to invest in the brand. I was very, very reluctant to do it. Anthony had to twist my arm. We set up the business back at our mum and dad's barn. We paid out to have it done up as offices downstairs and we put a showroom upstairs. I then went out and bought a load of second-hand fabric – the alarm bells should have started then, this was the beginning of it. I made about twenty or thirty different shirts and rebranded everything. The Gio-Goi logo was written in a new way. We made all the advertising look good. Anthony went out on the road as a salesman. We had Tracey in the office. We were trying to launch it on a shoestring – which you can't do. Anthony and Tracey would argue and our mum used to have to pull them apart. It was like being back on Benchill Road.

Anthony: The investor put in about £100,000 and we took £400,000 in orders over a very short period of time. We were trying to make a go of it and we picked up some momentum in the press. Then we had problems with the manufacturers who'd already been paid. It all looked rosy on paper but we were pissing in the wind. I even tried to get Alan McGee [*boss of Creation Records*] to back the label. He had signed Oasis and they were smashing it. We'd had money and now it was gone, that was part of our problem.

Alex Ferguson [*legendary and now retired manager of Manchester United*] was wearing Gio-Goi. We always wanted to meet United players to get them to wear Gio. You could always get a ticket or two off Ned, who did United's security, but you could never get to meet the players. We saw [*United player*] Clayton Blackmore in a pub in Altrincham. One of the boys stole his coat. It was rumoured we had stolen it to get his attention. This wasn't true – our pal robbed it and we took it off him because Clayton played for United. His car and house keys were in his coat and on them was a 0845 number to ring if they were lost and found. So we rang the number and said we have got Clayton's coat. We got it back for him. We said, 'We live in Altrincham, he lives in Altrincham. Can you set up a meet?' The next minute the phone rings and it's Clayton. He came to meet us and brought Remy Martin champagne brandy, champagne and tickets for a game to say thanks.

We then overwhelmed him with product. We sent thirteen Gio-Goi beanie hats back to the training ground. That was 1994 and Alex didn't stop wearing one of those hats for the next ten years – at every game. The treble in 1999, that hat was there. I met Alex in a restaurant and thanked him for supporting the brand. I also asked him why the hat had been with him for so long. He said it was his lucky hat and his wife washed it before every game. He said she always put it on the top of his case wherever he went. Every interview he did, every time that hat appeared on the telly I thought if only people knew – including Sir Alex. It still makes me smile.

Christopher: With the investment we made some stock and we had a go. We made about 10,000 pieces – we did some denim stuff and a hooded top with the logo 'University of Life'. I took the range to the Clothes Show Live *[at Birmingham NEC, February 1998]*. But by then the communication was starting to break down with our investor. The label was selling okay but we were having cash flow problems. The kid who we were working with put so much money in and then didn't want to invest any more dough. We were just too long in the tooth for this so we went, 'Right, fuck it.' It was coming up to Christmas and we needed some spending money. We downed tools and moved on. That's the problem with most investors – they want an easy ride. The reason we always seek investments in our projects is firstly we don't like using our own money and we generally think big, so we need someone with pots of money and balls, which, trust me, is like finding a needle in a haystack.

Anthony: He put the money in but he didn't get the return as fast as he wanted. That was the end of that one. I went back to selling tickets. I was living on my luck. I sold sunglasses for the Triads during the solar eclipse in 1999. We were doing clothes in a different way now. Ten thousand T-shirts turned up. I could move them. Every now and again something would come up. We had 20,000 pairs of Armani underpants at one time. We were buying and selling in Europe.

Christopher: Basically, we were back on the streets – doing whatever. Anthony and me were doing the grey market clothes together, that was the main focus – boxer shorts, polo shirts. I was back on the street grafting. Then I borrowed a few quid off Tracey and I bought a house to do up and sell. I was having my first kid. I knew I had to start getting proper work together.

Anthony: For the first time ever, we had time apart – eighteen months. I got my family in order and Chris got his family in order. We didn't see each other. It just became quite apparent that you were better off doing your own thing. He started buying houses, picking up bargains, doing them up and selling them on. He was not scared of getting his hands dirty. I went abroad on a couple of trips, met some people off shore and did a couple of things out of the country. I went to Florence to buy Stone Island gear to sell on the street.

Christopher: Anthony and I weren't speaking. We'd done a few moves together. I was doing some stuff out of Luxembourg – a strange place to be, I know. I can't remember what we fell out about – probably money. Gio had gone as far as I was concerned. I was not interested at all. I was not interested in fashion. I put on my marriage certificate, as my occupation, builder. I didn't want to know anything but going to work and doing up the houses. I was on my own and grafting. I did that for two years.

Then one day I get a phone call from Perry Hughes, an old friend, who was now managing Russell Watson [*the 'People's Tenor' whose debut album* The Voice *was a huge hit in the UK and US*]. Perry rang me from LA. They'd just got the theme for the *Star Trek* film [Star Trek: Enterprise*, 2001 – the song was called 'Where Will My Heart Take Me'*] and they couldn't find a stylist for the video and would I do it. I said no, not interested. But Perry is hard to say no to, very persistent and loveable. So I asked when it was. He said the video shoot was in London in a week's time. I'd never been a stylist but I knew how it worked – you get loads of clothes and take them to the shoot.

Tracey and me went to London. Tracey was ringing Paul Smith the day before the shoot but they wouldn't give us anything. So I ended up with one pair of shoes, black Chelsea boots, a pair of black jeans, one black three-quarter-length Crombie coat and a black V-neck T-shirt – that was it. They were used to seeing sixty or seventy garments on a rail. I took the stuff round to their apartment and I'd had a few bottles of wine. It was the first time I'd met Russell. Perry said no way will he wear that. I said, 'Get out of the way' and shouted Russell in. I said to him, 'There's your outfit for tomorrow, that's it. I don't really care. I'm doing this for Perry and that is the outfit you're wearing tomorrow and if you don't like it it's fucked.' Next day I got up, got to the studio and he was in the gear. He probably wore that outfit for the next six months. I knew it was right.

He was playing Wembley Arena, all over, 15,000-capacity venues. They asked if I'd style the show. I'd get him twelve outfits and do all the quick changes during the show. I did Carnegie Hall, Japan and Los Angeles. I sang as a backing singer at Wembley Arena for a bet. Perry was paying me good money but I was still doing the houses. I'd buy the house and live in it. I had them down to a fine art: twelve weeks from buying to finishing. So one day I'd be in hob nail boots knocking a wall down, the next I'd be on Savile Row picking suits. Photographers would ring me up and ask what the inspiration was for the photo shoot. I'd be covered in shit in the back garden with a tonne of bricks.

I got Russell in some far out gear that he'd never had picked himself, stuff like red satin suits [*worn when singing at the opening of the Commonwealth Games in Manchester in 2002*] and pink shirts. He was a big star. Although Perry was good at managing him and he had talent, no opera singer was wearing what I had him wearing. It was a breath of fresh air in that world.

Anthony: During the time we spent apart, I entered into litigation with Giorgio Armani. He'd brought out some perfume as 'Gio'. I registered our brand as two words, Gio and Goi, for perfume, a Class 3 trademark. I then sent a letter to Giorgio Armani's lawyers with egg and beans all over it. I said, 'Stop trading as Gio, we own the name.' Okay, I wasn't expecting them to stop trading, but I thought they might give us some money to fuck off.

Armani fell into my trap and wrote back. So I started litigation with them. They had scores of lawyers in Milan and Switzerland and I had my mate Dermot, who laid tarmac and could work a computer. I paid him £10 a letter and sent them out from a mailbox in Cheadle. This went on for two years. In the end we agreed to an out of court settlement. I can't speak about it because I signed a confidentiality agreement. It all got pretty tricky. They were doing a billion dollars a year with the name Gio. I had Gio-Goi registered as two separate words and if you put Gio-Goi on a rounded bottle it would look like Gio anyway. The documentation would be a great plus for Gio-Goi to use for any future sale. My plan had worked.

I was also keeping the registrations alive for the business, doing the dot coms. I updated all the intellectual property. We'd been let down so badly with the last episode, when the investor pulled out, but it was as a consequence of that deal that I did all this. I did what I felt was necessary.

I drove to Chris's house. He was building a lovely palatial house in Bramhall. Chris was bricklaying the wall. I said, 'It's taken me two years but I've beaten Armani's lawyers and I have all the trademarks.' He said, 'All right, but I've got to go to the builders' yard.'

Christopher: Anthony did a good job. I didn't give a fuck. It could have gone up in smoke for all I cared. I just didn't care. He did a fantastic job.

It was actually our mum who made us friends again. I was getting married and my mum said you have to invite your brother. My mum made me ring him and we became friends again. The Armani thing was done and dusted, we had a certificate – now what are we going to do? We'd been missing now for years. In that time nobody picked the phone up and offered help. Not one person. It was a lonely period.

Anthony: We were getting back on our feet, reintroducing ourselves. We made a book, a company portfolio, and I said to Chris, 'Right, we're going to sell the brand.' I said we should do it again but do it properly. Instead of trying to find a manufacturer and to sell it into stores, we did the book to showcase the brand to potential investors. We printed 200 and targeted *Drapers* [*leading fashion business magazine*] and various interested parties. The book was silver, large format, had a brief biography, a 'giography' I called it, and in it we spelled out what trademarks we owned. I'd done all the work on it. It was a detailed document of what Gio-Goi was and it explained that we were coming back, we were seeking investment, how we'd beat Armani, how we'd separated the name, details of all the dot coms . . . it worked. We were getting meetings and talking to magazines about what our intentions were. It was all about strategy. We were planning our re-entry into the fashion world. For me it had always been on the back burner – Gio-Goi had never gone away.

I was actually living in Spain on and off. My cousins had opened a sports bar in Fuengirola and I had a lot of friends on the Costa del Sol. I'd done a few bits of work and now I had brand new clothes and a brand new Mercedes convertible – and £5,000 spare cash to produce the Gio book. I was still doing tickets. I made some money at the European Championships selling tickets in 2004 in Portugal. I was back on the festival circuit, mixing, networking – gaining strength. It was about getting back out in the clubs, having holidays blowing money in Mexico and Cuba with my girl Rhianwen and learning to live again. Chris had some good luck with his houses. It was a slow climb, the coming together of Chris and me, and the closing of that dark period.

Christopher: I'd been out in America working for Universal Records with Russell and Perry and a few other artists. Russell was in New York having dinner with the Police Commissioner from LA. He was a big opera fan and he told me how his new boat was moored next to Armani's, George as he called him. George was having his boat repainted by Mercedes, in Mercedes black. I was thinking of Anthony in the Cheadle post office sending letters to Armani's solicitors. This police guy owned about ten shopping malls as well. We also went to John Gotti's restaurant on a regular basis while we were in New York with a couple of the cast from *Goodfellas*.

Anthony: Our friend was going out with Davinia Murphy and she'd had her car robbed I think. Our pal called us for help and we made some calls. We were instrumental in her problem getting solved and she got her car back. I was trying to sell the brand, so I decided Davinia's family owed me a favour. We were looking for a serious level of investment and her dad [*Alan Murphy, the Toilet Roll King, who made multi-millions manufacturing toilet roll*] was a big hitter based in the South of France. I flew over to Nice and was taken to Antibes, to his £20 million yacht. Alan Murphy drove from Monaco in his DB9.

I had a burning ambition to re-launch Gio-Goi. Everybody thought we were fucked. Gone. Nobody could believe we were back again. But we understood you couldn't launch it without a certain level of finance. We wanted to raise our game. We needed a certain type of investor, not someone who could pretend at it and put £100,000 in just because they wanted to be associated with something that was considered cool. We needed real investment. Alan was piped aboard for tea about eight o'clock and they put this meal out, all very flash. I showed him the book and explained what had gone on with Armani. He knew about the favour, that I was asking on behalf of what I'd done. I ate my tea and then Alan left me with the boat and staff because my flight was the following day. We agreed I could have the boat for three days any time. He was charging £15,000 a day, so I'd achieved a £45,000 free stay on the boat – which to this day I've never accepted. I wanted him to invest in the brand. I failed to get my investment from him.

Before he left I asked him to change some money. He gave me forty quid and told me to have a nice time on the boat, enjoy your stay, please don't drink beer on the deck and don't smoke. I got off the boat, got legless. Then I got talking to some people who were taking my picture because they thought I owned the boat. I got off in the morning and flew to Majorca to meet Rhianwen for a week and rethink my next move.

Basically we were back hunting. We were doing little flash collections, 100 shirts here, 200 there, pumping it up. There were other investment people looking at us. We were back in touch with Cream. Our story was getting better with age. There were more good things happening than bad things.

Christopher: I was in Hale village with Natalie and I bumped into a friend called Ash Taylor, who worked at French Connection. I asked if he had half an hour to chat about Gio-Goi. We agreed to meet in a café in Hale. He turned up with his friend Steve Black. We sat there and I said, 'Look, we want to sell the brand.' Steve loved the book that Anthony and me had produced and said he would try and help out.

I had the idea that if we had some Gio-Goi clothes on the shelves in the stores it'd be a lot more attractive to a potential buyer and we'd get more money for it. Steve liked the idea and he introduced me to his mate, Juls Dawson, to get that rolling. Juls was working out of Altrincham and a massive fan of Gio-Goi. When I met him I was looking at him for help, as we had been out of the game for so long. I spent a year working on Gio-Goi with Juls before Anthony really got involved. We set up an office in Altrincham and took some staff on – two girls, Caroline and Zoe – and Juls was going round the country making samples. I thought this kid knew everything about the business, but I was wrong. He knew how to sell gear, he was a fantastic salesman, but he didn't know about branded business or production. I was looking at him for the answers but straight away I was having these doubts. The samples he made were not the best. We could work on that.

Anthony: Chris had found someone to work with, so I didn't interfere. But I'd given Chris the ammunition to do his deal, the maintaining of the trademarks. It started with him making some clothes to assist the book. I was waiting for Chris to come up with the collection and then I'd be able to go back out and say, 'Here it is' and look for further investment. You can't launch a label unless you are properly financed. They say to launch a brand properly it costs three to five million pounds. We didn't have that in our back pocket.

Christopher: The next thing, Bread & Butter is on in Berlin, the big fashion trade fair [*2004*]. One thing we know how to do is put a wicked party on. So rather than go to the show with a load of clothes, I decided we'd do a party and that was how we'd re-launch Gio-Goi. I flew to Berlin and found a venue with Simon Farrell and paid for it. I built a catwalk back at the farm in Stockport and I got a load of plain garments out of my wardrobe. I had four of five T-shirts printed with Gio-Goi on. We invited 1,000 people and the venue fitted 250. We had a list of ten people who must get in, ten of the key people in the industry regarding investment.

On the night, at first the venue was completely empty and I was having palpitations thinking no one would come. The next thing it's rammed, banging. Three, two, one, the music comes on and all these male German and American models I'd auditioned in the day come down the catwalk in my clothes from my wardrobe and a printed T-shirt. Then the girls come out and they were in knickers and bra. I'd bought the knickers from Top Shop and printed Gio-Goi on the arse.

Anthony: We had no collection. Chris used all the gear out of his wardrobe. We turned the lights down, put a strobe light on and a smoke machine. They couldn't see the clothes properly but were all applauding. All the fashion industry turned up to see Gio-Goi. They had no idea what had happened to us. We'd disappeared off the face of the planet but you can only imagine the rumours about us. Lots of people came to look. G-Star left their own party to come to ours. Everyone in the industry rolled up and wanted to be seen at our party. They all got fucked up and we had a great night. We were on the front page of the Berlin newspaper the following day, photos of the girls walking round in Gio-Goi knickers. Bang. We were back.

Christopher: At the party my mate Danny Griffiths introduced me to this Scottish geezer David Douglas. He was frothing at the mouth. He said to me, 'Do you want to make some real money?' I was like, 'Yeah.' We'd put our fishing rods out and we'd got a bite.

Anthony: David Douglas had just sold his business for tens of millions. He was mithering us all night for things. He found what he was looking for at our party. There is always something for everyone at a fashion event. The next day I was on my way to the airport and he phoned me to say what a fantastic night he'd had. He said, 'If a bomb had dropped on your party there'd be nobody left in the fashion business.' He offered us £3 million there and then.

We went up to Scotland for a meeting where we agreed, in principle, to sell a percentage of the business for a price. For the record we would have accepted literally nothing. He actually offered us two million pound in cash there and then for the label and an earn-out of another million, I think. He'd sold a chain of major high street fashion stores and was now operating as Melville Capital. We refused, as we wanted to stay in the business. We had a point to prove out there in the fashion world and on the street. Melville were eager to get started now. We got a building round the corner from where we had started originally, a two up/two down with a nice dry cellar, on Oxford Road in Altrincham. It had once been a funeral parlour and the basement had been where they did the embalming. That's where we were. We put phone lines in, carpeted it and we opened for business.

We were fully funded, had a new office, the two girls were brilliant, Caroline and Zoe, and we had Juls and Simon. Melville brought a fella up from London, his MD – Mark Kilbourn, and put him in a flat round the corner. Melville knew about our reputation. When they came to Manchester, these people were away from their wives and girlfriends, so they'd be running around town. People were ringing me up: 'Who are these fucking idiots off their heads, all throwing your name about?' It wasn't exactly what I'd envisaged when I got into bed with a corporate investment company. I thought people with straight money had a bit more integrity.

Still, look on the bright side. We've come into a considerable amount of money. I've upgraded my car from a convertible to a

Range Rover Sports. We had a large percentage of the company still and we were on handsome salaries. We felt we could now take Gio-Goi places we couldn't before. We were away.

Christopher: I went to Hong Kong with a new designer and Douglas and Kilbourn to design a range. Almost immediately we sacked the designer and sent him home. He'd blagged it. We'd be in factories asking him to do stuff and he couldn't. So I ended up sitting and designing a full range. It was not a good situation. I rang Anthony and said, 'These fuckers don't have a clue.' That was day one but we were in and we had a deal. So finally, after about five weeks in Hong Kong, we came up with a range. It was polo shirts, T-shirts with graphics, jackets, and knitwear. We flew from Hong Kong to Turkey and did a load of shirts there. Melville knew a lot of factories and could pull favours in. We were only doing small numbers at this stage, but Melville were promising the factories the earth, saying they were going to do 10,000 units of this and that. When we went out with the range back in the UK and tried to sell it, only parts of the range worked. The shirts never got a reaction. When you're starting off, same for any brand, people don't want to be spending big money. All they want is some T-shirts to see how it goes. We'd done everything, including denim. There was nothing that stood out in that first collection because we were trying to find our feet, find our direction. At least we had finance.

We went back to Hong Kong and Turkey to do another range. I hired a new designer called Glen [*Dickinson*] and together we designed and made a load of hooded tracksuit tops with stripes across the chest. They were made out of tricot, a silky material. The style name was Penang. I also made some white jackets and cardigans. Douglas said, 'Cardigans? Who's going to wear cardigans? My granddad?' They also said the tracksuit tops would never sell but they were what really launched the brand again.

We ran them for two or three years, just changing the colours; we couldn't make enough of them. We sold hundreds of thousands of those tracksuit tops.

The designer Glen had his own company and we were paying him a retainer. Then we decided it was costing too much and we needed an in-house designer. He closed his company and came as an employee, working closely with me on the graphics. Simon Farrell was great at doing the sales. Juls was removed from doing production and now doing the sales.

The first order we got was for £34,000 off Republic [*high street retail chain*], who had about a hundred stores. The stuff was a week late and they wanted discount. I said I'd rather keep the stock than give them a discount. They told me to go away and build the brand. So now I had £34,000 of stock up my arse. It was a blessing in disguise, because we wanted to pitch the brand a lot higher than where Republic were. But we didn't know what we were doing at the beginning, so we'd try anything. From that moment, we did exactly what we did first time round – we started with the independent shops and the gear started flying. We were in some of the best shops in the country; people would go in a store and buy a Stone Island coat, a pair of Evisu jeans and Gio-Goi T-shirt. We couldn't stay in the basement office anymore because we were growing pretty quickly, so we moved back into town [*Manchester city centre*], into Fourways House [*in the Northern Quarter*].

Anthony: The investors at Melville were riding the crest of a wave, having just sold their business. They were out buying Ferraris and partying heavily, throwing money about. To be honest, it seemed to be a pet project for them. All we discovered about the investors was that they were becoming a headache. They weren't what they appeared on the surface. We were getting to know them more and finding out a lot of other things about them that wasn't all good.

Christopher: We were doing a lot of stuff to promote Gio. The first thing was we got the [*Gio-Goi-branded*] double-decker bus, painted it, had it done up like a club inside and took it to Glastonbury. We were doing stuff that other labels didn't really do. People would come up and say, 'What's the bus about? What does that mean on the side, Gio-Goi?' There'd be loads of people out of their brains partying on the bus. On the roof we painted, 'It's A Crime Not To Be Organised'. We knew the police would be able to see it in a helicopter as we parked it in our scrap metal yard next to the police heliport flight path. We were working with Mojofuel [*Manchester digital creative agency*] making little films for the Gio website. Amongst other things, we did one of kids in balaclavas and the gear peddling bikes around the streets at midnight. All menacing but cool.

Anthony: The double-decker bus was appearing all over the country at festivals and gigs. We needed comfort when we were travelling and there were plenty of stash holes. It was like a new War Wagon but with the brand on the side. It was a great form of advertising. It was the best club in Britain on wheels. People would use it to do private after-show parties.

Christopher: Damon [*Albarn*] out of Blur and Gorillaz was wearing the label. Footballers wore it and so did Mani, who was then in Primal Scream; all our old pals had it on. We were actively looking for music people to wear the brand. I heard this record on an evening radio show called *I Bet You Look Good on the Dance Floor*. I rang Anthony and said, 'Get in touch with these kids; they're going to be big.' He said, 'I've never heard of them'. I said, 'You've never heard of nobody.' Anyway, I left it and he never got in touch with them. Then three weeks later they were on their way to number one and Anthony is like, 'Oh yeah, we need to get in touch with these kids.' But at that point everybody wanted to get in touch with them. We were a couple of weeks late.

A similar thing happened to us with Coldplay. We were supposed to meet Coldplay at Glastonbury about doing their merchandise. I had meeting set up for three o'clock but I got absolutely out of my brain and never went. That's the problem with our industry: far too much rock 'n' roll.

Anthony: The whole world had converged on the Arctic Monkeys. Our friends were doing the security for them but they wouldn't compromise their business for us. We decided not to go to the Arctic Monkeys circus in London and we sent one of our boys, John Faulkner, my old pal and co-accused in Operation Bluebell, to follow the Arctic Monkeys on tour in France. They were playing Lyon. John got in the car and drove over there. We hadn't looked where Lyon was on the map – turned out to be a bit of a drive. The *NME* couldn't get backstage but John got backstage. He took pictures of all the band wearing the clobber. John had been hanging about with Babyshambles and he called us and said it wasn't very rock 'n' roll backstage at the Arctic Monkeys. They had Lucozade, Midget Gems, organic drinks and baby wipes, as opposed to syringes and tin foil and Rizla with Babyshambles, but getting a picture of them wearing the brand was a significant step for us.

The [*Bafta-winning*] TV show *Shameless* also started using our gear. [*Wythenshawe was used as a filming location for the Ch4 show. In 2000 Benchill had been named as the most deprived ward in England.* Shameless *continued to use the Donnellys' labels: Gio and Your Own [YO] until the series ended in 2013.*] Our story, and I hate to say it, is *Shameless*. There were lots of *Shameless* moments for us growing up. One time my mate walked in a pub with his pitbull and the dog was going mental. My other mate asked, 'Has it had a fuck recently?' No. 'Well, its balls are full. Give it here.' My mate then gave it a wank. The dog came and it hit a bloke's pint pot. Then a voice in the background says, 'Give it a cig.' I'm not proud of that but that was the sort of funny shit happening on our estate back then and no one cared and still don't, by all accounts.

Some of our mates wrote for *Shameless* too. When it first started, and it was fresh and different, we gave them a full wardrobe. For two seasons it just looked like the Gio-Goi show. You started seeing Gio everywhere. Not only did we get the money from selling the shares in the business to Melville but also we were overseeing the company marketing department.

11
TOO MUCH ROCK 'N' ROLL

Christopher: I drove up to meet our pal Max Beesley who was in Watford doing [*hit BBC1 drama*] *Hotel Babylon*. I took two big bags of clothes, one for him and one for his friend Robbie Williams. I'd had a chat with Max and he'd told me a story of how he'd been to Robbie's house and there was loads of Gio-Goi in his wardrobe. I said, 'We'll get him to wear it then.' Then we were doing an interview for *The Sun* and Anthony mentioned it, how Robbie had all the clobber. The interview was to accompany a photo shoot with Max in Gio-Goi but basically they bypassed everything and put the headline: 'Robbie's a Goi Boy' [*31 October 2005*]. I was up early to get the paper and when I saw it I was shocked. I thought Max was going to go mental. It went all over the world: 'Robbie signs fashion deal'. [*Max was quoted in* The Sun *as saying, 'I love the clothes and so does Robbie.'*]

Anthony: Robbie had supported us back in the day with Take That. The article appeared two days before his *Intensive Care* album came out, so there were cameras pointing at him from all around the world – he had a global audience and an eighty million quid record deal. I'd been thinking if we could get our brand on him for nothing, surely it would be of great benefit to us. Max was close to Robbie and he was a long-standing friend of ours. Max knows us better than most. He knows how cheeky we are.

We didn't announce that Robbie was the face of the brand. We said, 'We're back and this week we're doing something with Robbie' and they misinterpreted it. We ended up with newspapers all around the world saying, 'Robbie's a Goi Boy', explaining how he'd done a clothing deal to coincide with his album launch! EMI had a £20 million budget I believe to market the album but it almost became secondary to the clothing deal. Wherever Robbie went around the world, we went. I knew we were in trouble when I got a call from Australia asking if I wanted to do a licensing deal for Gio and they would buy me a Rolls-Royce immediately as a drink. A message got back to us that Robbie's people were totally unhappy. We were in the shit. If somebody had wanted to sue us they could have collapsed us. I sent a letter apologising. One half of me was scared but the other half was jumping with joy. We touched the world with that one. It had a magical impact. Robbie was cool and forgave us.

In the 'Robbie's a Gio Boy' Sun *article, Gio-Goi was described as 'one of coolest clothes labels in the country' and other bands wearing the label were listed as The Rolling Stones, Happy Mondays, Oasis, New Order and Primal Scream. It was also stated that Gio-Goi had provided last week's chart toppers Artic Monkeys with their outfit for their* Top of the Pops *debut. The article also featured the first picture of former Libertines star Pete Doherty, now with Babyshambles, wearing Gio-Goi. Since the start of 2005, after meeting at her thirty-first birthday party, Doherty was in a highly publicised on/off relationship with supermodel Kate Moss. In September 2005, the* Daily Mirror *ran photos of Moss snorting cocaine at a Babyshambles recording session.*

Christopher: We met Peter through our pal Brezzie when he was in Manchester with Babyshambles on tour. We organised an after-show party for them on our Gio-Goi double-decker because no one would give them a venue to party in. I gave him a Rudolf Dassler jacket, which was a collector's piece worth £1,000. We put Gio-Goi on it and took pictures. Those were the ones that appeared in *The Sun*. There was a big indie explosion going on. It was all indie. Everything was about Camden. Peter was all over the press. It was all about him and Kate. But because he was always in and out of court on a variety of drug charges no one would touch him with a bargepole. He was a perfect fit of us.

Anthony: We lapped it up. Guess what? If it's good enough for *GQ* it's good enough for us. Peter came to stay with me right after the Kate thing. He was at my house for three days hiding from the press. When he first got here he was with a journalist but Pete didn't know he was talking to a journalist. They rang me at five in the morning. I was still up. When they got to my house I said to the journalist, 'Who the fuck are you?' He was driving Pete's Jag. Pete said, 'Oh, he's helping me because I'm on the run from the press.' I said, 'He is the fucking press.' I then became part of the story. The guy said I kicked him up the arse and put him on the next train back to London. [*27 March 2006,* Evening Standard. *A two-page feature focused on the journalist's all-night drive to Manchester with Doherty. When they arrived at Anthony's home the journalist wrote: 'He takes one look at Pete's filthy hands, throws him in the bath, and pours us both a gin and tonic. "I've booked you a hotel room next to Mike Tyson, as much cocaine as you like, and a woman, yeah, and tonight you'll meet the Manchester massive." Then he gets on the phone to his sister and asks Pete to play something for her, while he dances clutching his groin around the living room. But Anthony's mood changes when I tell him I'm a writer. "No offence, son, but I'm a premier league cunt into stuff you don't want to know about. I don't like writers and I'd prefer it if you'd just fuck off." Fair enough, I say, but you could ask me nicely. Pete, looking slightly shame-faced, says, "That's Anthony asking nicely. Do you mind? We had a good run."'*]

I put Peter in the Great John Street Hotel where Mike Tyson was staying. That's when the press put we were singing in the bar – me, Tyson and Doherty. They said we were all together but Pete didn't come out of his room very much and did not even meet Tyson. When I came to pay him out of his room, I had to pay an extra cleaning charge of £120 because there was blood up the walls and everywhere because of what he was doing in that room. I put him in a Gio-Goi T-shirt and when we walked out the door, the press was there and he was papped getting in the car. We went back to my house and I hid him again. But the press started getting really hot. Everyone was looking for him and he was in my house off his barnet. I was in the middle of this big intense press hysteria – there were journalists banging on my mum's door. I told him to go back and square things off in London. He drove back, stopped at a service station and picked up a paper, one of the tabloids. In it there was a big feature a double page on me and Chris, with the headline: 'Keks, Drugs and Rock N Roll'. In it, it said we made Shaun Ryder and Pete Doherty look like naughty schoolboys. Peter was ultra-impressed and from then on we were thick as thieves. He wanted me to be his manager. I loved him and wanted to but he was absolutely crackers so I said no. But we now became part of the story.

Christopher: Peter was around all the time. He'd come up and stay. He was all over the papers with Kate. Then he'd be at the Admiral pub on Sunday afternoon in Ancoats playing his guitar to ten old blokes all sat having a pint of bitter. He was papped wearing a Gio T-shirt with the slogan 'It Is What It Is'. That was one of mine. I was doing the slogans and graphics. I did an interview and they asked me what happened to Gio-Goi first time around and I said, 'Too much rock 'n' roll, that's what killed it, too much rock 'n' roll and not concentrating on the business.' So we put out a 'Too Much Rock & Roll' T-shirt and it ended up selling shitloads, tens and tens of thousands. Another T-shirt said 'Those Without Vision Shall Perish'. I used the thing from Stuffed Olives, 'Once is all you need but it's seldom enough.' I also used 'Drug Free' again and that sold tens and tens of thousands. I would come up with the slogans and then sit with Glen and we'd do the graphics together.

In the early days we rarely saw Melville Capital. I think they were a bit embarrassed about their lack of knowledge in the branded market. We did a show in Berlin and even though they were in Berlin they never even came to the stand. But once it started firing, once it started making money, once the profile went through the roof, then they wanted to be involved, puffing their chests out, saying it was all about them. They brought a designer in called Steve Atkinson, who was quite well known for doing denim. Steve had worked at Firetrap so he'd worked in a very corporate environment and was used to critical paths and all that – 'this has to be done by this time, this has to be done by that time,' whereas we just didn't give a fuck, 'you got it when you got it' kind of attitude.

It seemed to us that Melville was trying to change the company and make it into this corporate thing. They started coming to Manchester more often. Steve went off and built this whole range and when it came in, it was not what Gio was about at that time. It was little button-down shirts, real skinny jeans, skinny black leather jackets, cool stuff but not what we were selling. It was a bit before its time. It was indie. The logo was of two guitars laid across one another in the shape of a cross. I knew it wasn't going to work. It was too much of a big step, too far forward from where the brand was at the time. So Douglas came to me and asked me to put a range together. Glen and me put a range together in a few days. We did basic stuff and that was what sold – graphic T-shirts, casual fits – not too high fashion. I called it White Label.

Anthony: I went to meet Pete in Bath with Brezzie. Pete was doing some recording. I said, 'We need to wind this up a bit more.' I said, 'Let's do a clothing range together.' Kate had just announced she was doing a range for Top Shop in a [*reported*] £3 million deal. It was the same principle as Robbie. There's a big campaign around Kate so why not do a clothing deal with Peter – he's the controversial one of the two. Reuters wrote that it was one of the cleverest marketing campaigns ever. Nothing could have prepared me for what was about to happen.

So we were in a pub in Bath discussing him doing a clothing range and he kept walking away and doing drugs in the corner of the room. He knows I don't like heroin. I kept telling him off: 'I don't mind you smoking crack or weed or drinking, but not heroin.' He keeps getting up and down, smoking crack. I got pissed and I must have blacked out.

In the morning when I got up he was still at it, doing the same, and that's when we actually nailed the deal. I went down with a typed piece of paper, a contract saying I would sign him from 2006 to 2009 and he would market Gio-Goi exclusively. I said, 'We'll do the clothes and we'll just put your name in the back of the neck, you don't do fuck all; we'll just say you designed it.' He is very scatty and unreliable, as well as being a beautiful and loveable person. He just quite calmly said, 'Yeah, no problem. Do what you want.' That's when I asked him, 'If you drop dead, now or later, and I'm with you and you're not wearing the brand, would you mind if I took your shirt off and put a Gio-Goi garment on?' And he said, 'Yeah, absolutely' and he gifted me his favourite set of rosary beads and posed in a 'Drug Free' T-shirt for a photograph.

I left with the contract, the photo and the agreement that I could photograph him dead should some Kurt Cobain incident happen or some sort of overdose. He was one of the most famous people in the world at that time. We had the crown jewels. He was controversial. Every day something was happening with him. Paul McCartney had a private meeting with him for two hours. Harrods were sending helicopters to pick him up and take him to parties. It was bizarre.

Dominique Vidalon and Reuters got in touch and I accidentally told them Peter had signed to do a clothing deal. They released it on the wire and it went crazy. I could not open my front door. It was like a scene from *Notting Hill*. The cat was out of the bag: the junkie, Moss's boyfriend, was doing his own clothing collection. The story went round the world. They said we must be insane dealing with him, but it just elevated the company globally and opened doors all over the world. Every time Kate did something, Pete was there, or vice versa, and between the two of them it was the biggest story in the world.

I picked him up one morning from Kate's house in St John's Wood. Pete came to the door; he had two hats on and a bottle of wine in his hand. He'd been up all night and everyone else was asleep. He asked me to drop him off at rehab. He was an outpatient. I had to fight the paparazzi and we got chased through London.

Christopher: We had piles and piles of samples of this indie stuff Steve had designed for Gio-Goi, so you know what? It's perfect for Peter, that's what he wears. So basically we blagged it. We said Peter and me had designed a range of clothes – it was a complete fabrication. We then announced we were doing a gig in Selfridges to launch the Doherty range. I went on tour with Babyshambles for a week filming to make a video and it was rock 'n' roll of the highest order, as rock 'n' roll as rock 'n' roll gets. I saw Peter as a tortured poet and he liked things we did, like 'Dodgin' the Rain 'n' Bullets'. He said we were modern-day poets, which we thought was great praise from an amazing songwriter and poet himself.

The Doherty/Gio-Goi collaboration was to be exclusively available from Selfridges in London from 7 December 2006 for thirty days and would be released to selected stores thereafter. To launch the range Babyshambles would play a gig on the seventh-floor car park of Selfridges on Oxford Street in London. The Monday before the launch, Doherty was fined £770 for possession of heroin, crack cocaine and cannabis in his latest court appearance. A question was put to Selfridges: Why was a respectable department store using a junkie with a tendency to get into fights to advertise their wares? 'He is the face of a brand we have in store,' said a spokesman. 'So it's not a direct association with Selfridges, it's a collaboration between him and the label.'

Christopher: So we managed to blag our way into this situation where we're doing a gig in Selfridges car park on Oxford Street with a load of samples that we couldn't sell. We drove from Bristol with Babyshambles the night before. There was a load of people at the Sanderson Hotel waiting for us. I was wasted because I'd just done a week on the road with them. I said to Anthony, 'All you have to do is make sure Peter doesn't disappear tonight.' I get up in the morning, phone goes, it's Anthony – Pete's disappeared. He had sneaked off in the night to a crack den. Anthony had followed him but Pete didn't want to leave the crack house and they had a bust-up.

Anthony: My bar bill at the Sanderson was £15,000. Dealers were following trolleys full of booze to my room. We were supposed to be doing that launch in-store at Selfridges. We should have done a private gig and taken money on the door. They didn't want us in the store because of the reputation of Babyshambles. Peter was ill; he was an addict not a criminal.

I went to meet the head of security and saw the guest list – MTV, BBC, Bryan Adams, the Sex Pistols, Kate Moss, and Alannah

Weston who owns Selfridges and Primark. There was an interest in the brand but there was more of an interest in Peter.

It was like Madchester all over again – here we are again with another load of drug-crazed lunatics. The security said to me, 'We can't risk a family coming in for a shopping experience and seeing him off his head in the middle of the store.' They wanted it but in the end they decided to do it in the car park. They get the publicity but they don't get the shit that comes with it.

Christopher: We're doing the gig at 2 p.m. and there was 500 people waiting from the press and there was no Peter. He was at least one hour and a half late. I was going ballistic. It was a disaster; people were saying they were leaving. Then Peter turns up. He said he'd been lost in the stationery department. He's a charming geezer, so you kind of think, 'Okay.' And then the bailiffs jumped out from nowhere and cornered him. They wouldn't let him go onstage because he had an outstanding fine. We have to pay the bailiffs a grand in cash. He then did three tracks which were electrifying – he'd not been to bed for two days. That was it – the launch of the range. We got what we wanted out of it. It was all over the world's press.

24 December 2006, The Sunday Times Style *magazine ran a large and prestigious feature on the Selfridges event and Doherty's relationship with Gio-Goi under the headline: 'Who's Keeping Pete Sweet?' The blurb read: 'Making Pete Doherty the front man for your menswear brand seems like asking for trouble. But if anyone can tame the wayward rocker it's the label's hard-nosed Mancunian owners.' The article described how Anthony had chased down Doherty the night before the Selfridges gig in a Jamaican shebeen and threatened him with a pool cue. Asked what made his relationship with the Donnellys work, Pete said, 'Ah, it's love. Love and intimidation, like all the best relationships.'*

The article also mentioned Doherty being interviewed by the CID over the death of Mark Blanco, a struggling actor, who fell to his death from the balcony of a London block of flats where Doherty was partying in December 2006. Doherty also said, 'Gio-Goi are on the fashionista manor. They've tumbled their gain. I love the clothes.'

Anthony: We were doing the photo shoot for the *Sunday Times* piece in Manchester and we were driving up the road and Peter was saying how uncomfortable he was. He was sat in the back seat. He lifted his shirt up and there was a bag coming out of his stomach. I said, 'What the fuck is going on? What's that? Oh my God, he is leaking.' He was saying it'll be all right. I said, 'Are you mad?' and I rang the hospital on my private health care plan. I told them I had a very famous person who needed attention but we needed to come in the back door. I told them it was Robbie Williams. I said it was an emergency. We walked in and they were shocked at who it was. They took him into a room. My phone went and it was Kate, 'What the hell is going on?'

I went into the room. It was an operating theatre – that surprised me. Pete was conscious with three people operating on him. He was looking at me and I said, 'It's Kate.' I passed him the phone on the operating table . . . it was surreal.

I paid the bill, £720. On it, it said, 'Pete Doherty, removal of alien implants' [*Naltrexone implants used to block the effects of heroin*]. I then took him to the studio where he did the photo shoot for the *Times Style* magazine like nothing had happened.

I've never met a more resilient human being, bordering on madness. He played football, he danced and he went on stage to do a gig at the Academy that night and announced to the crowd I had removed his implants.

Weeks passed and then he rang me from a gig and said, 'Come meet the missus in Brixton Academy.' The game was still on with the press – are they an item or not? He picked me up from the VIP area and took me backstage to meet Kate. Pete asked, 'Do you have some money for me?' I said, 'Yes, of course.' I went and got Rhianwen – the money was in her handbag – from the VIP area and went backstage. She and Kate got on well and as Rhianwen went to pass Pete the money, Kate took it instead.

Obviously, Pete would spunk it on drugs – he was deranged. I'd never seen anything like it. You felt like you were with Jimi Hendrix. This kid had a Ready Brek glow; people just wanted to be near him. I loved him and he loved me. People were always kissing his arse and with me it wasn't like that. Kate was a pleasure – really nice person. We got on.

Then there was a lull and I didn't see him for while. But I saw some pictures of him in a bar in Ireland with Kate and Shane MacGowan. I rang my pals in Dublin and asked them to go and find him and to tell him I wanted to meet him. I had to remind him we had a clothing range to publicise. My pals in Dublin went to where he was and put me on the phone to him. 'Peter, we need to do the photos for the collection, the gear's ready.'

Christopher: We ended up making up some of the range that Steve [*Atkinson*] had made to sell through Selfridges. Steve then became the head designer at Gio-Goi and I took a step back. Steve knew the value of what we did but he could play that corporate game as well. He was in the middle. Steve was in Manchester for a little while and when Gio-Goi opened an office in London he went there. Glen was down there before anybody, but inside the business it was getting very corporate. People started to get upset with me just turning up and taking Glen out. I got asked very politely could I not keep taking him out because he had a job to do. I would go down there weekly, so I rented a house in Camden. It was party central, nicknamed the 'Gio Mansion' – a £3 million pad on Camden Mews. Radiohead lived opposite. Pete was always popping in and out. It was like a railway station, people always coming and going.

Anthony: I was drinking with Pete's manager and he said, 'Look, we're doing this *Vogue* photo shoot for Dior [*Dior Homme by French fashion designer Hedi Slimane*] with Shane MacGowan's wife [*author/ journalist Victoria Mary Clarke*], Carine Roitfeld from *Vogue* and [*photographer*] Mario Testino.' He asked me would I like to get involved. I said, 'It's not a case of would I like to be involved. I've got the contract, he's signed exclusively to Gio, so he can't do this Dior shoot, but I am prepared to share the shoot with them because of course I would like to be on the cover of *Vogue*.'

That was it. They flew in with loads of jewellery and Dior's firm were just looking at us like, 'Oh my fucking God. What's happening here?' Mario Testino completely got us and was trying all our gear on, saying how wonderful it was. He loved us. All of a sudden the Dior was binned and it was all about Gio. It was a very drug-fuelled time. I was not in a good place mentally.

Christopher: Testino was one of the world's most famous photographers. I knew we couldn't take our normal jeans and T-shirts so I went digging through all the boxes of samples we had to find something which actually suited the photo shoot. I had some self-doubt sitting in the car on the way and Anthony was going, 'I've done my bit. It's over to you.'

It was all that lovey-dovey-kiss-everybody vibe. At first I was thinking, 'Is our product going to be right?' But as soon as I saw the Dior product, I thought, 'We are home and free here,' the blag was already done and dusted. We walked in and they had this long table that had all posh food on it. Anthony said, 'Fuck me, is this a wedding?'

They asked, 'What are you putting Peter in?' and the easiest answer to that was, 'Peter will wear whatever he's comfortable in

– we know all the stuff is right, that's what we're about.' We didn't know any of that stuff but that's what I said. 'Everything here is right.' And a lot of the shots that Testino actually used were all Gio-Goi product. We hijacked the whole thing. I filmed it all.

Doherty appeared on the cover of Vogue *in Gio-Goi in March 2007. He continued to lurch from scandal to scandal, often in Gio-Goi, but still seemed eminently blessed. In April it was announced Moss had become his fiancée. It was short-lived and by July the pair had broken up.*

Anthony: When they said they were getting married, we were making his suit. It was the saddest thing for me watching Peter self-destruct with Kate on his arm. We went to Glastonbury with them in 2007 and made them Gio-Goi bikes that they rode around on. I think we took the last pictures of them together. Although they had their problems I thought they looked great together. After that we were seeing less of him. His management were taking it more seriously.

The marketing budget for Gio around that time was vast and it was my intention to spend as much on marketing as humanly possible. I lived a very, very affluent lifestyle. I was going to Cream in Ibiza and turning up with twelve people and getting massive bar bills. I took my Range Rover over there and parked it in the sea on several occasions. It was general bad behaviour. I had the time of my life.

Christopher: We did a catwalk show with Ibiza Rocks [*in San Antonio's hottest new bar*]. We were getting loads of interest from all over. Dawn, who was one quarter of [*famously debauched Ibiza club night*] Manumission, had started Ibiza Rocks with her fella Andy. The business paid for Anthony to stay in Ibiza for the summer making connections. We collaborated with Ibiza

Rocks on some T-shirts and they were a big success. I made a decision that we needed to be in Ibiza with loads of branding. I got in touch with [*Cream boss*] James Barton, who was with us first time around. We struck a deal where I did his merchandise for exposure at his Ibiza night in Amnesia. I supplied them with load of graphics off the T-shirts, stuff like 'Peace, Love and Doves' and the next thing we were in Amnesia being flashed up on twenty screens. It was pumping, 7,000 people in there, with Gio-Goi on all the screens, the graphics spinning round. It was a big moment. Cream was the biggest superclub in the world.

We were still stocked in independents but we were also in large chains now. We were making a commercial brand but keeping it cool by doing the craziest shit with the marketing. I know for a fact other labels were having marketing meetings and showing all the stuff we were doing, all our videos, images, and saying we need to be like this brand. No one could touch us. [*Record label*] Def Jam wanted to have a meeting. I was in Vegas and they wanted me to fly to LA.

The world was closed first time around, mobile phones had only just come out, there was no YouTube. Now everything was open. Our pals were running All Saints, and they asked if we could do anything for them. We did a few little photo shoots. We shot them on the same day as Gio. We'd shoot Peter in Gio gear and then All Saints. We did two video edits, one for Gio and one for All Saints. [*The Donnellys also brought The Kaiser Chiefs, Rhys Ifans, The Kills and The Fratellis to All Saints.*] [*Superstar DJ*] Sasha wore Gio; we'd known him from day one. [*French producer and DJ*] David Guetta was interested in doing his clothing line with us. It was not about what the person did, it was about what they were. Why dress Alex Higgins? Because he was as rock 'n' roll as it got and that was what we saw the brand as. We dressed Mike Skinner from The Streets [*for Gio-Goi*]. They were playing Manchester and the lads came down to the office and we kitted them out. We sent a load of gear down to Mike and a [*branded*] low-rider bike to ride on stage. There's a video of him trying to ride it on stage. He smashed it into a speaker. Mike had gone from wearing polo shirts and T-shirts to wearing suits on stage so he didn't wear our gear. The rest of the band did. Mike wore it later on and sent us some pictures.

Anthony: We started getting sent random pictures from around the world. Sienna Miller walking in LA in a Gio T-shirt, Scarlett Johansson was wearing it, Mark Ronson, Jenny McCarthy – Jim Carey's wife – did a shoot in Hollywood. We hit it off with Kid Rock at MTV Awards and he loved our vibe. We were introduced to Jason Statham. It was a constant flow of people getting in touch. Sara Cox was into it, Fergie from the Black Eyed Peas liked the label: 'Can we get something over to the States?' Fergie then did a shoot wearing Gio-Goi. Amy Sacco from Bungalow 8 – she'd just opened a club in London; Victoria Hervey; Daniel Craig – he was just walking down the road and Gordon Smart saw he had a Gio coat on and in *The Sun* he put, 'Even James Bond is wearing the gear now.'

Because we'd been going down that indie front with Peter, we decided we had to resurrect that football terrace vibe. My mate Scully introduced us to Tom [*Meighan, the singer in Kasabian*] and took me to meet him in Leicester. The easiest place to meet him was sat on the seats in the bus stop outside a store that we supplied with clothes. Tom walking up dressed immaculately. We just had some beer in a bag. Kasabian had recently been offered a big deal from a major brand to model for them, so Tom and Kasabian were big news. We never went through the correct channels, it wasn't done through management; there was no hair or make-up. We walked in the store with Tom, he got his kit off, we cracked off 200 pictures and went to the pub. Tom said he liked the striped scarf I was wearing that Chris had got me for my birthday. He said it was like John Lennon's, and that was what I gave him, a scarf. He was as cool as he looks, a real gentleman, a real man's man. We have since become great pals with his manager Coyney [*John Coyne*], who we respect massively so all contact now goes through him.

Then I got it in my mind that I would target Rhys Ifans and Liam Gallagher to go with the Kasabian photos. I wanted to use a photo of them all showing the badge on the same Gio coat that was like a Stone Island type badge – it was more of a laddy garment than an indie garment. I'd made friends with Rhys on several pissed-up occasions. I'd supplied him with clothes for his band, Chrystal Peth, when they were making a video. He rang me to say thanks and said, 'If I can ever do anything . . .' He was photographed in a pub with the jacket on.

The same day Liam was in a pub in Primrose Hill. Liam was wearing a lot of our gear when Oasis first came out with *Definitely Maybe*. He wore it in the video for 'Live Forever'.

The first time Liam met Chris was in the heat of the Oasis thing. Chris was wearing a white plastic Stone Island jacket and Liam came over, pleased to meet us. He said, 'I love your coat.' Our style was always wearing the button-up, wear your coat high, and treat your coat as a jumper. Two days later Liam was in the paper with the same coat on. We were the first rocking that style. Liam copied it from us.

So Liam went to the toilets and did an impromptu photo shoot with the garment on. Now I had the three. I got in touch with Gordon Smart at *The Sun* and we were away again [*October 2007, the photos of the three stars in the same Gio-Goi jacket featured as a picture spread*]. That appealed to a whole different audience. We had more stars than Glastonbury on our books.

Christopher: The brand crossed all genres. You could go to the football and see a load of football lads in Stone Island and they'd have a Gio hat or a T-shirt on. That same day you could go see Peter play in town, or any indie band, and you'd see a kid in a black leather jacket, skinny jeans, a Gio T-shirt and a pair of winkle-pickers. At the same time we'd be sending gear to America for the hip-hop stars like the Wu-Tang Clan. It was the coolest brand around. Amy Winehouse wore the gear. She was famous for all the right reasons then. She was playing the Academy in Manchester and we'd done some ladies' T-shirts, vests and stuff. I didn't go down. I think Anthony took some stuff down and Amy put it on straight away and took a couple of pictures. She may have been friends with Peter at that time, I'm not sure.

Anthony: We bumped into her at a festival. Amy was on our bus and the tour managers said, 'We're in Manchester next week. Come down.' When it came to it, I was on the phone and I said to Rhianwen, 'Just go down there and have a chat with Amy.' Rhianwen and her mate went in and got talking to her. Amy was saying how lonely she was, then she stripped off good as gold and put the T-shirts on. They could clearly see she'd been self-harming. I went back and told the manager about the images, told him we'd airbrush the scars out. We did it and then we put the images in the paper.

I picked her up in a golf buggy six weeks later at V Festival. Peter had played a separate stage and then he'd gone on the bus to see Amy. We don't put the words with these photos but they said Amy was the face of our women's wear. She was a fan of Chris and me, she liked what we were about. Chris had got his bits going on too. He's working with Calvin Harris. I was walking in with David Bentley, Ledley King, Wes Brown . . . it was non-stop.

Christopher: A pal told us about this kid he was going to sign called Calvin Harris [*who recently created a new UK record with eight top ten hits from one album*]. I had his album, *I Created Disco*, nine months before it came out. Calvin came to the office because he wanted to design some clothes – tracksuit tops in really bright colours. I made all these tops for him and put his lyrics on them. I also did him a load of T-shirts when his first single off the album, 'Vegas', came out. We did all this stuff for him and in return we wanted pictures. His direct manager didn't want him to put any clothes on and I shoehorned him into this Gio T-shirt. While he was saying, 'I don't think my manager wants me to wear this' and his manager was saying, 'I'm not really sure,' I said to the photographer, 'Take as many photos of him as you can while I'm sorting this out.' He grabbed about sixty images. We actually went on to have quite a nice and long relationship with Calvin – he was wearing Gio for quite a while.

We catch them early and get our pictures early. A lot of the time it was me with my ear to the ground, or our close friends who worked for record labels. It was the same with The Enemy or The View, all of them.

Anthony: Keith Allen is a long-standing friend of ours. He rang me the day he first heard 'Smile' [*Lily Allen's debut hit single*]. He played it me from the car. He said, 'My daughter Lily is going to be huge.' She was on top of her game and we got the stamp of approval from her. Our partners at Melville said, 'The ladies' wear is not doing as well as the menswear. We really need a face. Can you do anything with it?'

My friend Scully rang Lily. I rang Keith. We jumped in the car with a camera and a few other bits and we went down to Keith's. He's got a beautiful place in the country. Lily was asleep, she got up, she came out, all relaxed, and we had a great night – and got the photos we needed.

'Sales are going through the roof,' Gio-Goi co-founder Anthony Donnelly, 42, told Reuters in an interview at the label's brand new London offices. 'In the last two years we have achieved what it takes other brands twenty years to do,' said brother and co-founder Christopher, 39. Gio-Goi now ranks among the top three selling streetwear brands in Britain. With a staff of about thirty, they moved to a new London office earlier this year, and the label is now selling in Greece, Spain, Germany, Switzerland, Italy and Benelux. It is also planning to tackle the United States and Japan soon. Pete Doherty, an icon of the new generation of rock musicians, has helped Gio-Goi capture the market of 'indie kids with skinny pants', said Christopher. The Donnellys say they were convinced Doherty, formerly of The Libertines, was right for their rock 'n' roll brand, as they often work with high-profile bad boys of the music industry. 'We target rock 'n' roll types. We have always chosen that route,' said Christopher, fondly displaying a framed Union Jack flag with the motto 'The whole world is our playground', a souvenir of the making of a Babyshambles video.

The Donnellys insist that they did not pay Doherty to wear their clothes, describing the contract they have with him as a 'gentleman's handshake'. 'We do not pay people to wear our clothes. That's one of our principles. A lot of people out there like Peter, Mike Skinner or Kasabian, they like what we are about, they get the clothes and association with the brand . . . Peter likes the clothes and we like him. That's it,' said Anthony. Gio-Goi is also currently dressing British singer Amy Winehouse for her world tour with their newly launched ladies' wear collection.

Christopher: The press were calling us the naughtiest label in the country. We were all over the world. We were stocked in hundreds of stores in the UK alone. We were in Brazil, Karachi, all over the world. In two years, turnover had gone from £30,000 to £575,000 to now we were turning over multi-millions. Sales in

2008–2009 were £19 million. At this stage we were looking at our partners Melville, thinking this is where they're going to come into their own. They always said, 'You watch, when the business gets to a certain point, you watch how we take it to the next level.'

12
FAST TRACK 100

Christopher: Anthony and me acquired a pub in Camden called the Prince of Wales. We didn't want a pub but we needed somewhere to do business. It became apparent that the corporate environment at the London office Melville had set up wasn't for us and it wasn't good for the brand or our reputation. We'd take Doherty to the London office and he'd be off his tits peddling a bike around and there'd be people sat around on computers. We thought it was hilarious but the MD was going, 'We can't have this.' Why? All the staff were laughing and loving it. They think they've come to work for this wild brand and the London office looks like a call centre. Why try and subdue a great atmosphere – we weren't a doctor's surgery.

So, these kids approached us and they said they'd done a deal on a pub but they couldn't complete because they had no money. So we said we'd do it. We put the money down for the pub and refurbished it with Brian Duffy. He'd been making the stands for our trade shows in Berlin and Barcelona. We refurbished the pub but kept the original style. I'd had my fortieth birthday there before we did it up. Everyone said they loved the pub as it was, but it was minging. We spent thousands on making it exactly the same. We put new carpets in but the same as were already in. We got all the furniture re-covered same as the original – it still had that old pub feeling. It was a great success. Finley Quaye did a night there called Cherry Cola, there was another great night called Shit The Bed, and we put our own nights on when we invited everyone out of the industry, say at Christmas, and thirty or forty clothing companies would come.

Anthony: It was an A-list haunt. Noel Gallagher, Sadie Frost, Pixie Geldof, Erin O'Connor, Carl Barat, Jade Jagger and David Walliams were there. We went in there and refurbished it. It was doing fuck all, it was three men on stools and the owner opened it when he fancied having a drink with his mates.

Noel came to the opening night. It was all good fun. If you asked for a vodka you got a bottle of vodka in an ice bucket and six glasses. It lost money but people came out of there very happy. It was voted the coolest rock 'n' roll pub in Britain by *Loaded*. Even our decorator was rock 'n' roll – Bobby Gillespie's brother, Graham. Jon McClure did a little set at the opening night. Steve Craddock played there. The Hawley Arms, where Amy drank, was round the corner. She'd come up to our pub. We kept bumping into her in the Monarch chip shop buying kebabs. The manager of our pub was dating Amy's stylist, so the relationship with Amy went on. Shit The Bed was a great night. There'd be Tom Wright, Mischa Barton, Alice Dellal, the supermodel for Victoria's Secret, Davinia Murphy and David Gardner – they'd lost a big diamond ring and they were on the floor looking for it one night. It was found and given back to them.

The label was becoming more mainstream. It was certainly not as underground as it once was and we were trying to balance a mainstream brand that was doing tens of millions and a cool underground vibe. That was what the pub was all about.

Christopher: At this point I'd stepped away from doing the clothes and was working more toward PR and marketing. After a

Method Man (Wu-Tang): YO.

GZA rocking Your Own.
Your Own Wu-Tang.

Idris Elba in the infamous Your Own [YO] bobble hat at the NME Awards.

Ben Grove jumping over Doyley in Manchester town centre.

Heidi at the V Festival.

Photoshoot for Your Own [YO] in New York.

Nico Mirallegro and Elliot Tittensor representing Your Own [YO].

Deadmau5 shoot for 'I Remember'. Camera man, Andy Rutherford, Chris, Greg Walsh and Aaron, who was Deadmau5 for the day.

Warren Brown, Chris, Dale and Aston at the Deadmau5 shoot.

Arthur and Stephen Graham on location at Deadmau5 shoot for 'I Remember', 2009, with the Mau5-YO Jag.

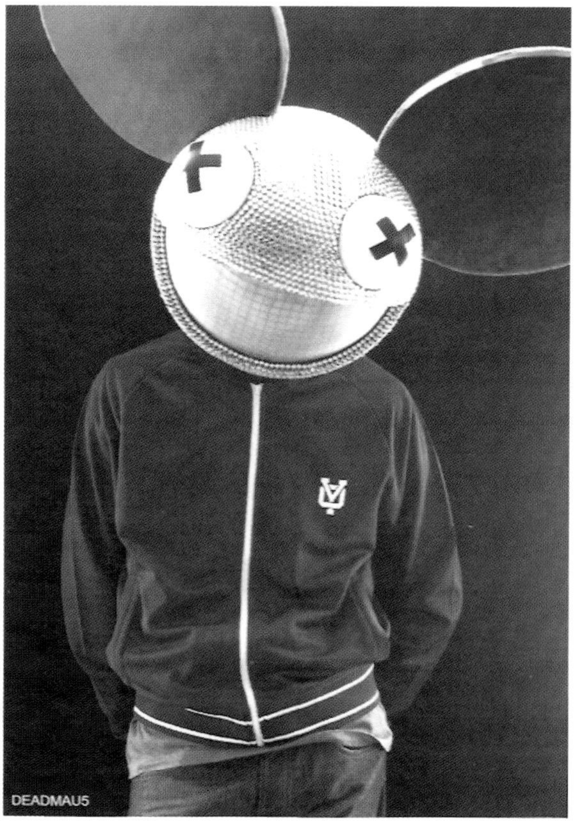

Deadmau5 in Your Own [YO].

Photoshoot in Miami 2013 in Yobot T-shirt.

Y-O logo carrier in Miami 2013.

Photo shoot with Jake Jacobs in Ibiza.

Nervo rocking the dusters backstage at Creamfields.

Anthony H. Wilson. The Legend. RIP.

How ironic – Chris dressed as a screw in his cameo role in Ben Drew's film *Ill Manors.*

John Cooper Clarke, iconic punk poet, and Chris at the after-show party for *Ill Manors*, after Chris tried reciting 'Chicken Town' (not very well).

Damien Hirst accepting
Anthony and Scully's
'Happy Wet Piss' painting.

Chris, Anthony, Gaz, Deano and Ben with the
Your Own [YO] tour bus on the way to Glasgow
Green for the Roses gig.

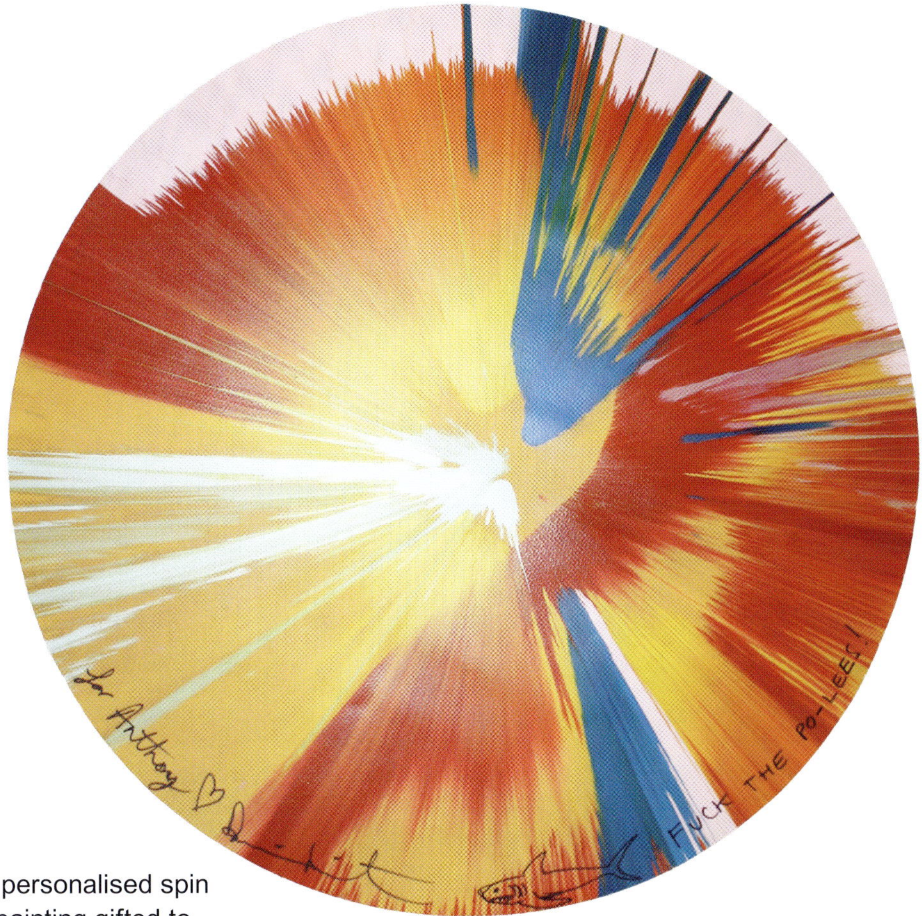

A personalised spin
painting gifted to
Anthony by Damien.

Chris shooting Cass Pennant's *Casuals* documentary at Gio-Goi's London office.

URBAN EDGE FILMS PRESENTS

CASUALS

80s casual classics
www.80scasualclassics.co.uk

A FEATURE DOCUMENTARY
Written & Produced by Cass Pennant
Directed by Mick Kelly

Running Time: 75 mins
Shot in HD, 16.09 Aspect Ratio

Check out more at our websites:

www.casuals.tv and www.urbanedgefilms.co.uk

Find our Facebook page
http://www.facebook.com/#!/pages/Casuals/200034230074017

Contact: Cass Pennant [illegible]

Programme from the *Casuals* documentary.

Leo Gregory on set filming *Hooligan Factory* featuring Your Own [YO].

Howard Marks, Radio 1 DJ Nick Grimshaw and Mike Pickering at an art exhibition curated by Anthony and organised by Tracey (art by Lennie Payne).

Jake modelling Your Own [YO] in London East End.

Your Own [YO] Cream Ibiza.

Shotty Horroh sporting Your Own [YO] in Manchester.

Anthony and Chris conspiring.

YO DUSTERS

Wretch 32 at V Festival.

Olympic Gold Medallist,
Luke Campbell at V.

Ed Sheeran at V.

Magician Dynamo.

Top 50 most influential Mancs in the *Manchester Evening News*. Featuring Anthony, fourth from the left in the back row, and Chris, second from the left in the second row.

Chris, Arthur and Anthony in the *Faces* book.

Arthur and Paul Massey at Arthur's yard. Taken from the book *Faces.*

Arthur and Billy Isaacs at the yard.

Chris and Oliver Wilson having a top laugh in Ibiza.

Chris and Ian Brown backstage after the Roses at V Festival 2012.

Ben Grove, Chris and Bez at Glastonbury.

Simon, Chris, Tracey and Nige (Wingman) at Formal Fight Club.

Chris and Mike Jennings having a pint after Chris won his fight.

June, Chris and Arthur after Chris's fight.

Chris and Tommy McDonagh outside the gym in Moston, Manchester.

Steve Black, best friend to Anthony and Chris.

Ash, Eddie and Steve – PRESENT London. Great friends, great memories, great future...

Anthony's long-time partner, Rhianwen.

Anthony's daughters, Carlie and Daryll, chilling in their dad's office.

Anthony's son, Dylan, at home.

Dylan Donnelly, the next Georgie Best.

Carlie and Daryll at Parklife.

Milo and Paris Donnelly, Tracey's son and daughter in Amnesia, Ibiza.

Chris's son, Leon, on his first modelling job for Your Own [YO].

The lovely Lola, Chris's daughter, modelling one of her dad's hats.

Chris's favourite picture of his wife, Natalie.

while that suited me, but at the beginning I wasn't happy with some of the clothes being made. But you personally can't like everything, can you? You have to let things go. But some of the slogans that they would put out on T-shirts began to annoy us. There was an old track out by E-Zee Possee and MC Kinky, 'Everything Starts With an E', and they put a T-shirt out that said 'Everything begins with an E' – just naff and obvious. We felt they were trying to turn Gio into something it wasn't and then they even started bringing people in to do marketing. Every brand in the country was copying us, the marketing that Anthony and me were doing, but the Melville corporate animal started saying we want to be glitzy and glam. That's not what it was about, but they started to take it down that road. The business had grown so big so quickly they couldn't cope with the finance . . . their arses had gone. They had started looking for other investors.

Anthony and me were being used as a smokescreen. Every manufacturer and investor who came along Melville would pull out the portfolio from the pub, pictures of Amy, Peter, Kate, Calvin, all the stuff we were doing . . . that's how they were selling it but we were being ostracised. That was a big mistake on their part.

Anthony: People loved the attitude and realism behind the brand. We had the company in that good a position Melville thought that they could do it without us. So they started to hire people in to do PR. We were running things to 2008 and now they wanted to paint us out of the picture. They asked us to dilute our shares because they had to put more money in. That was not our problem. That was their problem. We'd maxed them out. Gio was turning over nearly £40 million. I have no idea what happened to the money but they couldn't cope so they wanted to dilute us down. We told them to go fuck themselves. In my opinion, the MD was bullying the staff. I told him to leave the staff alone or I would bully him.

Then Melville went to see Pentland, a venture capital organisation, showing them all our marketing, all the things that the company was famous for. [*Pentland Group is a global brand management company with shares in Speedo, Ellesse, Berghaus, Boxfresh, Ted Baker, Lacoste and Kickers. In 2007 they had sales of £973 million.*] Melville were trying to raise money to take it to the next level – the £300 million turnover level that they said they could deliver.

We'd already sold shares to Melville for millions and then Pentland bought 51 per cent of the company for tens of millions. We went down there and did a deal, sold some shares . . . we were also on top wages. So now we're waiting for the global expansion of Gio – as promised. [*Pentland's chief executive Andy Rubin said, 'This is a very positive investment in a growing brand which is win-win for both sides. This is a strategic investment for us. We think Gio-Goi has been doing a phenomenal job.'*]

Christopher: Pentland must have said, 'Where's the pub? It's not in the business, the due diligence.' It was ours but they thought Gio-Goi had bought a pub. Pentland are huge, they own [*are majority owners of*] JD Sports and an opportunity came up for them to buy in. They came in for 21 per cent and another 20 per cent and another 10 per cent over a period of three years; they had these options. Pentland had heard and seen all this great stuff.

Melville's dream had come true: they were now partners with this massive, massive company. Melville now thought they were big time, but they were blagging it on the back of our success. They were trying to impress Pentland by making everything even glitzier. The sales catalogues became like telephone directories – and they were mostly full of shit. Melville should have made the back end of the business slick, so that the manufacturing and quality were right and the gear arrived on time, and they should have left Anthony and me alone at the front end, i.e. the pub, doing random stuff, going to Glastonbury, Ibiza and Miami. But they tried to make the front all slick and the back end was a shambles. We felt Melville were killing the brand and not being straightforward with us and the Rubins from Pentland. We felt they had a corner shop-type mentality. They didn't have a clue and everyone in the business hated them – well, anyone who mattered.

I wanted to sell out when Pentland came in. That wasn't a reflection on them, it was how I felt at that time about Melville. I wanted to get out. But Anthony was saying, 'How can this fail?' If our shares are worth millions now then with this massive company behind us they're going to take it through to £300 or £400 million turnover. He said, 'Instead of selling out and getting millions, in three years we can sell out and get tens of millions.' But I was of the opinion 'let's take the millions today'. Anthony didn't want to and everyone was saying the same – stay in – and I stayed in. The thing was, to the public the label was still current and credible. We still had an edge, Anthony and me were doing stuff at the pub, like the MTV *In 24 Hours* documentary with Pete Doherty, and the label was still cool.

Anthony: We met Juliet Denison from MTV at V Festival. She was outside the Louder lounge and couldn't get in. They asked us for help and we got them in and then we partied with them for a couple of days. We didn't know Juliet was the head [*of in-house development*] at MTV. I kept in touch with her and they were interested in doing something with us. At the time I was thinking Peter might die so I wanted to set something in stone with him. I'd been listening to 'The Long and Winding Road' by The Beatles and I'd call him and make him listen to the whole track –

we were both off our heads. I was saying, 'There needs to be an ending to this long and winding road of ours. We need to put something down as a testimony to our relationship. I would like to come and film you with us and do something that will stand out.' He later said it was a con but I cleared it with Peter and I rang Juliet and we started to discuss what to do [*for an MTV strand called* In 24 Hours].

Whilst shooting the MTV documentary with Peter we accumulated nearly forty-six hours of footage that has never been seen. He was going to do a gig at the pub and take part in a catwalk show we were putting on. The idea was for me to get all the artefacts from his house and build his house in our pub. I'd not been to the mansion he lived in but I'd seen his flat in Camden. I'd seen something from that flat on YouTube where he was in dire straits and the drug taking was horrific. He'd had a problem with people in London who'd robbed stuff from there. We arranged for some people to go and get him all his stuff back.

In the press they called him a troubled rocker. He'd been banged up, a junkie, all sorts . . . and the mansion was in a state. He was showing off the blood paintings he was doing and he even sang a song about Gio-Goi. He was our 'poster boy'. It was no secret that Pete was not everyone's cup of tea and had got issues. There was not another company that'd sell bulletproof vests when we did that and when we did the MTV thing there weren't a lot of people who would work with Pete. The documentary turned out great in the end. It became the second most viewed MTV programme ever behind *The Hills*.

Christopher: *Drapers* voted us as 'Young Fashion Brand of the Year'. We were often in *Drapers* – it was a weekly industry magazine and they need stuff to talk about . . . nobody was doing anything fresh apart from us. We didn't go to the awards show though. Anthony and me boycotted it as a fuck you to our partners at Melville. We just couldn't respect them. There was a big gap opening up now between our partners and us.

All these people who had not a lot to do with the brand wanted to go and stand on the stage to get this award. It was £10,000 a table and we bought three tables. When they accepted the award there were about twenty of them holding on to it. It was like when you went to a bring-a-bottle party when you were a kid and you and your mates were all holding on to one bottle of beer. At the same time we were number two in *The Sunday Times* Fast Track 100 [*December 2009. 'The companies that make up this year's Fast Track 100,' wrote* The Sunday Times, *'have shown they have what it takes to keep growing through the worst downturn in decades.' Only two firms in the top 100 had raised venture capital for further expansion in the past twelve months. Gio-Goi had seen their sales grow in the past year by 219 per cent.*]

Anthony: The Fast Track thing blew everyone's mind. Richard Branson invited us for dinner. I was asked to go to Dubai to host a party by a promoter on Sheik Khalifa's boat [*President of the United Arab Emirates*]. It was said to make Roman Abramovich's boat look like a bathtub. We were getting invites from everywhere. We were multi-millionaires – we'd been paid out. The reason I'd said we should hold on to something [*shares*] when Chris wanted to get out was because I expected Gio-Goi, now we were with Pentland, to do hundreds of millions.

It was obvious though that Melville was slowly but surely trying to take control from us.

At the Gio-Goi Christmas party there were hundreds of people. Everyone had a PA. We were only doing £40 million, we didn't need all these staff but Melville think they know best. We thought Pentland would do something when they bought in but they left Melville in charge. Melville started to try and launch other brands inside of this business. We felt they were abusing their power. It was an odd time. We'd already had a few million quid, so on one hand I wasn't arsed – we had enough to get by on – but on the other hand we didn't like Angus Morrison or David Douglas at Melville or what they were doing to Gio. And we still had shares.

So we'd be asking, 'Why aren't we doing £100 million in Germany like you said? Why aren't we in America when every store wants it? Where are all these big orders?' The independent stores were dropping off because of the shit they were producing. It was getting more difficult to do the marketing. We had a meeting with Pentland and said, 'You know we're not affiliated with these people outside work and we've watched them say they are us and now we're watching them steer the company down the wrong route. We're here to tell you we are sinking. We need to get rid of them.' No action was taken and it just got worse.

Christopher: I'd designed some shirts that looked like old '70s Simon Shirts and was reminiscing about the brand with David Douglas. A week later Douglas came in the office and said, 'I've bought Simon Shirts.' They asked me if I'd do the marketing but not Anthony; they were trying to split us up. I said that would never work. They launched it and I don't think it got past one season. They then got another kid in and his brand was called Felix Blow. They tried to launch it through USC and that fell on its face. I heard the kid never got his brand back. They made him design shit he would never have done – it was a very poor Superdry. Douglas and Morrison seemed to us to have a natural talent at failing miserably.

Partly because of them starting to do these new brands, we decided to start our own new label. We called it Your Own [*YO*].

That's when we did the Deadmau5 video for 'I Remember'. While I was working with Calvin Harris, I got a call from America off his management and they said, 'We've found this DJ who wears a mouse's head when he DJs and he's called Deadmau5, do you want to get involved?'

'Dead right. He sounds right up our street, crazy fucker with a mouse's head on. We're in.' That was the initial call. Then Deadmau5 came to the UK and I saw him play to twenty or thirty people.

Originally, I'd done a deal with Deadmau5's management on the merchandise, a fifty-fifty deal. I was in a good position. I was going to meetings with EMI's global merchandising but they didn't get it. I went to Amsterdam and met Footlocker to do a deal with them over it. They came to the UK and we met them in our pub, but the kid doing the production made a mess of it all – the gear turned out to be a load of shit. We had basically entrusted the production to a friend of a friend who had fucked it up.

Next, Deadmau5 was doing a show in Manchester and I rang the kid up and said, 'Where's the merch?'

'What merch?'

So I had to go out and get a load of T-shirts printed fast. I thought then, 'Working with this kid I'm going to make myself look like a tit.' I just went to Deadmau5 and said, 'Here's your merchandise deal back.' It felt like the right thing to do but in hindsight looking at how big he became it probably cost Anthony and me a fortune, all down to someone else. We always deliver but it's disappointing the amount of bullshitters out there in the fashion industry.

So at the start with Deadmau5 we were going to do his merchandise but we also wanted something to launch Your Own with and his management wanted something cool to launch him with. I got on great with Joel [*Zimmerman, real name of Deadmau5*] and he became a great ambassador for Your Own. He was very helpful at the beginning, but equally we helped launch him. He had a track coming out called 'I Remember' and we made the video with Colin O'Toole, a director from Manchester who'd worked with Ian Brown and many others. I was styling him for photo shoots. It worked for him. It worked for us. I did a lot for Joel. He wanted suits; I'd help him out. There was nothing in it for me apart from to get some product on him. I'd take him out shopping. We had a good relationship.

The video for 'I Remember' was up for an award against videos by Oasis and Keane. For my first video it was good. Our partners were upset because they were trying to launch new brands and the next thing we've got this amazing video being played on MTV with Your Own all over it – and they're supposed to be the people who know about making clothes.

The 'I Remember' video was planned as the first in a five-part series that we were going to do with Deadmau5 and Colin. At the end of the video it says 'to be continued' and my kids are playing a game of Mousetrap. When we came to do the second part I had a meeting with Joel and he said he wanted to have a load of sheep running through the town centre with mini-Deadmau5 on their back. That wasn't the plan. I said that's not for me and bailed. The next track was 'Ghosts N Stuff' and Colin flew to Canada and did it – Joel with a bed sheet around his head running around Canada. I think Colin just went along with it for the money. Gio-Goi was being pushed to one side now and internally everyone was moving in different directions.

Colin O'Toole: I met Chris at John Shard's photographic studio when I was doing a documentary about The Hacienda and we got talking and struck up a friendship. At the time Chris and Anthony were working with this artist Deadmau5, who was relatively unknown and were teaming him with the new brand

Your Own. I'm a filmmaker so I thought why don't we turn it into a short film. They roped in Stephen Graham, his brother Aston Kelly and Warren Brown and came up with this idea that is loosely based on Anthony and Chris. It was two mates who put a rave on, simple. I wrote the dialogue semi-based on their experience, and we got cracking.

Arthur had this warehouse round the back of Piccadilly and we had the run of the place. The opening shot we were in this unfinished building just off the Mancunian Way that had sort of been left to rot. It was all locked up, we tried to get permission to use it but it was taking ages so in the end, typically Donnelly, we let ourselves in. Arthur turned up with a pair of bolt cutters and we broke in, we got the shot, totally illegal and completely in the spirit of the video.

Anyway, all these police vans turned up and we thought, 'Bollocks, we're going to be arrested here, that's the end of the shoot.' The coppers were shouting at us to get off the site. It was quite mad, really – there were all these residents stood on their balconies watching this going on at 9 a.m. on a Sunday morning. Chris had a high-vis vest on so it looked like we had permission. The video got nominated for an innovation award at the VMAs and has had something like 20 million hits on YouTube – it has gone on to have a life of its own.

Anthony and Chris have genuine interest in interesting things and a unique way of going about things. They keep reinventing themselves and their drive and enthusiasm doesn't ever seem to waver. They have that uncanny knack of being in the right place at the right time. They worked with Deadmau5 before anyone knew who Deadmau5 was and a couple of years later he was the biggest electronic artist on the planet. At the time I just thought. 'What? This kid's a joke. He's got this stupid mouse head on' and Chris convinced me he was going to be this big DJ and artist and it turned out to be true. Some of the schemes you think, 'Why are they interested in that' and then it turns out to be massive. It's really interesting to watch.

Anthony: All our old pals have got involved with Your Own [YO] early doors. We had and still have tremendous support from all the buyers and plenty of celebrity endorsements. The Vaccines, Snow Patrol and Skream and Benga all wore Your Own [YO] on stage. [*Actor*] Nico Mirallegro and [*skateboarder*] Ben Grove modelled for the label. Chris had a meeting with The Prodigy to work with YO. Recently Idris Elba [*actor,* Luther *and* The Wire] wore YO at the *NME* Awards. Liam Gallagher took offence. He couldn't understand why Idris was wearing a YO bobble hat indoors. They had a bust-up at the after party at the Ivy club. [*MTV labelled the fight 'Brand Wars', claiming there was a row between YO and Liam's clothing label, Pretty Green.*] The people supporting YO [*the label has also been spotted on Ian Brown, Ed Sheeran, Wretch 32, Devlin, Stephen Graham, Jaime Winstone and Miles Kane*] are coming to us not because of the brand name but because they know us and appreciate our vibe. They support us and are happy to wear our clothes because of what they represent. It's not just about clothes. It's the history and the attitude.

Christopher: We are real. That's what it is. As well as the labels, we were looking at moving into management and considering buying a building to allow us to have retail space and office space for our management and production companies – all our businesses all under one roof.

I started the Formal Fight Club with Tracey and Simon Farrell. [*Champion boxer*] Michael Jennings [*who is now sponsored by YO*] took me down to his boxing gym, Collyhurst and Moston Lads, a club that is steeped in history. I started training there, sparring, with Mike and Thomas McDonagh, and I thought there needed to be an end game. So we formed the Formal Fight Club [*lavish star-studded white-collar boxing events*] and did our first show at the Midland Hotel. I think we had ten fights, 400 people came. It sold out. It grew from there. We've done four now; we're building a brand. It's become Tracey's thing. She's the female equivalent of Don King in the white-collar boxing world. We donate profits from FFC to the charity Forever Manchester. Tracey is an ambassador for the charity.

Anthony: Our main job though was Gio and we were still doing some amazing marketing, but it just wasn't working out with Douglas and co. The stylists looking after Kanye West came to see us and we were talking about doing something with Kanye. Then they said Rihanna was in town and would we like to style her. She was staying at the Chelsea Harbour Hotel, top floor. We took down some Gio garments, she stripped off and put two garments on. They got photos of her in a powder blue Gio Puffer jacket and not much else. That photo went around the world. She liked the brand. She wanted to be part of the story. Then when Rihanna came to Manchester to play the M.E.N. Arena we hooked up with her again. I took her to my local and we were all still in there at five in the morning, loads of silver limos outside, hundreds of people in the pub. Life was a rollercoaster.

Christopher: I was making a series of short films to celebrate our twenty-first anniversary in clothing. Colin [*O'Toole*] had mentioned something Gilbert and George had done. We planned to interview 100 people, not brand them, and ask them all the same series of questions. On the list we had homeless people, prostitutes, doctors, actors, musicians plumbers, solicitors . . . our sister, Tracey, did a brilliant job of putting together a real mix of people. We shot thirty-eight hours of footage. I told Melville and they said, 'What? You want to promote the brand by interviewing prostitutes and homeless people?' I said, 'Yes that's exactly what I want to do.' They went away on holiday and the guy who was in the middle between them and us, Joe Bowling, loved it and we signed the budget off – £35,000.

Colin and me filmed a prostitute down at the scrapyard and her answers were all really down and dark, she was a smack head. Then we asked her if she'd ever been in love and her face lit up – she was like a different person for a couple of minutes. Three months later she died.

We did one with [*recently deceased*] comic Frank Sidebottom [*real name Chris Sievey*]. He never spoke a word all the way into town and we watched him getting ready in the office, putting masking tape round his head, so he flattens his nose to get the voice. As he was putting his tape on he was starting to turn into Frank and then he changed completely – became the life and soul of the party. It was bizarre and amazing to watch at the same time.

I asked Mike Joyce of The Smiths what his most embarrassing moment was and if he'd ever been in love. We edited the films so that no one knew what the questions were. It was called *Live Who You Are*. It was an antidote to boring marketing. Melville never understood it.

We also made an album to go with the film. It was called *21*, a mix of House music of the past twenty-one years. Toolroom Records put the album out, a Gio-Goi album mixed by Graeme Park and Mark Knight. It was us thinking of something different to do for the brand. Me and Colin made a video for [*Toolroom artistes*] Mark Knight and Tiesto's 'Beautiful World'. There'd been a documentary on Ch4 about these young kids in Leeds who came from a really tough council estate but they did pom-pom dancing. Colin got in touch. We got them on bikes, in hoodies, looking proper scally, and then they broke into a warehouse and started rummaging through boxes. Next thing they're doing American cheerleading. We loved the video but Toolroom wanted to change it, make it grittier. They ended up with Tiesto playing in front of 100,000 people in South America with a 200-foot screen behind him showing the video.

Melville didn't like the films or the music. They were very square and seemed to have huge egos. They wanted the company to be about them. No one really saw the anniversary film. This was when we started to think about putting our own website together, *Donnelly24*. Melville weren't using any of the stuff we were doing. So we felt we had to put our portfolio out, all the work we'd done for Gio or Your Own [*YO*]. Our history was catching up with us. I was asked to take part in a film Cass Pennant [*former infamous leading face of West Ham's ICF hooligan firm turned author and filmmaker*] made called *Casuals*, a documentary exploring the early '80s terrace fashion. It was shown recently at the National Football Museum. We featured in the film *They Call It Acid,* named among the elite who gave birth to the Acid House movement.

Anthony: Melville bought into the brand but you don't become the brand just because you bought into it. I might be best friends with David Bowie and hang about with David Bowie but I'm not David Bowie. Gio-Goi is intrinsically linked with Chris and me because of the ups, downs and turbulence and everything else. But Melville thought it was about them. We also heard they were falling out with Pentland – maybe they discovered finally they wasn't what they said they was!

One day I went in to the London office and they was very hostile toward me. Gio-Goi was working and there were millions of pounds coming through the door – there were queues of people wanting to get involved from all over the world. I went in and there was this guy in the corner, the owner of Black Market Records. He'd been ringing to do a deal but he wanted to speak to us. What was happening was the phones and emails were being diverted to them instead of us. And they were trying to portray themselves as being the brand – it was never going to work. It became a constant battle. We had all this cool stuff going on and they were trying to hijack it. Superdry know how to market a brand and retain credibility. We should have become a label like them. We didn't have the right partners. They started to do Gio watches and trainers without consulting us. I was giving them murder because, to us, they were destroying the brand.

Christopher: Melville were also putting out Gio press releases that were utter bollocks, absolute tripe. [*E.g. Gio-Goi has three key DNA segments and therefore three consumers in mind. 'Contraband' is a premium line that fuses casualwear and denim with a rock 'n' roll spirit. Gio-Goi's 'Mainline' consists of urban casualwear and denim. The 'Trakstar' range is centered on the dance arena and consists of young casual sportswear with a fresh twist.*] We didn't even know who was talking this bollocks. The trainers they put out . . . Steve Atkinson is a great designer but Melville was putting people above him that knew jack shit. They were telling Steve what to make. Why have a great designer and then not let him design? I've got 600 pairs of shoes. If anybody in that business should have been doing the footwear it was me. I wasn't even consulted. Trakstar I came up with twenty years ago. It was supposed to be a more sporty range. We did it first time round. It was in the Intellectual Properties when we did the deal.

We were trying to do stuff that was credible but it was getting harder and harder to get Melville to accept what we wanted to do. I helped Plan B out. We helped to launch the [*No.1, 2x platinum*] album [*The Defamation of*] *Strickland Banks* at the Café de Paris. I'd heard a snippet of a track on the radio, 'Stay Too Long'. I phoned a pal who put us in touch with his management, Sam and Roy Eldridge, and I said I wanted to get involved. They came to the office and they were looking for a credible partner. So I said I'd help finance the album launch at the Café de Paris and we would arrange a photo shoot and content for the brand in return. They put me in touch with their stylist but he was a bit off-hand until I explained we were partners on this project. I think he thought I was going to try and plaster Gio-Goi over the back of Plan B's suit. Anyway, I put the branding in very discreet places for the launch, we did a photo shoot and we did a few things after that. Ben Drew is a top kid. He asked me to be in [*the film*] *Ill Manors*. I play a screw in the film.

Ben Drew, aka Plan B: It was when we were launching the *Strickland Banks* album back in 2010. It was the first live gig we'd done and we'd hired out the Café de Paris in Soho. We were filming the gig and we wanted the crowd to be dressed correctly, we didn't really want people turning up with hoods but we knew we couldn't really control that. Chris and Anthony got involved and as people were coming through the door, Chris was giving out polo shirts and other items of clothing for everyone to wear. It was compulsory that people would try and dress in that old-school Northern Soul way and the clothes they had at Gio at the time really leant itself well to that. We managed to get the whole crowd looking like it was from a bygone era; it was exactly what we needed. From that we really struck up a relationship.

It's weird in these industries to actually come across people that feel like they're from the same place as you. I know they're from Manchester and I'm from London, but I mean in terms of to meet a working-class person in the industry who's doing well. I like to see that. I think that's why we got on so well, it was instant. I felt straight away that I knew where they came from and vice versa. It was really refreshing to find people within their creative industry who weren't stuck-up and up their arse, they're just real and down-to-earth. And I really got that impression from Chris and Anthony.

With some of the ideas we had with *Strickland Banks* we had to finance our own stuff and Chris was always someone we could talk to about how we could do something with Gio-Goi which would, in turn, fit in really creatively with the *Strickland Banks* story. I had the support from the label with the videos but there was always extra content that we were looking to do; by hooking up with Chris and Anthony it allowed us to use that support to put those creative projects in place.

I knew about Gio-Goi before I met them because I'd seen the documentary with Pete Doherty on MTV. I was just into their stuff and it seemed perfect, if you find a brand you actually like and they want to work with you it's always going to be a good fit. I think Chris and Anthony speak to people on a real level, there's no bullshit. If you make an agreement with them you can be pretty sure that they'll stick to it and I think flakey people should steer clear, really. They are completely up front and men of their word, a bit like me. When I come across flakey people that don't stick to their agreements it really pisses me off. I think because of where we're from, if you haven't got your word you've got nothing. I can't speak for Chris and Anthony, but they come across as the kind of guys that don't want to have to deal with people who can't stick by their words, and I feel exactly the same. There were always possibilities with Gio-Goi; other brands seem to have a really rigid approach to what they're doing and you've just got to fit into it. Gio always left the doors open for us to try new creative stuff and come up with ideas and that was what always made it really exciting about working with them. I put a lot of cameos in *Ill Manors* of friends and people that I'd met along the way. For me it was a nice gesture to put Chris in the film. I wanted to show him that he'd helped us in the past and it was a nice nod to the fact that Chris had been there from the very beginning of the *Strickland Banks* project right up to *Ill Manors*, saying, 'Look, if you need anything I'm here' so it was nice to have his face in the film and let people know the connection.

Anthony: Melville didn't exactly jump for joy about the Plan B collaboration. I don't know why. Plan B was number one. Without consulting us they had decided, in their wisdom, that they were now going to open some high street stores. [*In October 2010, a store opened in Aberdeen, followed by one in Glasgow with plans for a Manchester store.*] We had no say in the stores. One shop should have opened on a par with Present in London, in a location that would have allowed it to remain true to its founders' beliefs. In these shops in Scotland, the changing rooms were all decked out in our imagery, so it was all about us and our friends wearing the brand, but there was no mention of us. I stopped talking to the partners. It seemed futile. In Glasgow, they turned up on their own and the people in the shop were looking at them like, 'Who are these two?' They put themselves in front of the label. They sold themselves on the imagery and history of the brand while trying to keep us out of the picture.

Now I thought that wherever we can take money from Gio, let's take it. To me now it was just one big cash cow. I was not interested in what Melville were making, or what they were doing. My passion for Gio had gone. I turned off. I went and sat in Spain for two years instead. I was constantly on holiday. Every month I made sure my money was in the bank and I did a half a day a month.

Christopher: Gio-Goi is Anthony and me. The other people involved seemed to be very jealous of our reputation. It became difficult to do things. You had to go through a load of red tape.

Something that was spontaneous, by the time it got through the red tape, the moment had gone. So you started to think, 'Is it really worth the aggravation?' The first store opened in Aberdeen. I was dead against it. But I asked Ben Drew to open the store. He said yes. He was on tour; I got him to do a detour and he played a full set for 200 people. It was a brilliant, intimate gig. Those were the kind of favours we could pull, but it was wasted on our partners at Melville. But we still had shares in the business. There was reason to plough on – there was an end game, an exit plan.

13
HERE WE GO AGAIN

Christopher: Through doing video stuff with Colin O'Toole and Daniel Wolfe on Plan B and Deadmau5, I got involved with doing a video for Chase & Status. The track was 'Blind Faith'. Colin and Daniel had written a script that was based on Anthony and me putting on Acid House parties. The track was late '80s, early '90s sounding, so Daniel thought there was no better person to get involved than me, to authenticate it.

I gave them a video copy of my twenty-first birthday party at the farm and they based the Chase & Status video around that. The production company who was working on the video had mood boards with white gloves, flares, dungarees and dummies. I said, 'That was where it went three or four years later, but it was not like that at the time. If that's the video you want to make, fine, but I don't want any involvement.'

I changed the whole thing and made it look real. I organised things for them with help from Tracey. The farm at the end of the video is where we did Joy. We shot the interior scenes in my dad's warehouse – same place we shot the Deadmau5 video 'I Remember'. I dressed the four or five main characters in my original clothes that I wore in 1988, clothes I'd kept. I even stood in a room and showed them how to dance to the music to make it look authentic. I also replicated all the old Gio-Goi stuff from memory. The stylist brought a load of stuff in from second-hand stores and we put a rave on in the warehouse. We gave 3,000 bottles of beer away, started it at 9 p.m. Monday night and let it roll. We didn't stop and start; it was a full-on party.

Daniel didn't turn up at the warehouse until three in the morning. He was filming at the farm. Colin was filming the party. It was all shot on old VHS, so it looked authentic. Chase & Status turned up and it looked like they had a buzz. They were there for a couple of hours; they got the shots that were needed and left because they were on a very tight schedule. We never got a chance to catch up on the night, as it was chaos. The party went on until ten in the morning. The video won all kinds of awards. The stylist took an award for best styling.

We had the video before anybody. It should have been there as soon as you went on the Gio-Goi website or Facebook or whatever, flashing, 'Look at what we've just done.' You couldn't even find it on the website! Then they were questioning the marketing! I'd say you've just had this great video. It was the biggest-selling record of 2011 apart form Adele. Where was it on the website? We had exclusivity to use that video before it came out. It was voted in the Top Fifty videos of all time, number forty-eight, and the Deadmua5 video for 'I Remember' was number twenty-four. For our first couple of videos we did okay. Melville didn't get it. I'm doing Chase & Status, one of the biggest dance bands in the world, and they want to do 2-for-1 boxer shorts.

Anthony: Then they opened a store in Manchester [*September 2011*] in the Arndale Centre. Chris did an opening party [*at Moho Live*] and got Park, Pickering and DaSilva out, all the Ecstasy granddads. You could not move for love or money; it was a huge success. The film *They Call It Acid* was shown. But the actual shop? I went there maybe three times. I wasn't made to feel welcome. The mood had got that bad between us and Melville that I didn't even feel like I had the right to go and make myself a cup of tea in the back of the shop. They were doing anything to keep the figures up – Gio was being stocked in lots of stores we didn't think it should be in. We felt Melville were running the label into the ground. All the top independents had dropped us.

Christopher: I didn't want to open a store in Manchester, more so than I didn't want to open the ones in Aberdeen and Glasgow. In the Arndale Centre – fucking shite. I'm not saying that about the Arndale, but for our brand image it was wrong. It should have been somewhere independent, a cool spot. They opened stores on Buchanan Street in Glasgow, the main street, the Arndale – the wrong locations for what the brand was about. We were now pretty sure Melville had completely lost the plot. We even heard they were trying to outmanoeuvre Pentland, get them to write off their investment. We went to Pentland and said to them, 'You've got two maniacs running the business.' We asked them to step in and sort it out. All the things that were attractive about Gio had been sucked out of it. It was becoming too much of chore and we were looking at outside ventures.

Anthony: My interest in art developed several years ago. With Gio-Goi becoming a pain in the arse I started to invest more time in Your Own [*YO*] and art. Does it matter about Gio? Wherever it ends up, does it matter? That history stays with us. I was going to London and booking art galleries. Howard Marks and Nick Grimshaw, Mike Pickering and hundreds more turned up at my first exhibition our Tracey organised for me. I was selling art I had accumulated on my own journey. I'd met Howard at the premier of the film *Mr Nice*. Rhys Ifans [*who starred in the film's lead role*] was an old pal. We had a good drink with Rhys and Howard after the private screening. I started selling art for a few months – it was interesting. That's when I decided I'd become an artist. If Damien Hirst can cut a cow in half and some fella can sell elephant shit, why not me? I wish I didn't have these crazy ideas always popping in my head. Rhianwen went out and bought an easel, canvases, some paint, and Scully and me got on it. We had shower caps and dressing gowns on; we were out of our brains. I'd convinced Scully we could become famous artists. My missus found us covered in paint lay under the kitchen table on our backs. We'd split a canvas and I'd painted half and he'd painted half. We called it 'Happy Wet Piss'. You could tell two people had painted it – one side looked like it was done by a horse with a brush, and the other by some sort of creature from the swamp.

In the meantime our new brand YO was supposed to have been doing something with Damien Hirst and my mate Tommy Dunn, but it had failed to happen. We were supposed to be doing a T-shirt collection that was pretty amazing but my friend Tommy, who organised it, kind of got it wrong. It wasn't a problem; all concerned were firm friends and still are. Damien was always there when we used to go to Glastonbury way back with Joe Stummer, Bez and Keith Allen. So I got in touch with Keith Allen when this T-shirt thing went tits up to call Damien on my behalf. We lost several thousand pounds on the project, as it wasn't properly endorsed by Damien. I then spoke to Damien and he said, 'Look, we're all mates' and we decided to gift each other. I gifted him the 'Happy Wet Piss' painting, all framed up off me and Scully, and he gifted me a fish in formaldehyde and a spin painting. He sent me a picture of him accepting our art. He thought it was mega because no one really did him any art like ours. Mine and Scully's painting has got pride of place in his office, I believe. That's something we are extremely proud of and Damien's a top bloke, a real gentleman. I love art and aim to continue painting – even though it's shit, what I paint is still art . . . right?

Christopher: While all this shit was going on at Gio-Goi a book called *Faces* came out [Faces: A Photographic Journey Through the Underworld *(Bernard O'Mahoney and Brian Anderson, True Crime Publishing). The Donnelly Brothers were featured among the Top Fifty villains, gangsters or 'faces' of the past fifty years. Also included were: Arthur Donnelly, Paul Ferris, Eric Mason, Frankie Fraser, Eddie Richardson and Freddie Foreman. In the book Arthur Donnelly is described as 'the Freddie Foreman of the North'.*] It was a serious book; there are some heavy faces in there. But it was about retired criminals. We're not in there for anything other than being Acid House organisers pictured with our dad, but Melville seemed intimidated and the gap grew wider.

My dad's done a lot for Gio and us in general. We did a photo shoot where we blew up some cars. We did it at the yard and he got the cars. It would take someone like Diesel six months to pull that together with the health and safety. We had one of my dad's pals in a hard hat with a hosepipe and that was it, that was our health and safety. When we worked with Brian Duffy, Brian had this crazy idea of displaying his furniture in an old caravan with Perspex sides. It had my dad written all over it. He got a caravan and took the sides off it, had it all made with Perspex so you could see right through. It's actually in Japan now in a museum and it was in the Tate Modern. It's got Gio-Goi wallpaper inside. He's in the Deadmau5 video. He plays the café owner. He only had one line to say, 'One full breakfast.' And he kept ad-libbing, 'One full breakfast – beautiful, beautiful.' He sorted all the beer out for the Chase & Status video and the warehouse. He's got his own fame with all the boys. Ian Brown loves him, all the lads do.

Tracey: Our dad is quite a complex character. His world is at the scrapyard with all the characters that call each day to see him. Then there's another side to him. He's quite open to new stuff. When he was in prison he learnt how to meditate, he then made me a meditation stool and sent me some books on meditation. He has the craziest stories to tell, like the time he was locked up in Walton Prison in the '70s pre-phone cards and televisions and he wouldn't get rid of his nits, as he used to race them to stop himself from getting bored. The grandkids love hearing stuff like that. It's a million miles away from anything that they know. I do think had he been steered in the right direction when he was a boy things would have been a lot different for him, he's a clever man. Thank God all the kids are removed from the crime we were raised around and are getting a good education.

Christopher: Gio-Goi was now totally commercial. We were getting slagged off in the press, called a 'chav' brand. I read one thing that talked about 'tribes of youffs' at Global Gathering, Ibiza and Marbella all Gio-Goi'd up to their eyeballs. When the youths of Great Britain went on the rampage in the summer of 2011 there was a noticeable amount of Gio-Goi being worn – and not just in Manchester riots. People were beginning to sneer at the label. It had become a load of corporate people trying to recreate what we did and doing it badly. They were putting shit like 'Party Hard' on T-shirts. We wanted to die with embarrassment.

Anthony: The Manchester store had only been open eight months and then it got closed down. Melville closed down all three stores [*in July 2012*]. They'd put a load of money into the shops and lost it. The financial director they employed allegedly seemed to have lost two million. [*In September 2012*] I officially left Gio to pursue other projects. I have been working on Your Own [*YO*] with some of the biggest retailers out there. Now there are a million brands out there all saying they are rock 'n' roll and all the other bullshit that goes with it, but not like us – we really have lived it. It took years just getting the brand YO registered, as you can imagine – YO is a great name for a brand and sounds as rock 'n' roll as it gets. The brand is having a great reaction in the US and Canada amongst electronic and rap artists and opportunities are coming thick and fast. We have offices in Times Square in New York that we can move into when we are ready for the States but it's all about timing and getting things right.

We went to the V Festival with the Your Own bus. We'd hired a Winnebago that was better than the Stone Roses bus apparently, so we haven't lost our attitude or style. We were joined by all the usual suspects . . . they call it networking. Wherever we go we seem to draw a crowd – maybe it's because of the fact that people know they can trust us and they can have a laugh safe in the knowledge that they won't end up in the paper doing something they shouldn't be doing. We had a brilliant time but left early to follow the Stone Roses' tour. Someone suggested giving the keys to the Winnebago to a kid who said his name was Nuts. He'd just been released from prison for arson. We asked him to return the keys to the driver. Once the beer had worn off and we had arrived at Stafford for the northern part of V, we were thinking it wasn't one of our better ideas. After a couple of days the bus company rang us and said it was the cleanest bus they'd ever had returned. Nuts had cleaned it top to bottom, clearly not as mad as he sounds – and obviously house proud. Never judge a book by its cover, note to self.

Christopher: It has been fun again doing Your Own. I actually feel more alive working on the new projects because it had been such a chore with Gio for the past two years. Working with people you have no respect for is not cool. With YO we can do what we want and it is working – YO is getting more and more attention. It's being stocked in credible independents, cool stores such as Present in Shoreditch that's run by our pals. It's about the vibe; a lot of brands are faceless.

One of my favourite sayings about Gio-Goi was one of Pete Doherty's. He said, 'When I wear Gio-Goi I feel bus stop' – as a famous person he can stand at a bus stop and no one is going to say anything. He's accepted.

With Your Own or any other projects we get involved in we are always going to need investment because of the scale of how we think: we think globally. We have begun negotiating with an investor based on the Gio-Goi model for YO. This time, however, we are retaining the control of the companies and the brands too – we are making sure we don't make the same mistakes that were allowed to happen with Gio-Gio. The investor said, 'I'm not buying into the brand, I'm buying into you two. Without you two that stuff on that rail doesn't mean anything. I'm buying in to what you two bring to the table.'

There are no other brands out there that approach things the way that we do. One of the first pieces of marketing for YO is we built a track around the 'Ten Commandments of Rave' speech by Stephen Graham from the Deadmau5 'I Remember' video. We used some world-class DJs, including Marshall Jefferson, on the track.

Anthony: A million brands now copy our Gio-Goi model. We're constantly looking to change and do things differently; we are always one step ahead of the game, we like to think. But how can we stay ahead when so many other brands replicate what we do? That's the challenge. We understand that we didn't invent the wheel by doing product placement and great marketing, but our style is unique to us. We are real and we have great history and a great story to tell. All those other brands who thought by doing what we were doing that they would become like us make me laugh . . . all these other labels saying, 'We are bad', 'We are rock 'n' roll', 'We are music' are not bad or rock 'n' roll or music – they are just following a trend. You have to eat, sleep and shit it to claim it. I have seen one brand, in particular, doing 'Category A' clothing – I have been a Category A prisoner. It is neither cool nor funny looking at spending the rest of your life in prison. I find it embarrassing to even talk to these people.

Our brand has become The Donnelly Bros. – a true adventure. There are no barriers for me and Chris, really, anymore. We have great friends in all walks of life. We are the same people we have always been, just now wearing a different label. The heritage comes with us on our journey. It doesn't become anybody else's just because they picked over some old bones that you left at the side of the road.

The other day we went to London to meet Mike [*McKay*] and Claire [*Davies*] of Manumission [*who had not hosted a club night since 2010*]. They had flown over to discuss their new venture, Cinemission, in Ibiza that is surely going to be the most successful club night on the island when it launches in 2014. We are collaborating with them on their merchandise exclusively. This deal is born out of respect and integrity and many years of the same experiences – this is what makes our thing work. Myself and Christopher do it effortlessly and that's why we will continue until we drop.

Christopher: So we were making a new brand out of YO whilst Gio-Goi was being murdered by Melville. Then all of a sudden, Douglas and Kilbourn started saying, 'We need your help.' Whereas for four or five years before when we were doing amazing things they didn't want nothing to do with us, now they were saying to me, 'We need a video like Deadmau5, like Chase & Status, like Tiesto. We need the next Plan B, the next Calvin Harris.' I was like, 'I can't believe it. You've had all that and got blasé – you didn't realise what you had.' The penny finally dropped with them like a ten tonne weight.

They needed me down in London all the time. I had no respect for them as businessmen; I didn't want to do it but I still had shares there. I did a few little bits. The gear they were making was shit. There was no soul in the business. They must have brought fifty creative staff in through the years, but it was those hard-core people who were there at the beginning and stayed loyal who really were Gio-Goi. They were the best people the business ever had, passionate people, but Melville had sucked the soul out of them all. It just wasn't a nice place to be. I went down once a week. I went in the office to say hello and then all my meetings I had in the bar downstairs. They looked pathetic and what they had done to the brand was tragic.

They were getting more desperate than desperate. The shops were gone. They were obviously struggling. Three years ago we had been number two in the *Sunday Times* Fast Track 100, the second biggest growing company in the UK. They'd now fucked it. They kept saying, 'Wait until you see what we do when this business starts selling, watch how we take it to the next level.' They took it down the toilet.

The last day [*January 2013*] I walked in the office and I saw them walking down the stairs. Their faces were that white they were almost blue. I heard them saying, 'He's here. He's here. Chris is here.' I asked what was wrong. They said the receiver was in, 'We've been put into liquidation.' I was told later that Douglas was in tears at the realisation at what had happened to the company. From there, within an hour, I had a meeting with Nokia about doing a load of stuff for Gio.

I went to the meeting an hour later with the Nokia marketing people and flipped it to Your Own. I was sat in my first meeting with YO an hour after Gio went under. The next day I came into our office in Manchester with a team of lads and stripped the office of anything to do with Gio and then refurbished it completely. Our shares were now worthless. That was it. Gone.

We lost a good few million quid in January 2013. All that work keeping it going for twenty-five years – court cases, gang warfare, police investigations and we never lost it. We entrusted Gio-Goi to them and they ran it into the ground and fucked it. Call us what you want but we never lost the brand on our watch.

Anthony: Melville Capital – we entrusted them with something we'd nurtured. We'd fought so hard to keep it alive and then for it to collapse like that was obviously painful – although I don't blame Andy Rubin from Pentland. It was Douglas and Morrison and Kilbourn. The bank pulled the plug, the bank was in for a few quid, and both sets of partners were in for a few quid. [*The administrators KPMG said the label was 'another victim of the recessionary environment'. It was the fourth retailer to collapse in 2013 following Blockbuster, HMV and Jessops.*]

The bank wanted their money back and was basically selling the company to the highest bidder. Everyone lost money. We lost our share value. We got caught in the crossfire. We said in our press interviews, straight away, that we hold the rights to the images and videos linked to the brand. I got on to KPMG through my lawyers and said that I would issue proceedings. I told them all the video content, the stills imagery, the celebrity endorsement, it all belongs to us. We made it clear any bidder would have to negotiate a deal separately with us to license the imagery – and the imagery was such a part of the brand's success. I was quoted in the paper as saying, 'It would be fantastic if the person that buys the brand marries the two pieces and puts the brand and the history back together. With the right backing it could be back where it deserves. For a buyer at the minute it would be like taking on Rolls-Royce, but without having the image rights for the Silver Lady on the bonnet.' Our history belongs to us. That can be evidenced beyond any doubt, that history continues with us.

Following reports that Sports Direct were considering buying the brand from the administrators, JD Sports Fashion bought Gio-Goi in February 2013 in a deal rumoured to be in excess of £4 million. Pentland is a majority owner of JD Sports.

Christopher: Out of the blue, we find out JD have bought it – and JD is part-owned by Pentland. From our point of view it looked a bit strange. The negotiations over Gio-Goi are still ongoing between us and Peter Cowgill [*Executive Chairman JD Sports*]. Hopefully there will be a happy ending. In the meantime we continue to crack on with our new brands. When all is said and done, we've been through more shit than most people. We have got balls of steel and tomorrow we can get up and have another go. Do you know why? We're still breathing.

In July 2013, the Donnelly Brothers struck up a private deal with Peter Cowgill. To be continued.

AFTERWORD

Working on this book has been an emotional rollercoaster, to say the least. Reliving the highs has been interesting but the lows have been low and quite difficult at times. Reading chapter after chapter almost seems like I've bought a book about the adventures and antics of two unruly lads from Wythenshawe who I've heard about – a different life and lifetime ago. But one thing I will say is that I have definitely lived all aspects of life – dark and light – and there's something to be said for that. For any number of reasons, this book only scrapes the surface of those experiences

Whether you like what you've read or not, we're all a long time dead. There are no apologies for any of the things that have gone on and nor do I expect any apologies from anyone else. I have no regrets other than losing close friends and family.

I have always been passionate about any projects I've worked on even if I've not seen eye to eye with my partners; the business always comes first. I have also met some amazing people along the way, some of whom I'm very proud to call my friends. I think you know in an instant how it's going to pan out when you meet someone new – good or bad. With me, if it's good it's for life and if it's bad, move on.

If I could pass on anything from my experiences it would be: be honest with yourself and others you value. Don't give up on your dreams no matter what – they'll keep you going when times are bad. There is nothing more important than health, family and friends. Have as many parties as possible and laugh.

Thank you to my wife and soul mate, Natalie. One love. Oh yeah, I can dance! ☺

Christopher Gene Donnelly

All my life I have worked tirelessly to achieve the best results that could be achieved from whatever I was concentrating on at any one particular time. Growing up I was a good kid. I loved my family and my friends dearly. I can say, hand on heart, I genuinely loved everyone I worked with, in whatever capacity they held within any of the work environments I was working with them in, be it crime, bootlegging, music, fashion . . . I put every ounce of effort into all of them. I would like to apologise for any pain I caused when I was younger and for the things I should have done that I never did, but these were the cards I was dealt and I played with what I had. I cannot help but feel that even though this book is colourful in the extreme, and there are some things I am not proud of, I never burned anyone that didn't burn me first.

I wouldn't wish what my family and I have had to live through on anyone – even the highs as well as the lows have been a drama. But I think our story proves what I always say: If you want something, you can get anything – just do it right.

At the end of the day you have to live with yourself, your conscience will always get you in the end.

Anthony Donnelly

ACKNOWLEDGEMENTS

Firstly, big thanks to all those who gave up their time to be interviewed or supply written testimonies – it means a lot to us.

Colin O'Toole conducted preliminary interviews with us, Tracey, Arthur and June Donnelly. He also interviewed Eric Barker, Harry Franco, Jeff Oughton, Graham Massey and Jack Dunkirk.

Becky Seward is responsible for the material gathered from Max Beesley, Howard Marks, Adrian Hunter, Peter Hook, Graeme Park, Kenny McGoff, Matthew Comer, Scott Kershaw, Tom Stubbs, Colin O'Toole, Oliver Wilson, Plan B, Darren Partington, Andy Carol, Bez, Eddie Prendergast, Cass Pennant, James Barton, Mike Pickering, Damien Hirst, Clint Boon, Jimi Goodwin, Matt Greenhalgh, Miles Kane, Pete Doherty, Chase & Status, Ian Brown, Jon McClure, David Bianchi, Deadmau5, Shaun Ryder, Mani, Stephen Graham, James Barnes, Keith Allen, Alan Erasmus, Scully, Carl Barat, Leo Stanley, Andy Rutherford, Gordon Mason, Ben Grove, Mike Moran, John the Duck, Juliet Denison, Bernard Sumner, Gordon Smart, Pat Carroll, Tom Meighan, Dean Skarratt, Karl Nielson and Stuart & Mark Knight.

Thanks to Sue Dean and Tracey Donnelly for their assistance in the organising of the imagery for this book, to the photographers – Matthew Comer, Scott Kershaw, Daniel Dempsey, Todd Graft,

Kevin Donnelly, Chris Kirkham, Marie Monaghan, Jim Whitworth, Annette Watkinson, Brian Anderson, Grant Fear, and Lisa Harrison Sherlock – and the artists Matt and Pat Carroll and Sarah Hardacre. For kindly supplying photos, thanks to Sparrow, John Faulkner, Anne and Jimmy, Brenda and Barry, Jackie and Janet Yates and Graeme Brown. Thanks also to solicitor Paul Dyson, and the two Michelles at Bailey Walsh, David Sefton, Mark Haddon PR, Mike at Mojofuel, Steve Black, the Barton family, Ash Taylor, George and Steve Demetrious, Campbell Brown at Black & White, Neil D. Murray QC and Kevin Pocklington at Jenny Brown Associates.

Author and journalist Simon Spence has balls of steel. We couldn't believe he had the neck to take our book on. The many hours we spent together were always a pleasure.

Special thanks to our family: in particular Tracey Donnelly – we couldn't have done it without you – and our mum and dad (for putting up with us). The future: Carlie, Daryll, Paris, Milo, Leon, Lola and Dylan.

Finally, may they rest in peace: Stephen James Yates, Anthony Cox, Tina Baguely, Christian Joyce, John Molloy, Ged Docherty, John Sullivan, Jack Grey, Michael Pollit, Julian Bradshaw, Tony Wilson, Rob Gretton, Colin Roffey, Tony Barton, John Yates, Granddad Jack, Jamie Calderbank, Paul Young, Aunty Sylvia, Aunty Rita, Aunty Jean and Uncle Alan.

INDEX

YOUR